THE LANGUAGE THAT MAKES GEORGE ELIOT'S FICTION

THE LANGUAGE THAT MAKES GEORGE ELIOT'S FICTION

KAREN B. MANN

THE JOHNS HOPKINS UNIVERSITY PRESS
BALTIMORE AND LONDON

The Johns Hopkins University Press, Baltimore, Maryland 21218
The Johns Hopkins Press Ltd, London

Library of Congress Cataloging in Publication Data

Mann, Karen B.
The language that makes George Eliot's fiction.

Bibliography: p. 211
Includes index.
1. Eliot, George, 1819–1880—Style. I. Title
PR4694.M36 1983 823'.8 83-257
ISBN 0-8018-3002-8

CONTENTS

PREFACE

As any enthusiast for George Eliot's fiction knows, excellent studies of her novels are numerous. They range from the work of first pioneers like Joan Bennett and F. R. Leavis, who awakened readers in this century to the aesthetic virtues of her works as a whole, to that of recent specialists like Felicia Bonaparte, who devoted an entire book to explaining one novel. The scholarship and the critical acumen of all those who wrote during the intervening period are formidable. Gordon S. Haight provided the basis upon which all other writers would depend in his edition of the letters and in his biography. Bernard J. Paris and George Levine traced the nineteenth-century intellectual influences upon George Eliot's thought. Barbara Hardy and W. J. Harvey wrote such sweeping formal analyses that all later critics would to one degree or another sit under their wings. From their work was able to grow a series of increasingly sophisticated analyses of Eliot's art as well as of her relation to earlier art and to the central preoccupations of her time. (Most notable among these are the studies by U. C. Knoepflmacher and J. Hillis Miller.) The collective accomplishments of Hardy and the critics who followed her had a dual effect upon criticism: more recent critics began to write articles analyzing single novels intensively and also more leisurely books explaining some generic, ideological, or historical aspect that provided the "key" to all of her fiction.

Yet, in all of this work, very few critics seemed to like George Eliot's style, even while they admired her artfulness. And most, even when they "liked" her, considered her quite serious if not downright prudish. Since I often found her funny and could not conceive of anyone's being able to reread her consistently if her style were so bad, I came to wonder whether that style—that is, the actual words, sentences, images, and so forth—was the element that triggered the responses of her admiring readers, either in itself or by means of the other fictional elements that had to be created through it. Further, while work had been done on the language of her fiction, it consisted of one excellent study by Reva Stump—now some twenty-three years old—which did not benefit from recent theories regarding language and discourse; and single articles that exposed how language works in one or another novel. There yet remained the task of examining how the novels as a whole might reveal George Eliot's diverse attempts to make language do what she wished as a medium between her and the world. This possibility, however, occurred to me only after I had begun my own intensive search for possible significance and consistency within one kind of language in her fiction. Hence, this book developed from a single issue, which I began exploring in 1975: the use of sound and music in Eliot's novels. As I gradually discovered other matters that lay "behind" and "beyond" her language of sound and music, I realized that many of the ideas that interested me most required that I analyze other segments of her language. As a result, my argument derives its organization from that initial impetus and its effects. Before explaining that organization, I should briefly outline the critical suppositions from which it finally emerged.

As a naive critic of Victorian fiction I originally faced the necessity of accommodating a liking for Romantic literature and for comedy with a liking for George Eliot. In addition, I had to understand, intellectually, why those likings existed outside of, if not prior to, academic interest in such works as "works of art." The texts that indirectly provided me with a justification for such apparently diverse tastes and that implied methods whereby to expose Eliot's own imaginative and comic (i.e., stylistic) possibilities were Geoffrey Hartman's *Wordsworth's Poetry, 1787–1814* and J. Hillis Miller's *Charles Dickens: The World of His Novels.* In order to emulate their work in the complementary world of George Eliot's fiction, however, I needed to comprehend their presuppositions and their later acts of literary criticism. At the risk of expressing a false (for them) intellectual genealogy, I offer the following critics as the most helpful in achieving that comprehension.

The most pervasive influence on my stance comes from critics and theorists whose essential quality is the limited nature of their own thirst for system; that is, critics who return again and again to the inchoate but powerful elements of literature and reality, despite the apparent adequacy of their own systems of explanation for those elements. These include Claude Lévi-Strauss (*Structural Anthropology*), Angus Fletcher (*Allegory: Theory of a Symbolic Mode* and "'Positive Negation': Threshold, Sequence, and Personification in Coleridge"), and Kenneth Burke (*Language as Symbolic Action*). Stated another way, Lévi-Strauss, Fletcher, and Burke seem capable of worshiping two gods—order and energy, words and world, time and space. In addition to them came Maurice Merleau-Ponty (*Phenomenology of Perception*), whose description of his own philosophy alternates between abstruse logical refutations of other systems and fascinating case studies of brain-injured individuals; in his work I discovered most forcefully the image of mind adjusting to world in order to grasp it and function in it.

Beyond these writers I perceived two different lines of literary criticism: the "realists" and "psychologists," who explored the nature and implications of mimesis, René Girard being the most recently notable among them; and the "linguists," who explored the constitutive and unavoidable reality of words *as words,* Morton W. Bloomfield and Roman Jakobson being the most clearly useful to me. The possible dichotomy between the focuses and priorities of the two groups became clearer as I discovered that the explanation of how plot or narrative works seemed to belong to the "realists" and "psychologists," and the explanation of how figurative language works belonged to the "linguists." My naive question remained, if not now expressed in terms of a liking for George Eliot's fiction, for Romantic poetry (figurative language), and for comedy (plot): Where do plots come from? Do they derive from language too? More specifically, where do Eliot's plots come from?

Other relevant theorists on narrative there were aplenty: for instance, Northrop Frye, Paul de Man, and the formidable group of essayists in the special issue of *New Literary History* devoted to narrative (1975). Of course, numerous critics of George Eliot's fiction had already shown what historical ideologies were formative in determining her plots: organicism, Comteism, Higher Criticism. Yet, despite the likelihood that such influences were real, I held the conviction (based upon Eliot's life, letters, and essays) that her first allegiance was to art as the truth of ultimate importance, and her second allegiance was, not to philosophy or ideology, but to "life"—whatever that was. So, to satisfy her, and to satisfy me, an explanation of "where her stories came from" required an accession to those two realities: language as that which constitutes her art, and the sensory world as somehow adequately grasped by that linguistic art. George Levine admirably describes such a temperament in *The Realistic Imagination:* "The impelling energy in the quest for the world beyond words is that the world be there, and that it be meaningful and good; the persistent fear is that it is merely monstrous and mechanical, beyond the control of human meaning. Realism risks that reality and its powers of disruption" (p. 22).

Finally, the node at which I could begin my exploration of George Eliot's fiction was one that had implications for all of these questions: the humorous remark, phrase, or even pun. Here artistic structure and reader response, sound and sense, doubled words and doubled realities, seemed inextricably bound up together, so that an adequate explanation of any part would require, and perhaps bring about, an adequate explanation of the other parts. Even more happily, such doublings seemed to require a narrative in order to discover or uncover their nature and impact; and if that was the case for my explanations, then it might well be the case for George Eliot's as well.

Implicit in the foregoing history of my own critical activity are assumptions about the means to, and even the existence of, meaningfulness in words and in the sensory world—assumptions that several recent literary critics have called into question. Although I have dutifully, if not faithfully, read both the theorists of deconstruction and poststructuralism and also critics who practice according to those theorists' inferences, I found both groups to be principally useful in checking any too hasty flight into outward reality as somehow determinative of the fictional world. I have never found them capable of shaking my conviction that adroit users of language want somehow to catch outward objects in their nets of words; this, I suspect, is also true for George Eliot. Precisely what I mean by this can only become clear in the extended argument that makes up this book.

The order of my argument and the methodology implicit in it derives from the preoccupations I have described. Because I believe that language is as crucial for George Eliot as it is for any Romantic poet, I have examined specific kinds of language not only as evocative of a particular sensory reality but also as constitutive of the elements usually considered to predominate in mimetic prose fiction. In other words, I have progressed within chapters from single incidences of figurative language to the largest units of fictional discourse, whether those are considered to be the embodied scene or the narrative's plot. Of course, certain metaphors are more central to particular elements of fictional structure than are others. Thus, Chapters 2 and 3 tell most about relations between character and setting as expressed through gustatory and spatial language. Chapters 4 and 5 explore the organizing principles of George Eliot's plots, as they emerge from the language of sound and of sexuality. The language of the drama examined in Chapter 6 explains most about point of view. Chapter 7 also concerns point of view—the novel-reader's—but since its own standpoint is outside the novels themselves, it serves as a fitting conclusion to the book.

Ultimately, I hope that the repeated movement in each chapter from linguistic expression to fictional structure does express what interests me most in George Eliot's fiction (or any fiction, for that matter): how does the author "generate" character, plot, and point of view as adequate embodiments in language of her stated meaning? In order to focus upon that issue—the generation of structure from the meaning expressed by language—I have had initially to take more or less for granted what George Eliot's "meaning" is. Baldly stated, I take it to be the problematic relationship between self and world. As such, it is the thread that runs through my entire argument. Of course, that meaning is redefined, if not defined, by my successive explications of Eliot's fictional methods. Nonetheless, it can serve as the ground note for those desiring a coherent thesis linking all of the chapters in this book.

Further, because my interest has remained centered upon the relations between certain figures of language and the conventional structures of fiction, I have not by any means provided complete and connected analyses of George Eliot's novels singly. For that the reader must go to the many excellent discussions of her novels already available. Indeed, it is only because of the inspiring work of other critics and scholars that I am able to make this contribution; their insights have provided the foundation, the real premises, of my argument. For all that I have learned from them—both those cited in this book and those whose ideas made the atmosphere in which I wrote—I am sincerely grateful.

I am equally if not more grateful to those real presences who assisted me toward the creation of this argument. First must come Thomas P. Joswick of the English Department at Western Illinois University for his theoretical, practical, and personal assistance during the past three years. To my former chairman, John Sekora, and the university administration, for the necessary reassigned time and a sabbatical, I am also most grateful. For the gift of time in another sense I would like to thank U. C. Knoepflmacher, Clyde de L. Ryals, and Lawrence G. Evans, each of whom taught me so well what I needed to know. The editors of two journals have graciously given me permission to reprint as chapters in this book somewhat revised versions of articles they had published. Chapter 2 appeared as "George Eliot's Language of Nature: Production and Consumption" in *ELH* 48 (1981): 190-216. Chapter 4 appeared as "George Eliot and Wordsworth: The Power of Sound and the Power of Mind" in *Studies in English Literature* 20 (Autumn 1980): 675-94. Chapter 3 is scheduled to appear in *Genre*, and the editors of that journal have kindly allowed its appearance here first. In all of this the assistance of the secretaries of the English Department, Helen France and Joann Loker, and of Carol Bradford as typist was indispensable, as was the care and advice of Barbara Tilly at the Johns Hopkins University Press. Last, I wish to thank my family, John, Jenny, Annika (and Nancy), for their patience—and, failing that, their resignation—in the face of my preoccupation.

THE LANGUAGE THAT MAKES GEORGE ELIOT'S FICTION

1

PREMISES

THE MOST DIFFICULT and yet most satisfying aspect of realistic fiction is its allegiance to two apparently opposed principles: art and life. Further, literary criticism thrives upon the energy produced between those two poles. George Eliot in particular has proved her greatness by the success of both the "art" and the "life" kinds of analysis of her fiction. In fact, the comprehensiveness of the work done on those matters of life that helped to shape her novels—philosophy, theology, science—and on those matters of art within them—plot, character, imagery—makes possible the following attempt to discover a more fundamental connection between the life she imitated and the art she created. My first premise is a simple one: if George Eliot chose to write fiction, she must have found in its structure and function something that was an essential part of her meaning and conceptions. I do not mean so simple and true an assertion as that which has made Eliot's fiction an example of "Dutch realism" in its care to represent everyday people undergoing common crises in a real world in order that we might understand and sympathize with them. Rather, I mean that the very structures of language and the literary art answered best her sense of the world, so that, whether she used those structures unselfconsciously or meditated upon their essentially linguistic character, she nonetheless found them to be her most fundamental means of grasping the world.[1]

The starting point for my argument is wordplay, because it is the smallest unit of literary language, but my conception of such play as a technique that causes the reader to hear one thing and conceive of two makes of it a kind of protometaphor, so that the completion of the first stage of my argument will depend upon an examination of metaphor as well. In fact, a discussion of this capacity of language to refer to not one but two realms (the realm of the world referred to and the realm of words themselves) brings about a doubling in my own argument. I wish to examine how George Eliot's fictional "language" is structured as well as how that structure seems to her to be also accurate for life.

A full exploration of the relationship between language and life required George Eliot to write numerous books and poems; any mapping of that exploration must also be extensive. In order to provide a schema for that territory, I offer a crucial metaphor linking nature and art in Eliot's own theoretical statements: the shell. Although this passage itself, and the subsequent quotations relevant to it, might seem too singular to justify the weight of argument, their contents and implications are repeated significantly in the fiction and will be examined in detail in Chapter 3. Here, in "Notes on Form in Art," she is trying to explain the relationship of artistic elements by using the natural image of the shell:

> Poetic Form was not begotten by thinking it out or framing it as a shell which should hold emotional expression, any more than the shell of an animal arises before the living creature; but emotion, by its tendency to repetition, i.e. rhythmic persistence in proportion as diversifying thought is absent, creates a form by the recurrence of its elements in adjustment with certain given conditions of sound, language, action, or environment. Just as the beautiful expanding curves of a bivalve shell are not first made for the reception of the unstable inhabitant, but grow & are limited by the simple rhythmic conditions of its growing life. ("Notes on Form in Art" [1868], *Essays,* p. 435)

Depending upon one's focus of discourse, the fundamental terms of Eliot's explanation can be variously stated: "form" and "content" (emotional expression, interestingly enough); repetition and diversification; animal and environment; growth and limitation. I wish to encompass at least approximately all of these possibilities by examining through the shell image itself an abstract relationship that may be discerned behind a whole variety of fictional units in Eliot's novels. Initially, this can be stated as the relationship between *energy* and *order* —terms that may apply equally to the natural and to the artistic universe.[2] In the passage above, Eliot appears to give priority to emotional expression as the driving force, the energy, behind art. And yet there is, even in the emotional energy she describes, a kind of prior order, for emotion has a "tendency to repetition" or "rhythmic persistence in [inverse] proportion" to the energy of thought, as well as to the impact of such "externals" as sound, language, action, and environment. If we turn from her direct explanation of artistic creation to her analogue from life, the nature of the process or situation she describes becomes clearer. The creation of the shell by the sea animal is a necessary response to both inner drives and external conditions: both the animal and the world about it are in movement, and the result, the work of art, is that delicate but visible interface between them —the shell.

A passage from an early letter, written by Eliot on June 4, 1848, elaborates upon the implications of this relationship. In this passage she reverses the metaphor by using the language of art to explain a natural or "real" psychological phenomenon:

> Alas for the fate of poor mortals which condemns them to wake up some fine morning and find all the poetry in which their world was bathed only the evening before utterly gone—the hard angular world of chairs and tables and looking-glasses staring at them in all its naked prose. It is so in all the stages of life—the poetry of girlhood goes—the poetry of love and marriage—the poetry of maternity—and at last the very poetry of duty forsakes us for a season and we see ourselves and all about us as nothing more than miserable agglomerations of atoms—poor tentative efforts of the Natur Princip to mould a personality. This is the state of prostration—the self-abnegation through which the soul must go, and to which perhaps it must again and again return, that its poetry or religion, which is the same thing, may be a real ever-flowing river fresh from the windows of heaven and the fountains of the great deep—not an artificial basin with grotto work and gold fish. (*Letters,* 1:264)

Importantly, this passage implies that poetry and religion are not systems of laws—forms of order—but forces—forms of energy (rivers and fountains). It also implies that such forces have access to a realm beyond this world of tables and chairs, whether envisioned as a heaven above or a deep below everyday human experience. The unnamed connection between such realms and the everyday world is imagination, conceived of as the "power" of mind. It is this faculty—the common link between self and world—that Eliot examines through the medium of her fiction, not only to point up its dangers (as much literary criticism of her work has amply revealed) but also to establish its fundamental necessity, so that human life will indeed not become an "artificial basin with grotto work and gold fish." The means for that examination is language.

Turning from the conceptions that George Eliot tries to convey through her use of such metaphors to the language of the metaphors themselves, we should consider the development of this shell image as she uses it in a variety of contexts; for not only do the internal relationships of this image offer insights into her convictions, but the other items linked to one another, either through a common metaphoric relationship to the shell image itself or through similarly constructed metaphors, become the central terms of her art.

My first extension of the shell image, then, derives from its multiple referents: shells protect kernels as well as encase animals. Eliot also made use of this image as a description of the work of art. In a letter to Anthony Trollope on October 23, 1863, she wrote:

> But I am much struck in "Rachel" with the skill with which you have organized thoroughly natural everyday incidents into a strictly related, well-proportioned whole, natty and complete as a nut on its stem. Such construction is among those subtleties of art which can hardly be appreciated except by those who have striven after the same result with conscious failure. (*Letters,* 4:110)

The implications of the nut image seem obvious enough, for they derive from the general nature of organic metaphors involving seed, root, stem, and blossom. The very conventionality of such metaphors for Romantic and post-Romantic literature would seem to depreciate the significance of Eliot's usage here. Yet, as later discussion will show, the very pervasiveness of such language, not only in her discussion of art but in her practice of it, provides a "fruitful" means of analyzing the form of her fiction and permits us to explore the connections between that fiction and the world. After all, the organic metaphor is one taken from nature and thus one whose structure should correspond to "reality."

Further, the use of the organic metaphor to denote internal as well as external reality remains viable today, as the following passage from a recent description of Freudian psychology makes clear:

> Now, in referring in this comparison to the Freudian theory itself, we want to evoke that image of the Ego fighting on two fronts: turned toward the outside, moderating appeals and assaults, turned toward the inside, channeling excessive and incongruous impulses. Freud conceived of this agency [the Ego] as a protective layer, an ectoderm, a cerebral cortex, a *shell.* . . . Yet the shell itself is marked by what it shelters; that which it encloses is disclosed within it.[3]

Nicolas Abraham, who uses this very description as a metaphor for the book he is reviewing (*Vocabulaire de la psychanalyse* by Laplanche and Pontalis), has entitled his essay "The Shell and the Kernel." Eliot, in trying to explain her own sense of human psychology, speaks of the "first seeds of dread and desire":

> What seems eminently wanted is a closer comparison between the knowledge which we call rational & the experience which we call emotional. The sequences which are forced upon us by perception, which establish fundamental associations, & are classed as knowledge are accompanied in varying degrees by satisfaction, & denial or suffering, to the organism in proportion as the established sequences are affirmed or disturbed. What is the difference with the sequences which are the subject matter of ethics? Only that the satisfaction or suffering is something more deeply organic, dependent on the primary vital movements, the first seeds of dread & desire, which in some cases grow to a convulsive force, & are ready to fasten their companionship on ideas & acts which are usually regarded as impersonal & indifferent.[4]

Further, Eliot finds not only the seed image appropriate for the "vital" movements of the human being, but she uses it to explain intellectual development as well; yet at the conclusion of her passage she shifts unobtrusively from germination language to the earlier containment language:

> In youth our minds are struck by instances which are the seeds of our future maxims or generalizations: in later life our minds are preoccupied with maxims into which instances are absorbed, melting into their corresponding generality.[5]

Thus, if early experiences produce general laws, these laws then later envelop the individual experiences. Whether these processes are identical or antithetical it is a part of my intention to discover.

Nevertheless, it is significant in itself that George Eliot feels compelled to use images and metaphors to explain her meanings. There is, for her, a way of knowing that is dependent upon one's grasp of metaphor and metaphorlike language. Thus, the reader of her fiction is well-advised to examine such language on two fronts: first, insofar as the literal referents can elucidate George Eliot's conceptions; second, insofar as the underlying structure of relations in such language can elucidate her sense of the structure of reality.

An example of my meaning is found in the following passage from George Eliot's Ilfracombe journal, written in July of 1856, when Eliot had just finished reviewing Ruskin's *Modern Painters* and was in the process of reviewing Riehl's *The Natural History of German Life.* In this passage she seems more concerned with theories of life than of art or society, as she and G. H. Lewes are at Ilfracombe to pursue his study of zoological specimens:

> From this end of the Capstone we have an admirable bit for a picture. In the background rises old Hillsborough jutting out far into the sea—rugged and rocky as it fronts the waves, green and accessible landward; in front of this stands Lantern Hill, a picturesque mass of green and grey surmounted by an old bit of building that looks as if it were the habitation of some mollusc that had secreted its shell from the material of the rock; and quite in the foreground, contrasting finely in colour with the rest are some lower perpendicular rocks, of dark brown tints patched here and there with vivid green. In hilly districts, where houses and clusters of houses look so tiny against the huge limbs of Mother Earth one cannot help thinking of man as a parasitic animal—an epizoon making his abode on the skin of the planetary organism. In a flat country a house or a town looks imposing—there is nothing to rival it in height, and we may imagine the earth a mere pedestal for us. But when one sees a house stuck on the side of a great hill, and still more a number of houses looking like a few barnacles clustered on the side of a great rock, we begin to think of the strong family likeness between ourselves and all other building, burrowing house-appropriating and shell-secreting animals. The difference between a man with his house and a mollusc with its shell lies in the number of steps or phenomena interposed between the fact of individual existence and the completion of the building. Whatever other advantages we may have over molluscs and insects in our habitations, it is clear that their architecture has the advantage of ours in beauty—at least considered as the architecture of the species. Look at man in the light of a shell-fish and it must be admitted that his shell is generally ugly, and it is only after a great many more "steps or phenomena" that he secretes here and there a wonderful shell in the shape of a temple or a palace. (*Letters,* 2:241–42)

What is most fascinating about this passage is its teasing implication that herein Eliot is considering not a metaphor for human activity but human activity itself; that is, she seems to find in the linguistic ganglion of animal/shell/landscape the fundamental fact of existence, not the means for understanding that fact. In addition, the shell image permits her to understand the relations between living organisms as expressions of energy and order and the fundamental conditions of time and space, for there are "steps or phenomena" that give duration to the completing of the shell, and the shell is itself a structure that exists in space.

The preceding brief analysis presumes an underlying set of relations which are a fundamental part of George Eliot's meaning in describing man as a "building, burrowing house-appropriating and shell-secreting" animal. These relations seem to define man's proper place in the natural order, insofar as man is indeed a species of animal. Yet the more metaphoric description of man as a "secreter" of buildings can easily come in conflict with Eliot's other "natural" language of seeds and organic growth. Eliot herself perceived the potential confusion such linguistic shifts could cause in the realms of thought and of action. In *The Mill on the Floss* her narrator examines that conflict in relation to the mental growth of Tom Tulliver:

> Whence Mr. Stelling concluded that Tom's brain, being peculiarly impervious to etymology and demonstrations, was peculiarly in need of being ploughed and harrowed by these patent implements: . . . I only know it turned out as uncomfortably for Tom Tulliver as if he had been plied with cheese in order to remedy a gastric weakness which prevented him from digesting it. It is astonishing what a different result one gets by changing the metaphor! Once call the brain an intellectual stomach, and one's ingenious conception of the classics and geometry as ploughs and harrows seems to settle nothing. (Bk. 2, ch. 1, p. 124)

I hope that a careful examination of these metaphors in George Eliot's novels will "settle" something: the relations among the various metaphors, especially the "natural" ones, and the relationship between those metaphors and the world to which they refer, should reveal a kind of structure for her fiction.

A quotation from William Blake, because he is himself a master of metaphor and because his work is the most pervasive and absolute presentation of the world as imaginatively centered, can serve as a keynote for the extended argument to come. Although George Eliot had her reservations about Blake's own mind, her sympathy with the viewpoints of such other Romantic poets as Coleridge and Wordsworth, as well as her astute awareness that the crucial issue for the nineteenth-century thinker was the relationship between mind and world, make Blake a useful touchstone by which to emphasize the more imaginative centers in her own work. Thus, in *The Marriage of Heaven and Hell,* where Blake is pursuing the very issues of order and energy with which I began, the following description of life occurs:

> Thus one portion of being is the Prolific, the other the Devouring: to the Devourer it seems as if the producer was in his chains; but it is not so, he only takes portions of existence and fancies that the whole.

> But the Prolific would cease to be Prolific unless the Devourer, as a sea, recieved [sic] the excess of his delights.[6]

Like the opposed metaphors of stomach and field which so confuse the issue of Tom Tulliver's education, Blake's "Prolific" and "Devourer" represent two contrary conceptions of human existence and of the natural order. According to the "Prolific" (and implied by Eliot's landscape image), man produces things, as a plant bears fruit. According to the "Devourer" (and likewise implied by Eliot's stomach image), man devours, as an animal eats that fruit. Thus, although both metaphors assert the "natural" character of man's existence, they entail opposed viewpoints and opposed philosophies of action.

In addition, we can find beneath these two sets of images a more abstract relationship, which is not unlike the relationship between mollusc and shell or seed and shell. Each depends upon the conception of *container* and *contained,* and these last two terms can enable us to extend our understanding of George Eliot's language to other images and metaphors that share that relationship. The importance of this conception to her work is evident in two significant passages from her last novel, *Daniel Deronda:*

> What [Deronda] most longed for was either some external event, or some inward light, that would urge him into a definite line of action, and compress his wandering energy. . . . [A]nd he dreaded, as if it were a dwelling-place of lost souls, that dead anatomy of culture which turns the universe into a mere ceaseless answer to queries, and knows not everything, but everything else about everything—as if one should be ignorant of nothing concerning the scent of violets except the scent itself for which one had no nostril. But how and whence was the needed event to come?—the influence that would justify partiality, and make him what he longed to be yet was unable to make himself—an organic part of social life, instead of roaming in it like a yearning disembodied spirit, stirred with a vague social passion, but without fixed local habitation to render fellowship real? . . . It is one thing to see your road, another to cut it. . . . He wanted some way of keeping emotion and its progeny of sentiments—which make the savours of life—substantial and strong in the face of a reflectiveness that threatened to nullify all differences. To pound the objects of sentiment into small dust, yet keep sentiment alive and active, was something like the famous recipe for making cannon—to first take a round hole and then enclose it with iron; whatever you do keeping fast hold on your round hole. (Ch. 32, p. 272)

> Deronda, having looked enough at the German translation of the Hebrew in the book before him to know that he was chiefly hearing Psalms and Old Testament passages or phrases, gave himself up to that strongest effect of chanted liturgies which is independent of detailed verbal meaning—like the effect of an Allegri's *Miserere* or a Palestrina's *Magnificat*. The most powerful movement of feeling with a liturgy is the prayer which seeks for nothing special, but is a yearning to escape from the limitations of our own weakness and an invocation of all Good to enter and abide with us; or else a self-oblivious lifting up of gladness, a *Gloria in excelsis* that such Good exists; both the yearning and the exultation gathering their utmost force from the sense of communion in a form which has expressed them both, for long generations of struggling fellow-men. (Ch. 32, p. 274)

The first passage shifts repeatedly between terms of external extension and terms of internal containment. Thus, Deronda desires a "line" of action, and the effect of taking that line is to be the "compression" of his energies. In addition, the passage draws upon the language of animals and plants in the references to anatomy and violets; both references rely upon the distinction between flatness and rotundity—scent being an invisible effect dependent upon the presence of circumambient air. Equally, Deronda desires both movement and stability, for he speaks—or thinks—in terms of habitations and of roads. Finally, and most importantly, the narrator herself offers a bit of humor regarding his dilemma in the anecdote of the cannon, in which enclosures depend for their success upon centers that are more than empty holes.

The second passage, less clearly metaphoric, justifies quotation, as it speaks of the alternate energies that correspond to the alternate spaces I have discussed. The yearning to escape and the yearning to be possessed, which are expressed here for Eliot in a literal church liturgy, constitute man's doubled condition. Both may be "selfish" in the sense that their center or starting point is the self. Yet Deronda's response is a giving up of self aided by two things: the musicality of the chants and the sense of order which both the chants and their history provide. Indeed, music is a crucial metaphor for examining George Eliot's sense of mind and world. A detailed discussion of these interrelated sets of metaphoric language and the conceptions they reveal can lead to other, larger fictional units of Eliot's novels. How do those containers of meaning—conventions of plot, perspective, point of view—relate to the energies they "contain"—humor, pathos? Can the structure (internal and external) and connotations of such pervasive metaphors accurately explain those relations as well?

2

THE LANGUAGE OF NATURE PART 1: PRODUCTION AND CONSUMPTION

> Mr. Casson's person was by no means of that common type which can be allowed to pass without description. On a front view it appeared to consist principally of two spheres, bearing about the same relation to each other as the earth and the moon: that is to say, the lower sphere might be said, at a rough guess, to be thirteen times larger than the upper, which naturally performed the function of a mere satellite and tributary. (*Adam Bede,* ch. 1, p. 13)

GEORGE ELIOT'S HUMOR has been the source of both praise and blame. For some readers, the comedy of her low characters is one of her best achievements as a novelist. For others, the heavy-handed sarcasm of her style, especially her use of circumlocutions to poke fun at base and obvious self-interest, is a defect deriving from her translating days. Yet Eliot herself felt the connection between prose fiction and humor to be fundamental. In her first effort at fiction it was her entertaining dialogue in the Cross Farm scene which struck George Lewes as the final prognostication of her success at novel-writing (*Letters,* 2:408). When she explained to her publisher John Blackwood the origin of *Silas Marner,* she, too, connected the genre and the mode: "I have felt all through as if [*Silas Marner*] would have lent itself best to metrical rather than prose fiction, especially in all that relates to the psychology of Silas; except that, under that treatment, there could not be an equal play of humour" (*Letters,* 3:382).

Assuming, then, a connection between humor and prose fiction, an examination of the structure and the subject matter of the joke about Mr. Casson will serve to begin a discussion of natural language as a source of both energy and order in George Eliot's novels. The structure of the anecdote seems obvious: the correspondence between body and planet is comic by reason of the incongruity of size, size being the point of the joke; thus, analogy—a technique long considered fundamental to Eliot's art[1]—results in humor because of the unlikeness of the objects of comparison. Yet the real humor of the passage is generated by a similarity on another level, which appears only because of the originally incongruous yoking: having compared Mr. Casson and the earth in terms of size or space, the narrator then sees a similarity in function or meaning, in that the smaller moon/head is a mere satellite of the larger planet/body. What had begun as an external comparison becomes an internal one—one that causes the reader to switch from viewing Mr. Casson in geographic terms to viewing him in appetitive terms, for it is clear that the second level of irony depends upon seeing that Mr. Casson's brain is ruled by his stomach.

There is nothing startlingly new about making use of externals to characterize internals, as this passage does. The very use of the body/cosmos analogy is sufficiently traditional in literature and philosophy to make this bit of wordplay about microcosm and macrocosm appear somewhat trite. Indeed, as long as we remain in that realm—the realm of words—we have no real problem understanding Eliot's intent. The difficulty comes for the literal-minded, who must wonder how man can be both a universe in himself and part of another universe. Man cannot simultaneously contain and be contained with regard to the same external object; further, in having to choose one or the other relationship, the literal-minded reader must choose between two attendant world views and moralities. According to the one, man is a whole, a center from which the rest of the world takes meaning; according to the other, man is a part, an element in a larger system, which determines his nature and function.

This is not the only instance of Eliot's use of wordplay to explore the relationship between inner and outer nature. In the following passage from "Janet's Repentance," one of the stories in *Scenes of Clerical Life,* she hints at alternative possibilities in the single term *consume:*

> The draper [Mr. Dunn] began to look forward to his next stock-taking with an anxiety which was but slightly mitigated by the parallel his wife suggested between his own case and that of Shadrach, Meshech, and Abednego, who were thrust into a burning fiery furnace. For, as he observed to her the next morning, . . . whereas their deliverance consisted in the fact that their linen and woollen goods were not consumed, his own deliverance lay in precisely the opposite result. (Ch. 10, p. 317)

This bit of humor begins in a comparison, as does the Casson passage; it is developed by the discrepancy, not in size but in significance, between the unmentioned burning of the martyrs and the stated burning of their clothes. Next, the very inappropriateness of the comparison generates further irony, for Dunn perceives a different meaning for *consume* than that of the Biblical tale: he intends *use* by the word, whereas the Bible presumes *destruction*. Finally, the relationship between the term *consume* and Eliot's other images and metaphors returns us to the question of internals and externals. *Consume* is a term associated with the language of eating and drinking (internalizing processes), yet in this passage it describes what happens to clothing, which is the external covering for the body.

The essential structure of such wordplay, then, is straightforward enough; but just as George Eliot is led by her initial insight concerning Mr. Casson's appearance to other insights generated by that appearance, the reader can be led from the jokes concerning planets, stomachs, and consumption to the implications of these terms themselves. Indeed, such terms are not simply the matter of infrequent humor but also the substance of many of Eliot's most serious insights concerning human nature. She uses the language of physical landscape and of animal appetite on both the literal and the metaphoric level to express the relationship between people and the world they "inhabit" (although the word itself implies only one of the two sorts of order possible). She even constructs an entire story—"Brother Jacob"—around one of those kinds of language. Before examining the results of that construction in "Brother Jacob," however, several distinctions between the use of the language of internal appetite and the other "natural" images of external landscape should be made.

Diction that refers to aspects of landscape or of appetite designates physical reality in the broad sense, so that when George Eliot uses terms from the natural world in order to define certain systems of order or natural laws, the implications of the language of landscape and the language of animals ought to be essentially similar. There are, however, two sorts of image included in the category "landscape": terms of visual/spatial reference, such as *mountains, seas, heights,* and *depths;* and terms of temporal/organic reference, such as *seeds, plants, flowers,* and *harvests.* Since the former have a more intimate connection with another group of images in Eliot's fiction—metaphors of pictorial or architectural significance—I wish to postpone their investigation until those too can be examined. Of primary concern here are the implications of examining mankind either through the language of plants, as in the description of Mr. Stelling's efforts to "cultivate" Tom Tulliver's mind with the ploughs and harrows of Latin and Greek, or through the language of animals, as in the narrator's defense of Tom's failure through the analogy of cheese and the stomach (see Chapter 1).

Considered collectively, botanical forms organize themselves easily accordingly to phylum and order and so fulfill the same artistic function as some animal images, namely, to denote certain specific qualities in Eliot's characters. There are many examples of this use in *Scenes of Clerical Life:* in "Amos Barton," Mr. Ely is a sly dog, and Bridmain is an elephant; in "Mr. Gilfil's Love-Story," Tina is a monkey; Janet Dempster, in "Janet's Repentance," is a tall Arum lily. Further, this sort of primitive iconography quickly compounds itself into a system or hierarchy that permits value judgments and, at the same time, implies the natural order that justifies those judgments. Thus, I presume, it is better to be a monkey than an elephant, and better to be an elephant than a fish. If we extend the hierarchy, not upward—where the rough "animals" of Bartle Massey's school try to become human (*Adam Bede,* ch. 21, p. 200)—but downward, into the plant kingdom, there is apposite humor in the fact that Rosamond Vincy was the flower of Mrs. Lemon's school (*Middlemarch,* ch. 11, p. 71).

Eliot's intentions extend beyond such allegorical correspondences, however. As her wordplay regarding Mr. Casson does, she moves from static external forms to dynamic internal functions. The natural order is not simply a system but also a process. For the landscape world, that process is usually termed *organic.* By this term a clear series of events is implied. In the first place, the seed or plant is nourished by those things that nature provides freely and that appear to be inexhaustible (if not always abundantly supplied): earth, sunlight, water. Destruction of the plant, when it does occur, is the result of forces outside the plant, as in the passage in which Eliot explains the oddities in Mr. Gilfil's nature through the image of the misshapen tree: "If you lop off their finest branches, into which they were pouring their young life-juice, the wounds will be healed over with some rough boss" ("Mr. Gilfil's Love-Story," "Epilogue," p. 244). Further, the relationship between the organization of the plant and the production of its fruit is fixed by the plant's very identity, so that one may tell the quality of the tree by that fruit, as Mr. Lyon explains in *Felix Holt the Radical* (ch. 5, p. 69).

Even where Eliot's characters are not plants but the sowers of plants, this same process is presumed. In a passage from "Janet's Repentance," which could as easily derive from any of the later novels, her conception of the organic natural process is apparent:

> [Mrs. Raynor] tried to have hope and trust, though it was hard to believe that the future would be anything else than the harvest of the seed that was being sown before her eyes. But always there is seed being sown silently and unseen, and everywhere there come sweet flowers without our foresight or labour. We reap what we sow, but Nature has love over and above that justice, and gives us shadow and blossom and fruit that spring from no planting of ours. (Ch. 5, p. 291)

In other words, the order of nature created by its organic energies is determined by the forward direction of time, the irreversibility of the process from birth through growth to maturity and then decay. That process is both the force of life itself and the order of that life. External conditions can alter or halt the progression, but they cannot reverse it. Even when we consider evolution as the larger organic process that determines Eliot's natural world, the generalization "ontogeny recapitulates phylogeny" implies its own obverse: phylogeny is ontogeny writ large.[2] This seems to be the case whether it is the individual, an aspect of the individual, or the larger community that is characterized as a plant:

> Why should they not take [Tina] to England, and bring her up there? . . . Besides, it would be a Christian work to train this little Papist into a good Protestant, and graft as much English fruit as possible on the Italian stem. ("Mr. Gilfil's Love-Story," ch. 3, pp. 151–52)

> [Said Dinah,] "But I'm not free to leave Snowfield, where I was first planted, and have grown deep into it, like the small grass on the hill-top." (*Adam Bede,* ch. 8, p. 77)

> Mrs. Tulliver was what is called a good-tempered person—never cried, when she was a baby, on any slighter ground than hunger and pins; and from the cradle upwards had been healthy, fair, plump, and dull-witted; in short, the flower of her family for beauty and amiability. (*The Mill on the Floss,* bk. 1, ch. 2, p. 13)

> Often the soul is ripened into fuller goodness while age has spread an ugly film, so that mere glances can never divine the preciousness of the fruit. But the years have not been so cruel to Nancy. (*Silas Marner,* ch. 16, p. 195)

> Since that Easter a great change had come over the prospects of

> Florence; and as in the tree that bears a myriad of blossoms, each single bud with its fruit is dependent on the primary circulation of the sap, so the fortunes of Tito and Romola were dependent on certain grand political and social conditions which made an epoch in the history of Italy. (*Romola,* ch. 21, vol. 1, p. 313)

> [Rufus uttered] "When the servant of God stands up to deliver his message, do you lay your souls beneath the Word as you set out your plants beneath the falling rain?" (*Felix Holt the Radical,* ch. 4, p. 54)

> [Dorothea] could only cry in loud whispers, between her sobs, after her lost belief which she had planted and kept alive from a very little seed since the days in Rome— . . . after her sweet dim perspective of hope, that along some pathway they should meet with unchanged recognition and take up the backward years as a yesterday. (*Middlemarch,* ch. 80, p. 576)

> [Mrs. Davilow's] delicate eyelids were pink, as if she had been crying half the night; and no one was surprised that, splendid as the match was, she should feel the parting from a daughter who was the flower of her children and of her own life. (*Daniel Deronda,* ch. 31, p. 263)

In these cases, and in the many similar ones, the single image of the plant can imply a whole fictional structure governed by forward directionality in its plot as well as the sympathy or pathos that can accompany that plot when the emphasis is on its inevitably mortal conclusion.

The term *pathos* introduces the first and most obvious distinction between Eliot's use of plant imagery and of animal imagery. Barbara Hardy has noted that the plant image tends to be poignant or pathetic, as it is in the characterizations of the female victims in the novels, Tina Sarti's portrayal being the first and most blatant example of this.[3] Animal images, on the other hand, are often ironic. Their usage derives from the tradition of Aesop and Chaucer. Equally a part of this sort of satire are the many real animals in her fiction whose thoughts and behavior provide a mocking commentary upon their more pretentious yet less wise owners; for example, Jet, the spaniel, is one of the first to suspect the Countess Czerlaski in "Amos Barton" (ch. 3, p. 73). When used in this way, animal imagery asserts simultaneously the reality of man's physical nature and the traditional literary evaluation of that nature. As George Clark says regarding the Aesopic tradition, animals can be "figures of man's corruption" that reveal a harsh and misanthropic point of view.[4]

In addition to the presence of references to Aesopic fables in George Eliot's fiction, there are also passages that draw upon another literary tradition regarding the creatures of the natural order. Although the point of view in Aesop is primarily ironic, the other tradition—that of Greek myth—expresses a sense of man's relation to nature in more dignified, even tragic terms. In virtually every one of Eliot's novels, mention is made of beings who are part animal or plant and part something else. From the ironic remark in *Adam Bede* about the unfair reputation enjoyed by Centaurs in history (ch. 12, p. 110) to the statue of Silenus that graces the hall of Transome Court in *Felix Holt the Radical* (ch. 43, p. 430), Eliot has found such "unrealistic" creatures to be expressive of man's mixed nature. In two significant passages, that mixed nature constitutes an imprisonment that does not allow a distinction between the entrapped self and the self that entraps:

> What was it, [Philip] wondered, that made Maggie's dark eyes remind him of the stories about princesses being turned into animals? ...... I think it was that her eyes were full of unsatisfied intelligence, and unsatisfied, beseeching affection. (*The Mill on the Floss,* bk. 2, ch. 5, p. 158)

> The poets have told us of a dolorous enchanted forest in the under world. The thorn-bushes there, and the thick-barked stems, have human histories hidden in them; the power of unuttered cries dwells in the passionless-seeming branches, and the red warm blood is darkly feeding the quivering nerves of a sleepless memory that watches through all dreams. These things are a parable. (*Felix Holt the Radical,* "Introduction," pp. 9–10)

These two passages are united by the nature of the energy that links inner and outer. In the first, Maggie is "unsatisfied," whereas the more generalized self of the second passage (Mrs. Transome is the real character being explained through the parable) is "fed" by warm red blood. Indeed, there are many possibilities for interpretation in the latter passage, for George Eliot conflates the language of plant (bush, branch, stem), animal (blood, nerve), and human psyche (passion, memory, dream) in an attempt to make an unseen and silent process visible and audible. The energy or power behind those processes is the converse of the hunger Maggie feels, for it is the need to express, to get what is inside out, a need whose satisfaction is nevertheless prevented by the self's own repression. Such passages as these return us to the central issue of the precise relationship between inside and outside which Eliot explores elsewhere through the language of seed and shell.

Apropos of taking such language literally, it is important to realize that George Eliot did indeed conceive of humanity as a species of animal. At the very time she was composing *The Mill on the Floss* and *Silas Marner* (novels intimately concerned with man's place in the natural order), she and George Lewes were enjoying the brisk sales of his *Physiology of Common Life,* in which Lewes examined the animal functions of man.[5] Further, in her revisions of Lewes's *Problems of Life and Mind* toward the end of her life she made explicit the importance in human beings of the animal urges for food and reproduction of the species.[6] Given these intellectual assertions, the language of animals—unlike the language of plants—seems in her novels to have a validity both literary and literal. The structural similarity between the organic processes of plants and the reproductive processes of animals appears to validate the use of organicism to explain human activity, for the importance of reproduction as a means of determining plot in her novels is obvious; yet the dominance of the appetite for food as an animal characteristic in her fiction results in a major shift in implication.

A passage from *The Mill on the Floss*—a novel otherwise patently concerned with the reproductive and genetic implications of man's animal nature—suggests what this shift in implication entails. George Eliot's explanation of the relationship between Wakem and Mr. Tulliver offers simultaneously the metaphor of appetite and the other kind of natural language that I have termed the language of landscape:

> To suppose that Wakem had the same sort of inveterate hatred towards Tulliver, that Tulliver had towards him, would be like supposing that a pike and a roach can look at each other from a similar point of view. The roach necessarily abhors the mode in which the pike gets his living, and the pike is likely to think nothing further even of the most indignant roach than that he is excellent good eating; it could only be when the roach choked him that the pike could entertain a strong personal animosity.... "Wakem was Wakem;" that is to say, a man who always knew the stepping-stones that would carry him through very muddy bits of practice. A man who had made a large fortune, had a handsome house among the trees at Tofton, and decidedly the finest stock of port-wine in the neighbourhood of St. Ogg's, was likely to feel himself on a level with public opinion.... [W]hy should [Wakem] hate [Tulliver]—that pitiable, furious bull entangled in the meshes of a net? (Bk. 3, ch. 7, p. 222)

The metaphoric shifts in the above passage make quite clear the crucial issues concerning the language of nature and the nature of man. At first the relationship between self and other is seen to be one of eater and eaten, with the comic possibility that one thinks as one eats. Soon, however, Wakem is not a devourer but a traveler, one who not only dehumanizes but deanimates those around him into so many stepping-stones. He has traveled to a house among trees within which we return to the language of consumption through the stock of port-wine. Further, what Wakem can offer to drink returns him again to the language of landscape, for the handsomeness of his house and the fineness of his wine put him "on a level" with public opinion in St. Ogg's. Finally, the narrator conflates animality and spatiality in the metaphor of the poor miller as a potent bull caught in his own labyrinthine net.

The language of animals as represented here is a language of appetite which describes not an organic or developmental relationship between self and other—as the language of plants does—but a repetitive and consumptive one. One result of this difference is that the reader's sympathies are not so clearly with the beast being nourished in this metaphor as they are with the plant in the other metaphor. For example, although Maggie Tulliver is generally a sympathetic character, the limitless appetite for delight which she manifests in *The Mill on the Floss* can reasonably give rise to interpretations of her character as vampire or destroyer.[7] Another difference between the two languages is that the narrative structure generated by the animal metaphor is less progressive than cyclical. The best way to explain what can happen in fiction as a result is to examine the little-discussed story "Brother Jacob," in which humanity is conceived of as a species of animal ruled by its stomach.

"Brother Jacob" appears to be a simple fable, told with obvious sarcasm, about the pretentions of one David Faux to a position in the world that is "easy to the flesh and flattering to the spirit" (p. 310). He is George Eliot's conventional egoist, imagining the world as "an udder to feed [his] supreme sel[f]" (*Middlemarch*, ch. 21, p. 156). Written in 1860—when George Eliot had just finished *The Mill on the Floss* and was preparing to write *Silas Marner*—David's history depends for its development upon the nature of parent/child relationships, the embarrassments of siblings, the primitive animal needs of humans, and the symbolic possibilities of gold. Yet it is not David who is the titular hero of the story, but Jacob, "a very healthy and well-developed idiot, who consume[s] a dumpling about eight inches in diameter every day" (p. 311). Indeed, although David provides the moral example that is usually associated with George Eliot's egoists, it is not he, who (in William Blake's terms, from *The Marriage of Heaven and Hell*) *produces* candies and confections, but his idiot brother who *devours* all the food that is available while threatening his "clever" brother with a pitchfork. This doubling of characters, with their alternative relationships to each other and the world as defined by their relationships to food, is a part of that repetitive or cyclic structure generated by the appetitive metaphor. Before examining that structure in detail, let me summarize the plot of this generally neglected short story.

David, the youngest son of hardworking parents, discovers the tedium of apprenticeship to a confectioner and decides to abscond with his mother's dowry to the new world, where he expects to become a brilliantly successful and wealthy man with relatively little effort. He hopes to steal the money and yet retain his reputation (and hence his future patrimony) by delaying his departure until some time after the money (carefully hidden away) has been stolen. His theft is complicated by the appearance of his idiot brother at the moment when he is burying the guineas, and he is forced to trick Jacob and leave suddenly in order to get away at all. When the story resumes he has returned to England, taken up an alias, and attempted to ingratiate himself with the best people of his new place of residence through a successful confectionery business, clever flattery of others, and prevarication about his own past. He is exposed once again by Jacob, who finds his way to David's store and represents the truth of his background at the very moment when David has convinced the best family in Grimworth to allow him to marry their daughter Penny. David loses his reputation, his girl, and his business, thus becoming "an admirable instance of the unexpected forms in which the great Nemesis hides herself" (p. 328).

The first sentence announces the general moral that this specific fable is to exemplify: "*Among the many fatalities attending the bloom of young desire,* that of blindly taking to the confectionery line has not, perhaps, been sufficiently considered" (p. 310, emphasis mine). David Faux, because of a "sweet tooth," feels that by becoming a candy-maker he can perpetually satisfy his own desires. His first lesson is that desires can alter, for "there is satiety for the human stomach even in a paradise of . . . sugared almonds"; further, "the tedium of life can reach a pitch where plum-buns at discretion cease to offer the slightest enticement" (p. 310). Because this fact is made clear in the first pages, both through narrative statement and through the turn of the plot in which David becomes dissatisfied in his apprenticeship, it appears that there is more to George Eliot's fable than this.

One could, of course, interpret the tale as an extension of individual greed and disillusionment to society at large, since the latter portion of the story concerns the corruption of the town of Grimworth by an appetite, not unlike David's, for good things without labor. Thus, the satire would lie in the greedy David's hoping to succeed by making use, in others, of the very appetities he desires to satisfy in himself. The people of Grimworth are exposed as fools misled by their desire to entertain well without the necessary domestic effort. The narrator, therefore, must describe "the gradual corruption of Grimworth manners from their primitive simplicity—a melancholy task if it were not cheered by the prospect of the fine peripateia [sic] or downfall by which the progress of the corruption was ultimately checked" (p. 317). This peripeteia consists in David's exposure as a fraud whose antecedents and prior experiences are not of the exalted sort he describes. The people of Grimworth, however, even if they are exposed as gulls, find refuge in their own moral superiority, so there is no anagnorisis for David or for them: "The rector disliked the sight of a man who had imposed upon him; and all boys who could not afford to purchase, hooted 'David Faux' as they passed his shop" (p. 328).

The real reversal of the narrator's initial generalizations, however, involves David's nemesis, his brother Jacob, who, despite the opening assertion of the tale, will never feel satiety. If the story begins, then, with a conventional (at least according to accepted George Eliot criticism) assertion of the failure of early aspirations and desires, it depends for its denouement upon an opposing view more in tune with that expressed through Carlyle's bootblack, whose desires are infinite. Brother Jacob in his own right replaces David as the representative of humanity, as its lowest common denominator. Jacob is an "idiot," without superior mental power (however much that power is mocked in the low cunning of his younger brother); he is Blake's devourer, who only loosens his grasp on his newly rediscovered brother when hunger prompts him "to seize a large raised pie" (p. 325). David is thus properly exposed by a brother whose appetite is more absolute than his own. The character of Jacob even suggests Eliot's own beliefs about the limits of the ability of education to divest human beings of their egoism. Further, David's recognition of the fact of "brother" is a necessary part of his exposure. That a man can himself be not only a devourer but also a victim of other devourers brings about a recognition of the painful (recall the pitchfork) otherness of the world.

The matter of brotherhood raises the further issue of family (i.e., biological) relations, which are a necessary part of the plot and therefore a source of insight about George Eliot's intentions. David begins by desiring not a part but the whole of his mother's legacy, a possible extension of the maternal capacity to provide food. He perceives his right to her possessions as natural and even "legal": "It is not robbery to take property belonging to your mother: she doesn't prosecute you" (p. 311). Indeed, not only does she not prosecute, but she and David's father are the only really admirable characters in the story—or at least the only characters who escape the general sarcasm. Mother love dominates in David's final exposure, for his mother's love results in her advertisement for David to claim his patrimony as well as in her search for the lost Jacob, just when David had hoped to keep the fact of his brotherhood a secret.

David's mother's guineas play an important role in the story in other ways. Like Silas's gold, they are capable of magical transformations and are meant to represent both the negative materialism of the unreformed egoist and the "golden gold" of human love given freely and untainted by selfishness or harsh judgments. In a crucial scene in which David must confront the primitive yet accurate perceptions of Brother Jacob, who can readily recognize his mother's "zinnies," David acts out a drama that reveals his fundamental desire and reintroduces the language of nature and food. He treats the money as seed, a metaphor apparent in Jacob's clutch upon them "as if they had been so many pebbles . . . in an attitude which promised to scatter them like seed over a distant bramble" (p. 313). David places the guineas in the ground, only to appear to unearth them as lozenges, a food that delights Jacob. In reality, the guineas are to be David's "seed money," and he is finally sufficiently confident of his powers for success that he is willing to take the guineas now and forego his later patrimony. His expectation is that "such a striking young man" will manage to win the affections of a princess of the West Indies who will shower him with presents beforehand, "after which, he needn't marry her unless he liked" (p. 314).

David is defeated in his trickery first by the degree of attraction that lozenges have for his hungry brother. Further, he is defeated by time, for he hopes to convince Jacob that a day must pass before the noisy but inedible guineas will turn into lozenges. David knows that Jacob's grasp of time is precarious (however strong his grasp of food and pitchforks may be) and that he might in his impatience unearth the guineas before David can abscond with them—as indeed he does. Finally, David draws a conclusion about the cause of his difficulties which underscores the nature of maternal legacies: "David had made up his mind not to steal any more, even from people who were fond of him: it was an unpleasant way of making your fortune in a world where you were likely to be surprised in the act by brothers" (p. 314). This particular brother, when he so surprises David on the following day, is a reminder of human animality; he is first a bull, then a wasp at a sugar-basin, and last an affectionate boa constrictor (p. 315). As the last metaphor makes clear, fondness is David's most threatening obstacle. Only Jacob's animal capacity for drink finally brings about the stupor that permits David to escape with his guineas.

This first chapter in David's experiences ends with a statement that summarizes his education in morality thus far; it also provides the clue to his later pseudonym and hints at the fundamental problem of fondness, which will again prevent his worldly success. Equally important, the assumptions behind his thought processes suggest the ambiguities of giving and receiving:

> He would never steal any more, but there would be no need; he would show himself so deserving, that people would make him presents *freely*. He must give up the notion of his father's legacy; but it was not likely he would ever want that trifle; and even if he did—why, it was a compensation to think that in being forever divided from his family he was divided from Jacob, more terrible than Gorgon or Demogorgon to David's timid green eyes. (P. 315, emphasis mine)

In the second stage of the story, David has returned as another person, one who will, he hopes, be given to "freely" by those who admire him. Again, however, David first appears not as a receiver but as a provider:

> It certainly made a blaze of light and color, almost as if a rainbow had suddenly descended into the market-place. . . . On one side there were the variegated tints of colored and marbled meats, set off by bright green leaves, the pale brown of glazed pies, the rich tones of sauces and bottled fruits enclosed in their veil of glass—altogether a sight to bring tears into the eyes of a Dutch painter; and on the other there was a predominance of the more delicate hues of pink, and white, and yellow, and buff, in the abundant lozenges, candies, sweet biscuits and icings, which to the eyes of a bilious person might easily have been blended into a faëry landscape in Turner's latest style. (P. 316)

The association of food and beauty continues when the narrator declares that David must visit the Palfrey kitchens in order to learn how his intended fiancée's mother makes her brawn, "[k]nowledge of this kind [being] like Titian's coloring, difficult to communicate" (p. 321). Even the proposed object of David's affection, Penny herself, has a name that connotes money. She also has a beauty that is like "a fresh whiteheart cherry going to be bitten off the stem" by the lipless mouth of David Faux, alias Edward Freely (p. 325). This building up of valuative terms has the usual ironic effect, for it reveals the pretensions of the characters and the baseness of their desires and at the same time hints of such baseness beneath even the most exalted of goals and ideals, such as beauty and love.

The scene of Jacob's reappearance is as crucial to David's final exposure as the burial of the guineas was to his earlier. Having abandoned his real home and family, David hopes to flourish on his own merits; yet he must nevertheless possess some home and family in order to do so. He thus invents relatives and creates his own habitat in the back of his shop. It is here that Mr. Palfrey is first brought to understand that David has a loving uncle in Jamaica, while another false uncle, an admiral, looks down from a portrait on the back parlor wall; and it is when the Palfrey family is grouped around the table in this very parlor, preparing amid muffins and buttered buns to discuss furnishings for the soon-to-be-married couple, that Jacob appears once again, like a heavy animal about to shatter the world that David has constructed. Jacob's reality as a hungry and affectionate idiot brother destroys David's future hopes and present business. Again, in the language of money, David's falseness proves what the real connection between self, self-image, and world is: "It is possible to pass a great many bad half-pennies and bad half-crowns, but I believe there has no instance been known of passing a half-penny or a half-crown as a sovereign" (p. 323). Had David remembered this lesson from his days in the Indies ("And so he had to fall back on the genuine value there was in him—to be content to pass as a good half-penny, or, to speak more accurately, as a good confectioner," p. 323), he might not have suffered the peripeteia this story recounts.

It is fortuitous that "Brother Jacob" incorporates gold into its organic and appetitive symbolism, for the question of value complicates any discussion of the physical nature of man. When the guineas in the story are seen as both seed and food, they imply the importance of production and consumption for human life. Even Mr. and Mrs. Faux accept the necessity of providing their children with material gold as a part of their patrimony; the more intangible portion of that patrimony—love and certain values—is the "gold" that David hopes to do without. In addition, he seems singularly without that other appetite that George Eliot so often incorporated into her conception of wedded love: sexual desire. In the West Indies and in Grimworth, David sees women as a means to an economic end rather than as a good in themselves, so there is particular irony in his being Penny's lipless devourer. In fact, although most readers find "Brother Jacob" to be strident satire, the word *irony* is indeed appropriate for the story. Eliot does not intend simply to embarrass us with our animal natures; she sees them as both our starting point and our limit. Human beings are animals as half-pennies are half-pennies; there can be no real success in trying to pass either off as something more exalted. The real issue of concern is to distinguish the "bad" ones from the true.

This can serve as a very broad generalization about George Eliot's use of the language of animals in her other fiction, when that use is connected with the issues of sustenance, nourishment, and consumption. As she herself says in "Amos Barton," her first story, "in bucolic society five-and-twenty years ago, the human animal of the male sex was understood to be perpetually athirst, and 'something to drink' was as necessary a 'condition of thought' as Time and Space" (ch. 1, p. 49). It is not simply twenty-five years before nor in bucolic society alone that such could be held to be the case. Animal need becomes for Eliot the common term linking most aspects of her art.[8]

The reality of appetite is clear enough in "Amos Barton." When her narrator presents the "conditions" of her story or problem, the matter of material needs is prominent: "Let him have a parish large enough to create an external necessity for abundant shoe-leather, and an internal necessity for abundant beef and mutton, as well as poor enough to require frequent priestly consolation in the shape of shillings and sixpences; . . . This was the problem presented by the position of the Rev. Amos Barton" (ch. 1, p. 44). In fact, most of the events in the story turn on food: Barton is discussed over tea at Mrs. Patten's; Amos lectures his charges at the College on "unleavened bread"; the clergymen in the area meet to discuss theological matters over dinner; Milly's best dress is ruined by the spilling of the gravy-tureen; the Countess leaves her brother, having quarreled with "her chicken and tart"; and Amos must finally leave Shepperton to go "where there's no good victuals to be had" (ch. 1, pp. 45–51; ch. 2, p. 63; ch. 6, pp. 91–97; ch. 3, p. 71; ch. 7, p. 98; ch. 10, p. 113). Obviously enough, those characters in the story who provide food (most notably the mother figure Milly Barton) are the more valued; even the metaphorical "sauce" that Nanny finally delivers to the Countess in order to reveal to her the true situation at the parsonage is productive, for the Countess does leave as a result of it (ch. 7, p. 104).

In the next stories of *Scenes of Clerical Life,* the metaphoric uses of such language tend to dominate. Tina Sarti finds Anthony's love-making a poison that seemed sweet while she drank it ("Mr. Gilfil's Love-Story," ch. 10, p. 194); Janet's moments of respite in her misery seem to her mother to be like "water-drops that visit the parched lips in the desert [which] bear with them only the keen imagination of thirst" ("Janet's Repentance," ch. 5, p. 290). It is in "Janet's Repentance" that the full irony of man's appetites becomes clear. In a bit of satire that has obvious similarities to Eliot's own "Brother Jacob," the Dempsters try to belittle Mr. Tryan by exposing the "animal" qualities and selfish egoism they presume lie behind his piety and efforts at spiritual reform. Their fake play-bill begins as follows:

GRAND ENTERTAINMENT!!!
To be given at Milby on Sunday evening next, by the
FAMOUS COMEDIAN, TRY-IT-ON!
And his first-rate company, including not only an
UNPARALLELED CAST FOR COMEDY!
But a Large Collection of *reclaimed and converted Animals:*
Among the rest
A Bear, who used to *dance!*
A Parrot, once given to *swearing!!*
A Polygamous Pig!!!
and
A Monkey who used to *catch fleas on Sunday!!!!*
Together with a
Pair of *regenerated* LINNETS!
With an entirely new song, and *plumage.*
(Ch. 9, p. 314)

Mr. Tryan's true spiritual worth comes, of course, not from converting animals but from recognizing human needs. He does not try to preach to the fasting on a full stomach (ch. 11, p. 324), and he thinks of the bodies of the poor, as well as their souls (ch. 12, p. 330). In addition, of course, he recognizes those appetites for which the language of eating and drinking can only be metaphorical. Thus, he speaks of Christ having "drunk the cup of our suffering to the dregs," and he has a yearning for "those pure human joys which he had voluntarily and determinedly banished from his life—for a draught of that deep affection from which he had been cut off by a dark chasm of remorse" (ch. 18, p. 362; ch. 27, p. 408). Even here George Eliot has a tendency to combine both the appetitive and the spatial—as chasms separate the thirsty from the water.

This pattern of usage and of intention continues throughout George Eliot's novels. A merely random sampling from the many possible episodes underscores this. For instance, Dinah Morris provides both food and comfort to Lisbeth Bede after Thias's death (*Adam Bede,* ch. 10, p. 96); Hetty's trials on her journey in hope and despair are exposed through her difficulties with food as well as fear (*Adam Bede,* ch. 36-37); Maggie and Tom Tulliver share food and love in a jam puff and must undergo psychological grillings at the Tulliver dinner table (*The Mill on the Floss,* bk. 1, ch. 6, p. 41; ch. 7, pp. 60-61); Dorothea first meets Casaubon at dinner, where Celia notices that he scrapes his soup spoon (*Middlemarch,* ch. 5, p. 35); Grandcourt reveals his personality through his teasing method of feeding his dogs while tormenting Lush at the same time (*Daniel Deronda,* ch. 12, pp. 90-91); and Deronda discovers the true spiritual value of the Cohens when he sees them at dinner (ch. 34).

My intention at this point is less to examine these instances in detail than to assert their pervasiveness. The language of animals and appetite is always available to George Eliot as an expression of fact and as a means of elucidating other "facts." This is probably the fundamental distinction between the natural language of plants and organicism and that of animals and appetite. The former remains relatively fixed in its implications, so that later narratives are not necessary in order to test its adequacy per se. That is, her sense of the "organic nature of life" is sufficiently given that, although later plots must come to terms with the implications of that "organic nature," those implications are outside the process by which her fictional structures are generated. I use the terms *structure* and *generate* intentionally, because it is the lack of movement from a single instance of organic language to its implications in either the world of things or the world of words which suggests to me that the changing form of Eliot's fiction is not affected as significantly by such diction.

Her fictional structures are, however, affected by the use of animal terms and imagery, because this language can be both literal and metaphoric. For example, the mere fact that humans must eat to live makes the appearance of kitchens and dining rooms in Eliot's fiction seem no more than a part of her realism. Yet whatever aspect of that literal fact the reader chooses to focus upon, said "fact" almost never remains merely literal. Just as Celia finds in Mr. Casaubon's way of eating soup a sign of larger, more intangible drawbacks, the narrator and the reader find in other literal uses of such language the germs of further conclusions or insights. This fictional technique is apparent in a crucial chapter in Eliot's most completely integrated novel, *Middlemarch.*

Chapter 2 of *Middlemarch* resembles "Brother Jacob" in that it is dominated by the language of landscape, food, and art.[9] The yoking of the sublime and the ordinary through such language generates exactly the irony that sustains *Middlemarch* and is intended in "Brother Jacob." The chapter opens with the phrase: "'Sir Humphry Davy?' said Mr. Brooke, over the soup . . ." (p. 11). The subsequent connection between Davy, a specialist in agricultural chemistry, and Wordsworth, a great poet of nature, consists in Brooke's having dined with each. Further, the contrast between Casaubon and Sir James appears first in the difference between the "blooming" appearance of the latter (p. 12)—which triggers Dorothea's comparison of such a man with a *cochon de lait* (p. 15)—and the pallor of the former, who "feed[s] too much on the inward sources" (p. 13). Casaubon and Sir James are, like the Blakeian contraries of the prolific and the devouring, contrasted through their associations with consumption and production. Despite his failure to amount to much as one of those mere "animals with a toilette" (p. 15), Casaubon is more obviously the one who eats in the chapter, and Sir James is "made of excellent human dough" (p. 15). In fact, from his interest in new schemes to improve farming productivity to his own natural metaphor for men and women as birch-trees and palms (p. 16), Sir James is identified with the straightforwardly organic aspect of the natural order. Moreover, in the later development of the plot, it is of course Sir James who is able to produce an heir, whereas Casaubon is finally unable to produce either literal or metaphorical children.

The language of food and drink is pervasive in *Middlemarch* on both the literal and metaphoric levels. From Fred Vincy's condemned appetite for "the best of everything" (ch. 12, p. 89) to Will Ladislaw's unfed hope for a chance to be united with Dorothea (ch. 51, p. 365), virtually every character hungers or thirsts after some sort of satisfaction; Joshua Rigg's soul thirsts for the joy of a money-changing shop (ch. 53, p. 381), and Dorothea thirsts to see Will (ch. 54, p. 393). The narrator herself suggests that such need is a condition of human nature when she uses the language of eating to characterize the passions:

> Our passions do not live apart in locked chambers, but, dressed in their small wardrobe of notions, bring their provisions to a common table and mess together, feeding out of the common store according to their appetite. (Ch. 16, pp. 123–24)

Even more suggestive is the description of Mrs. Cadwallader as a tiny insect devouring other, tinier creatures:

> Whereas under a weak lens you may seem to see a creature exhibiting an active voracity into which other smaller creatures actively play as if they were so many animated tax-pennies, a stronger lens reveals to you certain tiniest hairlets which make vortices for these victims while the swallower waits passively at his receipt of custom. In this way, metaphorically speaking, a strong lens applied to Mrs. Cadwallader's match-making will show a play of minute causes producing what may be called thought and speech vortices to bring her the sort of food she needed. (Ch. 6, p. 44)

The tax-pennies of this passage echo the pennies of "Brother Jacob" and raise a subject until now unexplored: If animal need is a fact of nature, then man's social structure ought in some way to take cognizance of it. In fact, the use of the body as a metaphor for the cosmos has traditionally included the state as a part of that complex of meaning. George Eliot is most conscious of this in the novel *Felix Holt the Radical,* whose announced subject is political and social issues. Most strikingly, although Felix seems finally to be a very bad political leader, he is an excellent user of metaphor, drawing frequently, almost compulsively, upon the language of animals and appetite to characterize his own behavior and that of others. It is evident from Felix's remarks that he does not condone the definition of either individual human beings or collective groups by the "stomach-and-pocket point of view" ("Janet's Repentance," ch. 26, p. 401):

> I thank Heaven I am not a mouse to have a nose that takes note of wax or tallow. (Ch. 5, p. 61)

> If I had not seen that I was making a hog of myself very fast, and that pig-wash, even if I could have got plenty of it, was a poor sort of thing, I should never have looked life fairly in the face to see what was to be done with it. (Ch. 5, p. 64)

> "That," says my phrenologist, "is because of his large Ideality, which prevents him from finding anything perfect enough to be venerated." Of course I put my ears down and wagged my tail at that stroking. (Ch. 5, p. 69)

> As long as three-fourths of the men in this country see nothing in an election but self-interest, and nothing in self-interest but

some form of greed, one might as well try to purify the proceedings of the fishes, and say to a hungry cod-fish—"My good friend, abstain; don't goggle your eyes so, or show such a stupid gluttonous mouth, or think the little fishes are worth nothing except in relation to your own inside." (Ch. 13, p. 153)

"Let a man once throttle himself with a satin stock, and he'll get new wants and new motives. Metamorphosis will have begun at his neck-joint, and it will go on till it has changed his likings first and then his reasoning, which will follow his likings as the feet of a hungry dog follow his nose. . . . I'd sooner be Paley's fat pigeon than a demagogue all tongue and stomach, though"—here Felix changed his voice a little—"I should like well enough to be another sort of demagogue, if I could" (Ch. 5, pp. 66–67)

It is tempting to conclude that it is his very condemnation of the animal nature of man that brings about Felix's downfall. His attempts to separate his animal nature from his thinking nature (and so to deny the former) result in exactly those sorts of repressive behavior that are exhaustively exposed in the portrait of Maggie Tulliver. As George Eliot writes concerning Felix's abortive attempt to prevent mob action, "It was on this sort of influence [definite will and an energetic personality] over men whose mental state was a mere medley of appetites and confused impressions, that Felix had dared to count" (ch. 33, p. 326). Whatever his intentions, destruction of life and property is the result. If we are not to fault the construction of the novel, we must assume that Felix's effective disappearance from its action until his marriage to Esther at the conclusion is an indication that it is to this very recognition that Felix must be brought. Indeed, the last reference to animals in the novel is made by Felix, who seems to have comically accepted his animal status: "Felix, however, grumbles a little that [Esther] has made his life too easy, and that, if it were not for much walking, he should be a sleek dog" ("Epilogue," p. 487).

The general character of the language of animals and appetite, then, is obvious enough on a superficial level. As a form of order, such language permits the creation of a hierarchy of beasts/characters whose value can be known from their species; as a form of energy, such language describes the drives for satisfaction that determine action:

> [Johnson] was not going to be ruined, though Jermyn probably was: he was not a highflyer, but a mere climbing-bird, who could hold on and get his livelihood just as well if his wings were clipped a little. And, in the meantime, here was something to be gained in this Bycliffe business, which, it was not unpleasant to think, was a nut that Jermyn had intended to keep for his own particular cracking. (*Felix Holt the Radical,* Ch. 37, p. 365)

But such meanings depend upon perceiving language as more or less referential, so that its effectiveness as communication depends upon the appropriateness of the comparison, the reality of the idea behind the words.

A more subtle use of animal metaphor is such a complete transference of the terms of appetite from the physical to the psychological realm that the effect is less one of comparison than of identity. A good passage for demonstrating this is the one that describes the meeting between Grandcourt and Lydia Glasher at Gadsmere in *Daniel Deronda* (ch. 30). The interaction of mental state and social gesture in this scene is representative of George Eliot's most praised fictional style; thus, it may also show how much that style may be linked with the metaphors, not only of appetite, but also of landscape and music. As in "Brother Jacob," the fundamental dramatic tension in this chapter derives from the familial structure that is parodied in the Grandcourt-Glasher connection.

The first real mention of the terms of appetite occurs in the description of the diamonds that Grandcourt wishes to retrieve for Gwendolen:

> These particular diamonds were not mountains of light—they were mere peas and haricots for the ears, neck, and hair; but they were worth some thousands, and Grandcourt necessarily wished to have them for his wife. (P. 254)

Here, in a serious mode, is a conflation of food and value like that of the guineas and lozenges of "Brother Jacob." These diamonds—a fitting representation of the life that Gwendolen imagines herself to hunger after—are indeed without the ability to nourish.

At the same time that Lydia and Grandcourt are carrying on their battle of wills over Lydia's future, the children provide a further counterpoint to the examination of animal appetite. There is a rich bloom on the cheeks of the girls, although their mother is now emaciated; the boy, meanwhile, plays with a Noah's ark, "occasionally licking the spotted [animals] to see if the colours would hold" (p. 255). The perpetrator of this innocent, if inappropriate, consumption of exteriors is quickly banished to the garden to play with the dogs on the gravel, for it is Grandcourt who has arrived, instead of a miller with the boy's donkey. Equally literal, if not so comic, is the necessary meal which this "family" must undergo: "The hours had to go by; there was eating to be done" (p. 258). The real devouring is of a more sinister and psychological sort. In a true perversion of Blake's prolific and devouring contraries, Grandcourt discovers that the "standing banquet for his delight in dominating" which Lydia's melancholy and dependent position provided now places him in a relationship that has its "ugly obverse": "There is no quailing—even that forced on the helpless and injured—which has not an ugly obverse: the withheld sting was gathering venom" (pp. 255, 253). Indeed, although Grandcourt seems clearly the "devourer" here, he must discover the unpleasant fact that he himself is providing food for Lydia's revenge:

> And yet [Lydia] could not bear to give up a purpose which was a sweet morsel to her vindictiveness. (P. 261)

> Amidst such caressing signs of mutual fear they parted. The effect that clung and *gnawed* within Grandcourt was a sense of imperfect mastery. (P. 262, emphasis mine)

What Grandcourt has discovered is the reflexive nature of human need: that which he consumes can equally consume him, that which he imprisons can send "suckers" into his own life (p. 260). Of course, the appetite that is being anatomized here is not gustatory, but sexual, and the full implications of that animal reality will be examined later in connection with family relationships in general.

Metaphors of consumption, then, perform two distinct functions, which are simply the poles of the twined aspects of metaphor itself; one emphasizes the likeness of the objects so linked, and the other emphasizes their distinctness. Thus, in passages such as that which delineates Grandcourt's psychological needs and physical situation, there is what Wallace Stevens calls an "appositeness" of metaphor, so that "the effect of analogy is the effect of consummation."[10] As Stevens goes on to say with regard to such metaphors, "There is always an analogy between nature and the imagination, and possibly poetry is merely the strange rhetoric of that parallel: a rhetoric in which the feeling of one man is communicated to another in words of the exquisite appositeness that takes away all their verbality."[11] In other words, in reading the passage about Grandcourt and Lydia, we are not consciously aware of the essentially metaphoric quality of language because of its appositeness.

Contrarily, there are metaphors that announce their disjuncture, so that, as Walker Percy declares, their peculiar feature is "mistake"—"[their] beauty often seems proportionate to [their] wrongness or outlandishness."[12] This is perhaps why writers about language, such as Morton Bloomfield, declare that poetic language "calls attention to itself."[13] In prose fiction, George Eliot is able to "call attention" to the literary character of her language through the intransitive quality of certain metaphors,[14] through the presence of irony in her tone, and through actual discursive examination of her own terms. These manifold techniques are perhaps analogous to what Henry James used in his "Conversation," which served as a review of *Daniel Deronda,*[15] for they permit her to speak in manifold voices providing a linguistic version of her desire for multiple points of view. A final passage from *Daniel Deronda* illustrates this effect:

> "But Mr. Hans said yesterday that you thought so much of others you hardly wanted anything for yourself. He told us a wonderful story of Bouddha giving himself to the famished tigress to save her and her little ones from starving. And he said you were like Bouddha. That is what we all imagine of you."
>
> "Pray don't imagine that," said Deronda, who had lately been finding such suppositions rather exasperating. "Even if it were true that I thought so much of others, it would not follow that I had no wants for myself. When Bouddha let the tigress eat him he might have been very hungry himself."
>
> "Perhaps if he was starved he would not mind so much about being eaten," said Mab, shyly.
>
> "Please don't think that, Mab; it takes away the beauty of the action," said Mirah.
>
> "But if it were true, Mirah?" said the rational Amy, having a half-holiday from her teaching; "you always take what is beautiful as if it were true."
>
> "So it is," said Mirah, gently. "If people have thought what is the most beautiful and the best thing, it must be true. It is always there."
>
> "Now, Mirah, what *do* you mean?" said Amy.
>
> "I understand her," said Deronda, coming to the rescue. "It is a

truth in thought though it may never have been carried out in action. It lives as an idea. Is that it?" He turned to Mirah, who was listening with a blind look in her lovely eyes.

"It must be that, because you understand me, but I cannot quite explain," said Mirah, rather abstractedly—still searching for some expression.

"But *was* it beautiful for Bouddha to let the tiger eat him?" said Amy, changing her ground. "It would be a bad pattern."

"The world would get full of fat tigers," said Mab.

Deronda laughed, but defended the myth. "It is like a passionate word," he said; "the exaggeration is a flash of fervour. It is an extreme image of what is happening every day—the transmutation of self."

"I think I can say what I mean, now," said Mirah, who had not heard the intermediate talk. "When the best thing comes into our thoughts, it is like what my mother has been to me. She has been just as really with me as all the other people about me—often more really with me." (Ch. 37, pp. 350-51)

This exchange among the Meyrick girls, Daniel Deronda, and Mirah serves several purposes for George Eliot. The ostensible function is to elucidate Daniel's discomfort at being perceived only as a savior, although there is a true reflection of his relationship to Mirah in the story of the tiger being saved from death by Bouddha. Further, of course, each character's response to the myth reveals his or her nature. The Meyrick girls, who are often comic, choose to read in a "perverse" way, seeing the story from the point of view of Bouddha instead of the tiger; they also insist upon a psychological examination into motive and a conformity to the canons of realism, for Mab suggests that a starving Bouddha would not mind being eaten, and Amy offers that this reality must be accepted if it is true. Mirah, as is consistent with her other behavior, chooses only to exalt the beauty of Bouddha's sacrifice and quickly goes on to justify a belief in the beautiful as a belief in the ideal. Finally, Daniel, in his desire to once again "come to the rescue," tries to explain the "reality" of the ideal as a justification for Mirah's response to the story.

What occurs next in the discussion has a particular bearing on the subject of metaphor and appetite. Mirah finds that there is no alternative way to express her conception of the story's meaning, so, at the end of the conversation, she is reduced to offering simply another parable—"it is *like* what my mother has been to me." Yet her seriousness seems to come off less well than the livelier responses of both Daniel and the Meyricks. They show more wit and intelligence in their exegesis of the tale, and the very terms of their remarks echo mine (order and energy). Amy suggests that the act of allowing oneself to be eaten would "be a bad pattern"; in response, Daniel insists that the beauty lies in the flash of fervor embodied in the image. In other words, Amy perceives a kind of moral order implicit in the parable, whereas Daniel focuses upon the energies of love and sacrifice which are meant to be displayed. Indeed, Daniel's reference to fervor seems to be directed more toward the fervor of the artist in providing the exaggerated image, so that the "word" of the artist will carry the energy of passion with it.

Yet, Daniel's definition of the act that the image mirrors as a "transmutation of self" comes as a sudden alteration of the significance of the myth. Until this phrase occurs, it appears that Bouddha and the tiger exist as separate entities, one of whom "eats" the other. Deronda asserts, however, that it is not the one who is eaten who disappears, but the one who eats, for if Bouddha is transmuted into the tiger, then he is the tiger, and the tiger is no more; paradoxically, the one who eats is eaten in the process. Once again, then, George Eliot relies upon the language of appetite to explain the paradoxical relationship between inside and outside because that relationship itself can only be presented metaphorically. It is crucial that the result of combining what is external and what is internal to the self be neither the negation of the self nor the negation of the world but instead the creation or metamorphosis of the self so that the new self is both an advance upon and a repetition of the old self. This is the crucial factor for Daniel when Mordecai offers him his spiritual wealth, much as Bouddha offers his body to the tiger (ch. 63, p. 566). Against Mordecai's assertion that nothing Mordecai has written be called his, so "what is mine shall be thine," Daniel declares the importance of affirming one's spiritual parentage by quoting every thing "in the name of him that said it." For, although Mordecai appears to be practicing self-abnegation, his blending of himself into Daniel is also a kind of domination; as he says himself, "for he whom I longed for afar, was he not you whom I discerned *as mine* when you came near?" (p. 566, emphasis mine). Most readers would agree that what Mordecai seeks through his diffusion is dominion. The final irony of the Bouddha passage itself is a further reflection of this. Even the gentle Mirah, who had argued against any selfish motive in Bouddha's sacrifice, finds in the later parable of the maiden who loved the king a similar kind of triumph. When Mordecai suggests that by dying in place of the woman the king loves, the maiden shows "surpassing love, that loses self in the object of love," Mirah responds:

> "She wanted the king when she was dead to know what she had done, and feel that she was better than the other. It was her strong self, wanting to conquer, that made her die." (Ch. 61, p. 553)

This change of focus from the appetite to devour to the compulsion to dominate or overwhelm exemplifies that duality that has always been inherent in the shell image as a representation of the relationship between self and world. The connections to other images and realities that are revealed by this new focus lead to that other area of "natural" language—terms of landscape and space.

3

THE LANGUAGE OF NATURE
PART 2: EXTERIOR AND INTERIOR SPACE

GEORGE ELIOT'S METAPHORS deriving from animal appetite reveal clearly a concept of the self which also defines the relationship of that self to the world. Human beings not only "eat" nature, however; they also "inhabit" it. Thus, it is important to explore that other kind of natural language, the kind that concerns not organic nature but spatial or landscape nature, to discover what literal and metaphoric references to the world may add to our sense of Eliot's art. Here, as well, the image of the shell provides a starting point, for a shell is an object that demarcates two kinds of space (interior and exterior) and incarnates two crucial geometric figures (center/circumference and orbit).

The shell satisfies many of George Eliot's needs with regard to the relationship between inner and outer precisely because it represents a changing relationship, containing within itself the principles of both stability and growth. In this it has a clear advantage over other representations of self and other, which rely only upon the static concept of placement or containment. For instance, the discussion of the differing sensibilities of Mirah and Mordecai in *Daniel Deronda* makes use of the nutshell-and-water image, but the implications of the metaphor are not complete enough:

> In that mood [Mirah] once said, "Shall I tell you what is the difference between you and me, Ezra? You are a spring in the drought, and I am an acorn-cup; the waters of heaven fill me, but the least little shake leaves me empty." (Ch. 52, p. 495)

The "fountain" here is intended as an expression of Mordecai's feelings

—of the emotional force of his personality, which, many readers will be ready enough to suggest, flows without let-up in the novel. And whether Mirah's presentation of herself is accurate or not, she conceives of her inadequacy as a lack of inner resources; this lack makes of her self no more than an empty shell. Thus, on the one hand, we have energy without limit, and on the other, limits without energy. The same difficulty is projected through the same sort of image for Catherine Arrowpoint and Klesmer:

> Here was the safety of full cups, which are as secure from overflow as the half-empty, always supposing no disturbance. Naturally, silent feeling had not remained at the same point any more than the stealthy dial-hand, and in the present visit to Quetcham, Klesmer had begun to think that he would not come again; while Catherine was more sensitive to his frequent *brusquerie,* which she rather resented as a needless effort to assert his footing of superior in every sense except the conventional. (Ch. 22, p. 178)

Here the liquid is quite clearly a metaphor for emotion, and its overflow seems desirable. Additionally, George Eliot sees the relationship between such internalities and their containment in temporal terms, which are expressed here through the image of the circular clock dial, much as the temporal growth of the sea creature is marked by the expanding circles of its shell. Finally, of course, we see the conflict between such *circular* spatial terms and the more "conventional" vertical hierarchy to which Catherine herself mentally refers at the end of the passage.

The most important aspects of the shell image itself are center and circumference. There is within the shell a center of life, the animal creature who secretes the shell as he inhabits it. It is the supposed absence of this internal "source of being" which Mirah was bemoaning in the quotation above. Eliot's use of similar imagery for both Grandcourt and Gwendolen suggests, however, that such an absence is not possible for humans—that each of us has such a living center:

> Grandcourt's thoughts this evening were like the circlets one sees in a park pool continually dying out and continually started again by some impulse from below the surface. The deeper central impulse came from the image of Gwendolen; but the thoughts it stirred would be imperfectly illustrated by a reference to the amatory poets of all ages. (Ch. 28, pp. 236–37)

> "Strange and piteous to think what a centre of wretchedness a delicate piece of human flesh like [Gwendolen] might be, wrapped round with fine raiment, her ears pierced for gems, her head held loftily, her mouth all smiling pretence, the poor soul within her sitting in sick distaste of all things!"... [thought Deronda]. (Ch. 35, p. 309)

Such centers of self are vital in both senses of that word: indeed, Mordecai argues for their necessity in social terms that are really only an extension of this concept of self to the selfhood of nations and of humanity at large:

> In the multitudes of the ignorant on three continents who observe our rites and make the confession of the divine Unity, the soul of Judaism is not dead. Revive the organic centre: let the unity of Israel which has made the growth and form of its religion be an outward reality. Looking towards a land and a polity, our dispersed people in all the ends of the earth may share the dignity of a national life which has a voice among the peoples of the East and the West—which will plant the wisdom and skill of our race so that it may be, as of old, a medium of transmission and understanding. Let that come to pass, and the living warmth will spread to the weak extremities of Israel, and superstition will vanish, not in the lawlessness of the renegade, but in the illumination of great facts which widen feeling, and make all knowledge alive as the young offspring of beloved memories. (Ch. 42, p. 400)

Mordecai (who cannot, of course, necessarily be identified with George Eliot) summarizes here the implications of the spatial image of the center and circle. It is the center that defines the form of the circle and the circumference that provides protection to those within its bounds. The image also has a temporal significance, for the circle is not a fixed limit but an ever-generated interior space that has the property of progenitiveness, as implied by the two terms "plant" and "offspring" above.

If centers and circuits are necessary, they nonetheless offer the possibility of disharmony. Both the external and the ideal boundaries thus defined present possibilities for discrepancy between the space marked out and the needs at the center of that space. These difficulties seem, nevertheless, to depend upon the arbitrariness of the circumference—that is, on its failure to conform any longer to the circuit marked out by the central self. For instance, Gwendolen begins by assuming an adequate space for herself in the "circuit round Wancester," but that circuit quickly becomes the locus of Grandcourt's evil influence, from which she tries to "wheel away"; her effort is unavailing because Grandcourt finally has "a ghostly army at his back, that could close round her wherever she might turn" (ch. 9, p. 65; ch. 28, p. 237; ch. 36, p. 337). During the struggle between these two strong selves, Mrs. Davilow notes that the world she and her daughters inhabit may indeed not correspond to their capacities, for as she states upon Gwendolen's return from Leubronn, "[h]ere we are at Offendene with a great shell over us as usual." The chapter concludes with Gwendolen's remark that she, however, is "stifled" (ch. 26, pp. 218, 219).

The shell can express either the discrepancy between the needs of self and the opposing factual presence of the outside world or the discrepancy between the old self and the new. In this regard the shell image is better suited to George Eliot's needs than either the fountain or the cup image alone. Although all of the above instances derive from *Daniel Deronda,* her last novel, this use of the shell extends throughout Eliot's earlier fiction as well:

> [Said Lucy,] "It *does* seem out of keeping that I should ever live in a great place like the Park House—such a little insignificant thing as I am."
>
> "But people are not expected to be large in proportion to the houses they live in, like snails," said Maggie, laughing. (*The Mill on the Floss,* bk. 6, ch. 2, p. 324)

> Ineffable moment! when the man you secretly hate sends you a Latin epigram with false gender—. . . attempts at poetic figures which are manifest solecisms. That moment had come to Politian: the secretary had put forth his soft head from the official shell, and the terrible lurking crab was down on him. (*Romola,* ch. 7, vol. 1, p. 117)

> On the other hand, the 'Duffield Watchman' saw in this signal instance of self-liberation from the trammels of prejudice, a decisive guarantee of intellectual pre-eminence, united with a generous sensibility to the claims of man as man, which had burst asunder, and cast off, by a spontaneous exertion of energy, the cramping outworn shell of hereditary bias and class interest. (*Felix Holt the Radical,* ch. 8, pp. 113-14)

> "Dear Dodo, do throw off that cap. I am sure your dress must make you feel ill."

> "I am so used to the cap–it has become a sort of shell," said Dorothea, smiling. "I feel rather bare and exposed when it is off." (*Middlemarch,* ch. 55, pp. 399–400)

> [Said Lydgate,] "I must do as other men do, and think what will *please the world* and *bring in* money; look for *a little opening* in the London crowd, and *push myself;* set up in a *watering-place,* or go to some southern town where there are plenty of idle English, and *get myself puffed,*–that is the sort of shell *I must creep into* and try to keep my *soul alive in.*" (*Middlemarch,* ch. 76, p. 563, emphasis mine)

> All four [Meyrick girls], if they had been wax-work, might have been packed easily in a fashionable lady's travelling trunk. Their faces seemed full of speech, as if their minds had been shelled, after the manner of horse-chestnuts, and become brightly visible. (*Daniel Deronda,* ch. 18, p. 147)

As these passages reveal, the shell image presents for the self the double difficulties of protection and freedom. The shell may give order and definition to the energies inhabiting or embodied within it, but it must equally allow for the expansion of that center's influence; that is, either the shell must expand, or the creature must be able to survive temporary shell-lessness. In other words, the space that the shell encloses should not be static but dynamic; it should be perpetually defined as such by the equal pressures of internal and external life.

Additionally, however, there is the necessity not only to continue to exist within that space but also to progress over time, and George Eliot relies on the circular image to express this conception of duration. For instance, as the epigraph for chapter 12 of *Daniel Deronda* she quotes a passage from Shakespeare's *Henry IV, Part I,* wherein time is marked out by the circular movement of the clock hands: "O gentlemen, the time of life is short;/To spend that shortness basely were too long,/If life did ride upon a dial's point,/Still ending at the arrival of an hour" (p. 90). The circular motion of the clock hand mirrors that larger circular motion through both space and time which is the movement of earth and sun. That circuit, like the expanding curves of the bivalve shell itself (her metaphor for poetic form from "Notes on Form in Art" quoted above) inscribes not a circle but a spiral, for the arrival of each hour or dawn does repeat the previous day's pattern but also advances upon the time and place so "repeated." Thus, the ultimate spatial pattern for the relationship between center and circumference may be the spiral or the moving circle of the orbit.

A passage from Coleridge's "Rime of the Ancient Mariner" helps to explain this assertion:

> In his loneliness and fixedness [the Mariner] yearneth towards the journeying Moon, and the stars that still sojourn, yet still move onward; and every where the blue sky belongs to them, and is their appointed rest, and their native country and their own natural homes, which they enter unannounced, as lords that are certainly expected and yet there is a silent joy at their arrival. (Marginal gloss, lines 263-71)[1]

The peculiar pleasure embodied in the journeying stars derives from their movement as an appointed round, which makes of motion not a wandering but an infinite return, so that each moment in the journey is a perpetual egress and a perpetual arrival, as if all points in space were thresholds to be crossed with joy rather than fear.[2] Further, an orbit really has two centers, not just one, for there is the "center" around which the orbit circles and there is the orbiting object itself. What is fascinating about Coleridge's lords of the blue heavens is that they not only move along an appointed path or track which has its own circular pattern, but also make every point along that path a center and a home because of their presence there. Thus, whether we look to George Eliot's remarks on setting—

> [The shepherd's] solar system was the parish. (*Felix Holt the Radical,* "Introduction," p. 2)

or on character—

> "You [Lydgate] are a sort of circumnavigator come to settle among us, and will keep my [Farebrother's] belief in the antipodes." (*Middlemarch,* ch. 17, p. 131)

or on theme—

> "And so, Master Marner, as I was saying—for there's *windings* i' things as they may carry you to the fur end o' the prayer-book afore you get back to 'em" (*Silas Marner,* ch. 10, pp. 131-32, emphasis mine),

the underlying "diagram" into which her fiction lapses is the arc carved out by two centers of energy or being. Even the supposed fixedness of a horizon becomes expressive of this, when the narrator remarks of Gwendolen at the conclusion of *Daniel Deronda* that "she was for the first time feeling the pressure of a vast mysterious movement, for the first time being dislodged from her supremacy in her own world, and getting a sense that her horizon was but a dipping onward of an existence with which her own was revolving" (ch. 69, p. 607).

Equally, when characters in Eliot's fiction look up at the heavens, their response is a version of what I described earlier (with regard to Deronda's response to the Jewish chants) as the paradox of taking in that which is outside while giving out that which is within. Thus, Janet Dempster, in her "starlight walk," feels like a "soul, *dipped* in the sacred waters of joy and peace, [which] *rises* from them with new energies, with more unalterable longings" ("Janet's Repentance," ch. 25, p. 398, emphasis mine). The tension of her contrary energies and longings is given specificity in the sentences preceding these, in which the metaphor of the child and the father serves as a representation of the double centers (father and child) that determine the onward path: "She felt like a little child whose hand is firmly grasped by its father, as its frail limbs make their way over the rough ground; if it should stumble, the father will not let it go" (p. 398). From this perspective there is, in Daniel Deronda's efforts to get "outside himself," a kind of violation of the very order of things: "He was forgetting everything else in a half-speculative, half-involuntary identification of himself with the objects he was looking at, thinking how far it might be possible habitually to shift his centre till his own personality would be no less outside him than the landscape" (ch. 17, p. 140). Although his immediately subsequent rescue of Mirah might qualify as a selfless shift of his attention to the plight of another, that rescue does presuppose a self to do the rescuing.

An exploration of the language of landscape and space in Eliot's novels is necessary, then, to understand her conception of "being in the world." Spatial language, like the organic language discussed in chapter 2, can be literal and conventional as well as metaphorical and paradoxical. Implicit in this language is Eliot's discovery and metamorphosis of a linguistic or figurative unit by means of which she grasps reality and then presents it artistically.

Let us begin with an instance of wordplay regarding space in *Adam Bede:*

> "Well, Mr. Poyser," [Mr. Craig] said, before the good slow farmer had time to speak, "ye'll not be carrying your hay to-morrow, I'm thinking: the glass sticks at 'change,' and ye may rely upo' my word as we'll ha' more downfall afore twenty-four hours is past. Ye see that darkish blue cloud there upo' the 'rizon—ye know

> what I mean by the 'rizon, where the land and sky seems to meet?"
> "Ay, ay, I see the cloud," said Mr. Poyser, "'rizon or no 'rizon. It's right o'er Mike Holdsworth's fallow, and a foul fallow it is." (Ch. 18, pp. 174–75)

It seems gratuitous for George Eliot to have Mr. Craig, the gardener who hopes to woo Hetty Sorrel, pause over the word horizon during his lesson on reading the weather. Yet his definition and Mr. Poyser's response exemplify alternative world views possible in Eliot's fiction. Craig's definition emphasizes the shifting nature of the horizon, an imaginary boundary where land and sky "seem" to meet—a boundary that moves with the movement of the perceiver. Mr. Poyser's response about the location of the cloud in question relies upon fixed landmarks, namely, Mike Holdsworth's fallow, over which the cloud now stands. These two modes of spatial relation sufficiently characterize the alternately absolute and relative systems by which the self defines its place in the world. The absolute method, that of Mr. Poyser, relies upon horizontals and verticals, upon up and down, far and near. The relative method is more ambiguous, like the Romantic optical tradition from which it derives. The one depends primarily upon the real external existence of landscape, the other upon the nature of the eye (I) that views the landscape.

The term *horizon* appears in other places in George Eliot's fiction, often used in a metaphorical rather than a literal sense. For instance, it occurs in a crucial passage in *Middlemarch,* one that is frequently used to embody George Eliot's conception of the proper moral stance:

> But [Lydgate] had none of those definite things to say or to show which give the way-marks of patient uninterrupted pursuit, such as he used himself to insist on, saying that "there must be a systole and diastole in all inquiry," and that "a man's mind must be continually expanding and shrinking between the whole human horizon and the horizon of an object-glass." (Ch. 63, p. 468)

Lydgate himself had, at the start of the novel, "seen Miss Vincy above his horizon almost as long as it had taken Mr. Casaubon to become engaged and married" (ch. 11, p. 70). From the use of the word "above" here, it appears that horizons (although "absolute") are indeed only ideal limits, for they are traversed by others whose very appearance, and hence existence, argues for the reality of a world beyond the individual's own point of view. Hence the concept of horizon asserts simultaneously the reality of space and the limits imposed on that space by the perceiving self.

A further characteristic of horizons, their circularity, "rhymes" with George Eliot's interest elsewhere in curves and centers. In fact, her preoccupation with this particular geometric configuration lies behind her significant choice of the pier-glass metaphor in *Middlemarch*. Her parable about that pier-glass, a *locus classicus* in discussions of her moral vision, is deliberately altered from the original example offered to her by an "eminent philosopher" among her friends (ch. 27, p. 194)—if N. N. Feltes is right in attributing the gift of the metaphor to Herbert Spencer and John Ruskin.[3] Both men had explained optical selection by means of the example of moonlight on water. That Eliot chose a pier-glass rather than the sea for her experiment merits examination.

Feltes quotes both Ruskin's and Spencer's descriptions of the optical effects of moonlight and their conclusions concerning them; both assert that the dark parts of the water are not truly "dark" but only incapable of reflecting the moonlight because of the position of certain wavelets. Ruskin speaks of "a long line of splendour . . . seen on the waves under the moon, reaching from the horizon to our very feet," while Spencer adds that this "bar of light" will move as the observer moves along the shore of the water.[4] Thus, Ruskin emphasizes that the darkness is not really dark, for the moon shines on all the water equally, but Spencer emphasizes that the brightness is not really bright, for it exists only when the observer exists. Yet both presume the separateness of the observer and the source of light. George Eliot, on the other hand, replaces the moon (itself only a reflection of light) with a candle as a "centre of illumination" and replaces the body of water with a mirror. At first, this seems to emphasize the egoism of the observer, who is not viewing an external world but is seeing only self.[5] Yet those scratches in the mirror do have objective existence, and the self is a source of energy (light). By eliminating Ruskin's transcendent moon and Spencer's limited scientific observer, Eliot achieves a particular kind of irony. Unlike the irony Feltes perceives to be dramatic ("The tone of George Eliot's discussion embraces both respect for 'the serene light of science' and the wonder of 'Lo!' but because the reader is not a part of the experiment the whole passage is tinged with irony."),[6] Eliot's is a more embracing irony born of paradox: the very light that permits us to see is that which limits or even distorts what we do see.

There are two other significant aspects of Eliot's choice of optical experiment. The first concerns her attitude toward the sea, which has vital associations for her—associations that would inappropriately complicate the meaning of the metaphor. The second, geometric, point concerns the alteration from Ruskin's and Spencer's bar or line of light to the circle of scratches in *Middlemarch.* In moving from one to the other we move from one- to two-dimensional space. The point of the moon and water example, of course, is that a whole body of water exists beyond the line of light as a kind of horizonless expanse of which the observer, like Gwendolen Harleth in *Daniel Deronda,* is unaware. Eliot's ego, however, derives its safety from a slightly different source, in that it is enclosed within a circle of meaning that places that ego at its center. It may be some proof of the truth of this metaphor for Eliot that she reverts to it in characterizing Ezra Cohen's response to Mordecai: "[Daniel] was received with . . . a slight air of wondering which even in Cohen was not allowed to pass the bounds of silence—the guest's transactions with Mordecai being a sort of mystery which he was rather proud to think lay outside the *sphere* of light which enclosed his own understanding" (*Daniel Deronda,* ch. 46, p. 428, emphasis mine).

Indeed, "enclosure" is an aspect of space in George Eliot's landscape, moral as well as physical, for spatial language is significant for her in literal and metaphorical terms. Thus, the actual universe that her characters inhabit is characterized by extension, by far and near and high and low, by the directionality implied by those terms, much as Mr. Poyser defines the location of the cloud in the passage above. Yet there is also the more ambiguous relationship between inside and outside, interiors and exteriors, which, although it too has a literal reality in her fiction, often becomes generative of particular insights when such relationships are seen to be metaphorically intended. Of course, the language of extension can be metaphorically intended as well, but its usage seems fixed and traditional. It is necessary, nevertheless, to clarify Eliot's use of both kinds of language in order to appreciate the special importance to her of those spaces that seem so fundamental to her conception of being in the world.

George Eliot remarks upon the fundamental reality of the physical world in *The Mill on the Floss;* in noting Tom's joy in returning home after his first term at school, the narrator of the novel declares that the "pattern of the rug and the grate and the fire-irons were 'first ideas' that it was no more possible to criticise than the solidity and extension of matter" (bk. 2, ch. 1, p. 135). Yet the relationship between man and his environment cannot be reduced to those terms alone:

> Extension, we know, is a very imperfect measure of things; and the length of the sun's journeying can no more tell us how far life has advanced than the acreage of a field can tell us what growths may be active within it. A man may go south, and, stumbling over a bone, may meditate upon it till he has found a new starting-point for anatomy; or eastward, and discover a new key to language telling a new story of races; or he may head an expedition that opens new continental pathways, get himself maimed in body, and go through a whole heroic poem of resolve and endurance; and at the end of a few months he may come back to find his neighbours grumbling at the same parish grievance as before, or to see the same elderly gentleman treading the pavement in discourse with himself, shaking his head after the same percussive butcher's boy, and pausing at the same shop-window to look at the same prints. If the swiftest thinking has about the pace of a greyhound, the slowest must be supposed to move, like the limpet, by an apparent sticking, which after a good while is discerned to be a slight progression. Such differences are manifest in the variable intensity which we call human experience, from the revolutionary rush of change which makes a new inner and outer life, to that quiet recurrence of the familiar, which has no other epochs than those of hunger and heavens. (*Daniel Deronda,* ch. 58, p. 530)

This passage combines several of George Eliot's most significant conceptions of landscape with her other language of appetite and art. The opening sentence remarks on the dual nature of travel as an expression of both space, or extension, and time, or duration. The second sentence moves in "another direction" suggested by the conclusion of the first, wherein Eliot implies the distinction between external acreage and internal or potential growth. Thus, a man's *external* journeying may bring about internal developments—developments associated with language, stories, and poems. Such mental traveling becomes more vivid by its contrast to the stability of the elderly man whose sameness of life is also emphasized internally and externally by the sameness of food (the butcher's boy) and of viewpoint (the prints in the window). Further, although Eliot appears to offer in her simile regarding thought and movement an analogy based on extension, her real interest seems to be more in the variable inwardness or "intensity" of the experience than in the rate of forward movement. She concludes by reverting to two "natural" phenomena (hunger and heavens) that permit an expression of externality and internality which incorporates these other contraries of difference and sameness, movement and stability discussed earlier with regard to the shell image. The heavens themselves move, of course, but by the "stability" of that movement they permit mankind to determine its own position or place. Yet, although the importance of the journey in Eliot's fiction is well documented, and although that importance seems to validate the significance of extension and direction as aspects of her real and fictional worlds, the degree to which apparent onward movement is transformed into enclosure and entrapment suggests again that her concern is with inside and outside as much as with here and there. Further, even her conception of journeying depends as much on starting points and circles as it does on extension and directional movement:

> Man can do nothing without the make-believe of a beginning. Even Science, the strict measurer, is obliged to start with a make-believe unit, and must fix on a point in the stars' unceasing journey when his sidereal clock shall pretend that time is at Nought. His less accurate grandmother Poetry has always been understood to start in the middle; but on reflection it appears that her proceeding is not very different from his; since Science, too, reckons backwards as well as forwards, divides his unit into billions, and with his clock-finger at Nought really sets off *in media res.* No retrospect will take us to the true beginning; and whether our prologue be in heaven or on earth, it is but a fraction of that all-presupposing fact with which our story sets out. (*Daniel Deronda,* ch. 1, p. 1)

In examining George Eliot's stories, we must begin with that large segment of what she asserts is "all-presupposing fact": the three-dimensional world that man inhabits. Insofar as this world is indeed characterized by extension, it appears to function in her fiction as a map or grid against which we can clearly define the position or direction of the self. This grid may be literal, like Farmer Poyser's landscape, or metaphorical, as in the tradition of Milton's *Paradise Lost.* In consonance with that literary tradition, Eliot often plays linguistically upon the paradoxes of high and low, near and far, as terms denoting not physical but moral situation or movement. Thus, early in *Scenes of Clerical Life,* she treats comically the often inverse ratio between this-worldly and other-worldly heights:

> Mrs. Phipps . . . had invested part of [her] reputation for acuteness in the supposition that Mr. Bridmain was not the Countess's brother. Moreover, Miss Phipps was conscious that if the Countess was not a disreputable person, she, Miss Phipps, had no compensating

> superiority in virtue to set against the other lady's manifest superiority in personal charms. Miss Phipps's stumpy figure and unsuccessful attire, instead of looking down from a mount of virtue with an auréole round its head, would then be seen on the same level and in the same light as the Countess Czerlaski's Diana-like form and well-chosen drapery. ("Amos Barton," ch. 4, pp. 76-77)

Like the language of organic nature, this sort of spatial language implies a stable and essentially one-directional order. From this stability George Eliot is able to derive in a serious mode the conviction expressed in the quotation from Tennyson's *In Memoriam* that serves as the epigraph to chapter 43 of *Felix Holt the Radical:*

> Dear friend, far off, my lost desire,
> So far, so near, in woe and weal;
> O, loved the most when most I feel
> There is a lower and a higher!
> (P. 411)

She is also able to derive the comic inversions of value hinted at in the passage concerning Miss Phipps quoted above; these inversions make up a large portion of the humor in *The Mill on the Floss.* In that novel it is consistently Mrs. Glegg who, because of her unshakeable convictions regarding the stability and propriety of her own values (an attitude not unlike Milton's), draws upon the language of up and down to define the moral relations of the novel. In one instance out of many, "Mrs. Glegg had on her fuzziest front, and garments which appeared to have had a recent resurrection from a rather creasy form of burial; a costume selected with the *high* moral purpose of instilling perfect *humility* into Bessy and her children" (bk. 3, ch. 3, p. 183, emphasis mine).

Accompanying this sort of metaphorical language is that more paradoxical sort concerning movement, not simply from one position to another, but from one whole space to another. That is, our sense of landscape is not the perception of a stable and complete world that permits predictable measurement and movement, but the perception of possible other spaces that may imply the transformation of our present space, or at least our liberation from the apparent limits of the present space. Indeed, chapter 43 of *Felix Holt the Radical* contains this other sort of language regarding enclosure and exposure. Here Harold and Esther are discussing physical transformations of the Transome estate even as Esther is contemplating the moral imperatives regarding the inheritance of that estate. George Eliot's term for the "confusions of right and possession" is provocative: "labyrinthine" (p. 413). It seems only appropriate to assume that the subsequent discussion of the physical landscape is a commentary on this moral confusion. As an improvement of the estate, Harold suggests thinning certain trees, for "if they were divided into clumps so as to show the oaks beyond, it would be a great improvement" through the creation of "an idea of extent that is lost now." Esther agrees, because "one likes a 'beyond' everywhere" (p. 416).

This exchange incorporates the two aspects of space that need to be examined. First, it implies that the wider the space, the greater the improvement—enclosure or entrapment being tantamount to imprisonment in a labyrinth. Clearly, such will not necessarily be the case for George Eliot, although the details of her qualification of this assertion are important. Second, the passage concerns the relationship between natural space and humanly created space—and my very sentence implies an important distinction between nature and man in this regard. In fact, these two aspects are not really separable, for an examination of the wide expanses of landscape in Eliot's fiction will lead to an appreciation of those preferable, humanly created enclosures; they return us to the idea of the centered space by means of the archetype that forms a contrary to the labyrinth: the temple.

Given George Eliot's presentation of man as a species of animal, we might expect her primary interest to be in his "home" in nature. Yet her first work of fiction, *Scenes of Clerical Life,* is emphatically a work of interiors, however much her characters in those scenes may wander about the landscape or become locked out of their houses. It is in her first full-length novel, *Adam Bede,* that Eliot extensively examines man's place in the natural order; her most complete commentary on that place is Hetty's two-part journey in hope and despair.[7] What we find there (as in the journey undertaken for the opposite reason by Jane in *Jane Eyre*) is that the natural world alone is not our home. When Eliot treats it as such in her novels, there is always the mediating presence of human habitations:

> [Raveloe] lay in the rich central plain of what we are pleased to call Merry England, and held farms which, speaking from a spiritual point of view, paid highly-desirable tithes. But it was *nestled* in a snug well-wooded hollow, quite an hour's journey on horseback from any turnpike, where it was never reached by the vibrations of the coach-horn or of public opinion. (*Silas Marner,* ch. 1, p. 53, emphasis mine)

> The busy scenes of the shuttle and the wheel, of the roaring furnace, of the shaft and the pulley, seemed to make but crowded *nests* in the midst of the large-spaced, slow-moving life of homesteads and far-away cottages and oak-sheltered parks. (*Felix Holt the Radical,* "Introduction," pp. 5-6, emphasis mine)

Thus, abandonment in a large and inhospitable natural landscape implies other kinds of psychological, social, or moral alienation and brings with it the sense of being lost in a space that is without meaning, order, or comfort. For instance:

> [Janet's] life was a sun-dried, barren tract, where there was no shadow, and where all the waters were bitter. (Janet's Repentance," ch. 16, p. 350)

> Marner did not want to punish him, but only to get back his gold which had gone from him, and left his soul like a forlorn traveller on an unknown desert. (*Silas Marner,* ch. 5, p. 94)

> "And thou, Romola, didst wring thy hands and seek for water, and there was none . . . and the plain was bare and stony again, and thou wast alone in the midst of it." (*Romola,* ch. 36, vol. 2, p. 51)

> Solitude in any wide scene impressed [Gwendolen] with an undefined feeling of immeasurable existence aloof from her, in the midst of which she was helplessly incapable of asserting herself. (*Daniel Deronda,* ch. 6, p. 45)

The accurate and obvious conclusion to draw, especially from the last example, is that such expanses seem to announce the radical disjuncture between the size and importance of the individual and the immensity and power of the surrounding universe. Deserts provide no sustenance and no human companionship. Their scale is inappropriate to human comfort. People in such environments thus die of inanition or, in slightly different terms, of their distance from their kind—a distance clearly defined in horizontal terms.

There is, however, a different example of the anxiety over space, with different implications. This anxiety centers on the eternal and unchartable sea. Critics have already made much of the use of water imagery in *Middlemarch,*[8] but I find it interesting that only in that novel, in *Scenes of Clerical Life,* and in *Felix Holt the Radical* does a literal body of water not play a significant part in the plot. (I could argue that water is indirectly present in these works through the deaths by drunkenness of Dempster, Trounsem, and Raffles.) In Eliot's other works, difficulties with water, be it the sea itself or its relatives, the river and the pond, are plentiful. Hetty considers drowning herself in a pool; Maggie and Tom do indeed drown; Dunsey Cass steps into a quarry pool; Romola sets off suicidally in a rowboat on the sea; Mirah attempts drowning in the river, and Grandcourt fails to escape drowning in the sea. Why water should pose so actual a threat to human life is thus an important question. John Arthos, in speaking about *The Mill on the Floss* (the most watery of Eliot's novels), asserts the connection of death by water with self-destruction, finding that the flood is brought on by the very imagination of Maggie Tulliver.[9] There is indeed in sea imagery a justification for such linkage, since the original Narcissus myth and later manifestations (most obviously the crows-nest section of Melville's *Moby-Dick*) represent self-destruction through excessive self-absorption. This is perhaps a crucial difference between water and land imagery as projections of a wasteland: the desert is part of the iconography of the world, but the sea is part of the iconography of the self.

Even more important for my purposes is the actual nature of death by water. On the desert, metaphorical or otherwise, George Eliot's characters are threatened by a lack of food—there is nothing to swallow, or whatever is provided is bitter and unwholesome. On water, the landscape itself can "swallow" a character, and what seemed a solid, horizontal surface, or even a floor for the overarching height of sky, reveals hidden depths that envelop the self. In another sense, in drowning one dies from swallowing too much—as the three drunkards Dempster, Trounsem, and Raffles do. That the sea may be the inner self seen suddenly outside the self only compounds the confusions of inside and outside.

This paradox may find resolution in the metaphor concerning water discussed earlier. If the sea is indeed the frightening expansion of those water images—fountains and rivers—that have been George Eliot's means of presenting the force of emotion, then indeed death by water does become destruction through the uncontrollable or unordered needs and energies of the self. Geometrically speaking, on the one hand, a world barren of such energies is a wasteland in which the self is reduced to a point; on the other, the excess of such energies is expansion of that point into a flood that overwhelms three-dimensional space. Two passages from *Scenes of Clerical Life* exemplify these contrary difficulties:

> We are poor plants *buoyed up* by the air-vessels of our own conceit: alas for us, if we get a few pinches that empty us of that windy self-subsistence! ("Amos Barton," ch. 2, p. 52, emphasis mine)

> Even anti-Tryanite prejudice could not resist the fact that Jane Dempster was a changed woman—changed as the dusty, bruised, and sun-withered plant is changed when the soft rains of heaven have fallen on it—and that this change was due to Mr. Tryan's influence. ("Janet's Repentance," ch. 26, p. 401)

These passages make use of the pressures of water without and air within—the opposing forces of expansion and ingestion—as a means of expressing a conviction about the essential realities of internal and external space; the equal pressures (i.e., forces), like those that create the sea shell, create and sustain the plantlike self.

Nevertheless, the physical landscape of nature remains an actual and inherited part of man's environment, and it is apparent that the plant image still keeps us at one metaphorical remove from man's own literal condition. When we turn from that landscape, not to man's own interior, but to those structures that he creates outside himself as a "building, burrowing house-appropriating and shell-secreting" animal, we can discover other, complementary aspects of George Eliot's conception of the relationship between self and world. In that regard, it is appropriate that her first sentences as a novelist describe a "temple," for "Amos Barton" begins with Shepperton church, a place whose description encapsulates many of her later conceptions regarding enclosed and inhabited space. In this passage, Eliot is concerned with the apparent contrast between the regularity and order of the new church and the heterogeneity of the old, especially as they differ in windows, roofs, and exteriors. But equally significant is the difference in the sense of internal space:

> Then inside, what dear old quaintnesses! which I began to look at with delight, even when I was so crude a member of the congregation, that my nurse found it necessary to provide for the reinforcement of my devotional patience by smuggling bread-and-butter into the sacred edifice. There was the chancel, guarded by two little cherubims looking uncomfortably squeezed between arch and wall, and adorned with the escutcheons of the Oldinport family, which showed me inexhaustible possibilities of meaning in their blood-red hands, their death's-heads and cross-bones, their leopards' paws, and Maltese crosses. There were inscriptions on the panels of the singing-gallery, telling of benefactions to the poor of Shep-

> perton, with an involuted elegance of capitals and final flourishes, which my alphabetic erudition traced with ever-new delight. No benches in those days; but huge roomy pews, round which devout church-goers sat during 'lessons', trying to look anywhere else than into each other's eyes. No low partitions allowing you, with a dreary absence of contrast and mystery, to see everything at all moments; but tall dark panels, under whose shadow I sank with a sense of retirement through the Litany, only to feel with more intensity my burst into the conspicuousness of public life when I was made to stand up on the seat during the psalms or the singing. (Ch. 1, p. 42)

The new church has an "innutrient" exterior surface (p. 41); the old was a place inside which people could eat "bread-and-butter." Instead of the strict horizontals and verticals of the new church, the old has the curves and figures of antique sculpture. Most importantly, instead of the rather blank open space of the free seats in the new church, the old has an appealing movement from retirement to exposure which satisfies the young narrator's double desire for safety and excitement. George Eliot shows here, then, her appreciation for enclosed space, and yet for movement.

In her next scene, "Mr. Gilfil's Love-Story," Eliot pays even more extensive attention to architectural space, this time of the secular sort. Chapter 2 begins the "enclosed" narrative of Gilfil's youth with a slow and careful placement of figures in a landscape that is both natural and artificial. The heat of the sun—an echo of inhospitable deserts—is repulsed by the protective, leafy elms, so Tina Sarti can make an exterior parlor, complete with cushions, "in the favourite spot, just on the slope by a clump of laurels, where [she and Lady Cheverel] can see the sunbeams sparkling among the water-lilies, and can be themselves seen from the dining-room windows" (p. 132). Here, at least, the inside has been brought outside, and conversely, the outside covers that which is within, for Tina's highly civilized dress covers a girl with "the eyes of a fawn" (p. 133). Further, when Eliot shifts her point of view from outside the house to inside, she again turns from the persons to the surrounding space:

> Any one entering that dining-room for the first time, would perhaps have had his attention even more strongly arrested by the room itself, which was so bare of furniture that *it impressed one with its architectural beauty like a cathedral.* A piece of matting stretched from door to door, a bit of worn carpet under the dining-table, and a sideboard in a deep recess, did not detain the eye for a moment

from the lofty groined ceiling, with its richly-carved pendants, all of creamy white, relieved here and there by touches of gold. On one side, this lofty ceiling was supported by pillars and arches, beyond which a lower ceiling, a miniature copy of the higher one, covered the square projection which, with its three large pointed windows, formed the central feature of the building. The room looked less like a place to dine in than *a piece of space enclosed simply for the sake of beautiful outline;* and the small dining-table, with the party round it, seemed an odd and insignificant accident, rather than anything connected with the original purpose of the apartment. (Ch. 2, p. 134, emphasis mine)

Although I think George Eliot appreciates the beauty of this room, there is about it a coolness that derives from the discrepancy between its function (as a place in which people satisfy their hunger) and its size, and between its visual appearance and its human occupants. This last is expanded upon through the echo of the terms of the room in the physical description of Captain Wybrow: "Nothing [could be] more finely cut than the transparent nostril and the short upper-lip . . . , but the defect was on the side of that delicacy and *finesse* which was the distinctive characteristic of the whole person, and which was carried out in the clear brown arch of the eyebrows, and the marble smoothness of the sloping forehead" (pp. 135–36). Through a kind of play upon the convex surface of Anthony's head and the concave surface of the room, the interior space of the dining hall conveys the emptiness of Anthony's own interior.

Cheverel Manor is not really Anthony's building, however; it is the result of Lord Cheverel's desire to "[metamorphose] his plain brick family mansion into the model of a Gothic manorhouse" (ch. 3, p. 147). His pattern for this is to be the cathedral. The house is "Gothic" in an entirely unintended sense, however, for it becomes "haunted" by Tina's murderous thoughts and Anthony's abrupt death. This is a crucial clue to George Eliot's use of habitations as "temples." In order for a defined and delimited space to be such, it must have some indwelling spirit that provides a center.

A fitting contrast to the artificial elegance of Cheverel manor, because by implication it has such a center or presiding genius, is the parsonage where Milly Barton lived: "A loving woman's world lies within the four walls of her own home" ("Amos Barton," ch. 7, p. 99). More extensive is the description of another humble home from Eliot's last novel:

The small front parlour was *as good as a temple* that morning. The

> sunlight was on the river and soft air came in through the open window; the walls showed a glorious silent cloud of witnesses—the Virgin soaring amid her cherubic escort; grand Melancholia with her solemn universe; the Prophets and Sibyls; the School of Athens; the Last Supper; mystic groups where far-off ages made one moment; grave Holbein and Rembrandt heads; the Tragic Muse; last-century children at their musings or their play; Italian poets—all were there through the medium of a little black and white. The neat mother who had weathered her troubles, and come out of them with a face still cheerful, was sorting coloured wools for her embroidery. Hafiz purred on the window-ledge, the clock on the mantelpiece ticked without hurry, and the occasional sound of wheels seemed *to lie outside the more massive central quiet.* (*Daniel Deronda,* ch. 20, pp. 154-55, emphasis mine)

There are a number of directions from which to approach (and depart from) this passage. In the first place, Mrs. Meyrick, the mother here, recalls all those other women whose spirits had created homes that are temples—from Mrs. Poyser to Romola, even to Mrs. Vincy of *Middlemarch.* Those women who are not mothers but carry out a kind of mothering activity create similarly sacred worlds: Janet for Mr. Tryan in "Janet's Repentance," and Maggie for her father in *The Mill on the Floss.* This last novel repeats a second aspect of the quoted passage regarding the Meyrick parlor, namely its conception of the relationship between inside and outside:

> As for Maggie, she was peculiarly depressed this morning: she had been called up, after brief rest, at three o'clock, and had that strange dreamy weariness which comes from watching in a sick-room through the chill hours of early twilight and breaking day—in which the outside daylight life seems to have no importance, and to be a mere margin to the hours in the darkened chamber. (Bk. 3, ch. 3, p. 187)

> Maggie in her brown frock, with her eyes reddened and her heavy hair pushed back, looking from the bed where her father lay, to the dull walls of this sad chamber which was the centre of her world, was a creature full of eager, passionate longings for all that was beautiful and glad; thirsty for all knowledge; with an ear straining after dreamy music that died away and would not come near to her; with a blind, unconscious yearning for something that would link together the wonderful impressions of this mysterious life, and give her soul a sense of home in it. (Bk. 3, ch. 5, p. 208)

The "center" for Maggie's world here is her father, much as Milly Barton's family is the "center" of hers. Such a center provides both a presence (a filling of the enclosed space) and an order (a place from which to measure). In this regard, the Meyrick parlor constitutes a temple of a particularly satisfying sort, for it provides security in its central quiet while it does not imprison, for the air and sunlight come in through the window; in addition, the past is present in the surrounding audience of great art upon the walls.

George Eliot's remarks in her Ilfracombe journal may clarify the last issue regarding such spaces. In that journal (*Letters,* 2:241-42) Eliot began her meditation by noting the discrepancy in scale between our created homes and our "natural" home, so that "one cannot help thinking of man as a parasitic animal—an epizoon making his abode on the skin of the planetary organism." The term "animal" then generates a list of functions regarding "making one's abode," which themselves begin to reveal the ambiguities inherent in such activity: if we are "building, burrowing house-appropriating and shell-secreting animals," then we hollow out solid space, or we invade it, or we create it by giving out that which is within. Even the present participial form of these verbs underscores the importance not simply of the fact of the habitation but also of the energy necessary to create that habitation. When Eliot finally settles for the "shell-secreting" aspect of such human activity, she ends with two terms that introduce and perhaps justify close scrutiny of the human habitations of her last novel, *Daniel Deronda:* "Look at man in the light of a shell-fish and it must be admitted that his shell is generally ugly, and it is only after a great many 'steps or phenomena' that he secretes here and there a wonderful shell in the shape of a temple or a palace."

It is in *Daniel Deronda* that George Eliot concerns herself most directly and extensively with the possibilities of space as a means of examining man's place and function in the world. In none of her other novels does she pay such close attention to exterior and interior spaces as they are occupied by civilized people. From the gaming room at Leubronn, through the peripatetic archery match at Cardell Chase, to the room for Mordecai within the Cohen home, which exists behind their shop, Eliot shows a conscious awareness of the places man creates or appropriates. The most elaborate of these descriptions of place, of course, is Abbott's and King's Topping—a double name that echoes the "temple or a palace" phrase from Eliot's journal entry some twenty-two years before.

There are several parts to Sir Hugo's estate, each of which has something to offer to George Eliot's iconography of space. There is the drawing room into which Gwendolen and Grandcourt step with such dignity; the library where Deronda works; the dining room, which was once the abbey refectory; the kitchen, which alone is in a state of perfect preservation; the stables, which were a part of the original church; and the cloister, which consists of both the enclosed ground, so important to Deronda in his youth, and the upper gallery, where the New Year's dance takes place. The crucial problem for the plot of the novel concerns the tensions between the present owner, Sir Hugo, and the future owner, Grandcourt. It is really Gwendolen, of course, who is most aware that she and her husband are "appropriating" this world, and her recurrent fear is that someone other than she is the spirit or presiding genius of the place. Her most acute sense of this comes during the visit to the stables, which were once the church. Critics of Eliot's fiction have already explained the social and moral implications of this degeneration of function.[10] The stables, transformed in purpose and hence in spirit, gain further resonance from the horses, whose presence reminds us of our animality—indeed, the space at the abbey that most closely corresponds to this in form and quality is the kitchen, so that even here Eliot reminds us of our own "insides" and our fundamental appetites. The discussion that occurs within the stables seems to repeat this connection, for the remarks and gestures of each character are an index to the interior, spiritual qualities of each.

Daniel Deronda's attitude seems to be a kind of moral yardstick for the company in the stables, but although his reverence in this place is important, the cloister at the abbey is truly his natural home. An examination of it summarizes all the aspects of space that have hitherto been touched upon, from landscape, to habitations, to centers, to spirits of place.

> This cloister was built of harder stone than the church, and had been in greater safety from the wearing weather. It was a rare example of a northern cloister with arched and pillared openings not intended for glazing, and the delicately-wrought foliage of the capitals seemed still to carry the very touches of the chisel. Gwendolen had dropped her husband's arm and joined the other ladies, to whom Deronda was noticing the delicate sense which had combined freedom with accuracy in the imitation of natural forms.
>
> "I wonder whether one oftener learns to love real objects through their representations, or the representations through the real objects," he said, after pointing out a lovely capital made by the curled leaves of greens, showing their reticulated under-side with the firm

gradual swell of its central rib. "When I was a little fellow these capitals taught me to observe, and delight in, the structure of leaves." (Ch. 35, p. 316)

The cloister, like the Meyrick parlor, provides both protection from externals, with its "greater safety from the wearing weather," and access to them, through the "arched and pillared openings not intended for glazing." Further, in its decoration the cloister makes the beauty of nature more permanent, much as the greenery in the niches in the gallery overhead conversely makes that more interior space a "bower" (ch. 36, p. 331). Finally, Deronda himself calls attention to the natural curves of the foliage, which echo the curves of the arched openings: the leaves curl inwardly and yet swell outwardly, the central rib suggesting both architecture and anatomy. Moreover, the cloister is a more accurate representation of Deronda's self than the abbey stable, because it is more connected with the external, natural world, and because its "genius" is more human and less divine. After all, it is here that Daniel first learns of his possible identity, or at least of his identity insofar as that is determined by his parentage. When lying on the grass and indulging his eagerness "to know how time had been filled up since the Flood" (ch. 16, p. 121), he discovers by accident an analogy between his own condition and that of the illegitimate sons of popes and cardinals—appropriate enough fathers for him to consider in a cloister. The possibility of illegitimacy changes Daniel's inner world, "as happy careless voyagers are changed when the sky suddenly threatens and the thought of danger arises" (p. 123). These references to water may well be related to those other moments of destruction through drowning discussed earlier. Luckily for Daniel, of course (and further proof of the inappropriateness of the abbey image itself for his identity), he later discovers that his true father is not a popelike figure. Thus, the cloister again becomes a representation of his own youthful self, not his hidden ancestry.

The significant achievement of that self in its relation to the outer world is stated by Deronda himself in that passage: "I wonder whether one oftener learns to love real objects through their representations, or the representations through the real objects." In the cloister, the presence of external physical nature has been mediated by human art, and the result is more enduring through the reciprocal and contrary relationship between the given object and the human response to it. Nevertheless, the apparent stasis that this reciprocal relationship implies can really no more resolve the dilemma of space for George Eliot than can the apparent clarity of the organic imagery discussed in Chapter 2. There remains, like the infinite appetite that opposed the organic language, a fact of physical space that reiterates the problem of the accommodation between self and world. When the narrator in *Daniel Deronda* remarks comically that "[t]his was the period when the broadening of gauge in crinolines seemed to demand an agitation for the general enlargement of churches, ball-rooms, and vehicles" (ch. 8, p. 64), she is suggesting that humans cannot avoid, in the creating and inhabiting of their own spaces, impinging upon the space outside of themselves.

Nevertheless, the reader can come to understand George Eliot's beliefs by means of those segments of her fiction which concern natural landscape and human habitation, either literally or figuratively. Certain fundamental images and relationships appear in her novels from first to last, although it seems clear that the process of examining those is an ongoing one for Eliot herself; what may be a random comparison in her early work later becomes conscious food for reflection and finally even the underlying structure for extensive portions of her later novels. Much as Daniel Deronda comes to realize more clearly the "nature" of nature through the forms of the sculptor's art, George Eliot comes to realize more clearly the nature of nature through the forms of the writer's art.

As an additional proof of this assertion, the reader may look to Eliot's use of art itself in her fiction. Significantly, however, the art that predominates is not writing, or even painting and sculpture, but music. The reasons for this link together the recurrent problems (both ontological and ethical) apparent in man's condition as an appetitive animal inhabiting a three-dimensional landscape. Through music, which has already appeared at least tangentially in several of the passages quoted above, Eliot is able to transcend or transform the conflicts between self and world.

4

TOWARD PLOT: THE LANGUAGE OF SOUND

> Yet with health's nectar some strange thirst was blent,
> The fateful growth, the unnamed discontent,
> The inward shaping toward some unborn power,
> Some deeper-breathing act, the being's flower.
> After all gestures, words, and speech of eyes,
> The soul had more to tell, and broke in sighs.
> Then from the east, with glory on his head
> Such as low-slanting beams on corn-waves spread,
> Came Jubal with his lyre: there 'mid the throng,
> Where the blank space was, poured a solemn song.
>
> ("The Legend of Jubal," p. 23)

GEORGE ELIOT'S CONVICTIONS regarding the significance of sound and music can be documented not only through their pervasiveness in her fiction but also through her extrafictional comments and actions. For instance, as early as 1840 she particularly admired one of Wordworth's poems, "On the Power of Sound" (*Letters,* 1:68).[1] Importantly, this poem is contained in that section of his *Collected Works* entitled "Poems of the Imagination." Further, George Eliot herself chose the same topic some years later for one of her better efforts at poetry, "The Legend of Jubal." It is apparent in both Wordsworth's and Eliot's conception of sound that the possibilities inherent in that metaphor permit them to express an ordered, or "harmonic," relationship between self and world.

It is important to note the links between sound and George Eliot's other dominant language of consumption and space. In the quotation from "The Legend of Jubal" above, these metaphors begin to coalesce by means of their common focus upon certain orders and energies as the fundamental conditions of existence. The lines quoted draw upon the language of appetite, of organic growth, of sea, and of space. But the anxieties that can result either from man's insatiable appetite or from the world's alien largeness are avoided here because the resolution of these anxieties—music—is, although "sensible," nonetheless intangible. Because of this, the power and ordered harmony of music permit Eliot to transform those metaphors that announce man's physical limitations into expressions of his spiritual possibilities. Although her characters (Maggie Tulliver, for instance) can indeed have insatiable mental appetites, the sustenance they receive through the ear is not necessarily a devouring. Neither is the filling of surrounding space with music an entrapment or a suffocation, because that space remains permeable, the waves of sound (like the waves of light) expressing a medium rather than a limit. That medium transforms the relationship between self and world from a mechanical relationship into a vital one, because it incarnates a twofold capacity: the power of mind to hear the living world speaking to a human being, and the subsequent power of mind to answer that external voice. What Eliot has done through music, then, is to transfer the ground of her interest from the physical to the mental world, although she takes with her the problematic relationship of inner and outer, production and consumption—expressed now in terms of yearning and possession or of influence and impression. Of course, the power of her own fiction is dependent here, too, upon the degree to which she perceives the powers of mind and music to be both literally and metaphorically significant.

In order for the language of sound and music to have significance for George Eliot, it must embody truths concerning both internal and external nature. Obviously, the world is made up of sounds, and people are capable of hearing those sounds. Certain qualifications must be made, however, especially when the world of sound is presented in language that is clearly metaphorical:

> For there is seldom any wrong-doing which does not carry along with it some downfall of blindly-climbing hopes, some hard entail of suffering, some quickly-satiated desire that survives, with the life in death of old paralytic vice, to see itself cursed by its woeful progeny —some tragic mark of kinship in the one brief life to the far-stretching life that went before, and to the life that is to come after, such as has raised the pity and terror of men ever since they began to discern between will and destiny. But these things are often unknown to the world; for there is much pain that is quite noiseless; and vibrations

that make human agonies are often a mere whisper in the *roar of hurrying existence.* (*Felix Holt the Radical,* "Introduction," p. 9, emphasis mine)

If we had a keen vision and feeling of all ordinary life, it would be like hearing the grass grow and the squirrel's heart beat, and we should die of *that roar which lies on the other side of silence.* (*Middlemarch,* ch. 20, p. 144, emphasis mine)[2]

First, then, we may associate raw sound with existence itself; sound is a proof of the reality of external life and of its vitality. Yet its largeness and apparent lack of order are announced by the term "roar" —a word that also implies its frightful destructiveness. For this reason, Eliot precedes the passage quoted from *Middlemarch* above with the remark that "perhaps our frames could hardly bear too much" sensitivity.

Our frames, our course, are so "ordered" or constructed that we can indeed hear; this means that, in the language George Eliot has most recourse to, we can become conscious of or "vibrate" to influences from the roaring existence around us. The following passages reveal the range of relationships which Eliot expresses through the term "vibration":

When suddenly the great bell in the palace-tower rang out a mighty peal: not the hammer-sound of alarm, but an agitated peal of triumph; and one after another every other bell in every other tower seemed to catch the vibration and join the chorus. And, as the chorus swelled and swelled till the air seemed made of sound—little flames, vibrating too, as if the sound had caught fire, burst out between the turrets of the palace and on the girdling towers. (*Romola,* ch. 36, vol. 2, p. 40)

Among all the human beings present, there was perhaps not one whose frame vibrated more strongly than [Baldassarre's] to the tones and words of the preacher; but it had vibrated like a harp of which all the strings had been wrenched away except one. (*Romola,* ch. 24, vol. 1, p. 351)

[Philip writes] "I have felt the vibration of chords in your [Maggie's] nature that I have continually felt the want of in his [Stephen's]." (*The Mill on the Floss,* bk. 7, ch. 3, p. 439)

The vainest woman is never thoroughly conscious of her own beauty till she is loved by the man who sets her own passion vibrating in return. (*Adam Bede,* ch. 15, p. 129)

> But by this time the effect of the Tractarian agitation was beginning to be felt in backward provincial regions, and the Tractarian satire on the Low-Church party was beginning to tell even on those who disavowed or resisted Tractarian doctrines. The vibration of an intellectual movement was felt from the golden head to the miry toes of the Establishment. ("Amos Barton," ch. 2, p. 67)

> Here, with the nearness of an answering smile, here within the vibrating bond of mutual speech, was the bright creature whom she had trusted—who had come to her like the spirit of morning visiting the dim vault where she sat as the bride of a worn-out life; and now, with a full consciousness which had never awakened before, she stretched out her arms towards him and cried with bitter cries that their nearness was a parting vision. (*Middlemarch,* ch. 80, p. 576)

Each of these passages suggests that the influence of what is external to the self is not a devouring or an invasion, but a "resonance." The "frame" of the self is stirred to activity by the activity outside the self; indeed, as the passage about Hetty from *Adam Bede* seems to imply, that stirring becomes the means whereby the self actually becomes "conscious" of its own reality. As a logical, metaphorical extension of this concept, Eliot frequently portrays the characters in the novels as musical instruments, responsive to the invisible vibrations of the world in which they live. Hetty Sorrel is like Memnon's statue, vibrating only to "certain shortlived sunbeams of morning" (*Adam Bede,* ch. 9, pp. 83–84), and Dorothea Brooke puts Will Ladislaw in mind of an Aeolian harp (*Middlemarch,* ch. 9. p. 59). Daniel Deronda, in speaking to Mordecai about his sense of "inherited yearning," applies the metaphor to mankind in general: "The ancestral life would lie within them as a dim longing for unknown objects and sensations, and the spell-bound habit of their inherited frames would be like a cunningly-wrought musical instrument, never played on, but quivering throughout in uneasy mysterious moanings of its intricate structure that, under the right touch, gives music" (*Daniel Deronda,* ch. 63, p. 565). The language of appetite ("longing") and order ("intricate structure") in this passage is by now familiar. Further, the doubleness of self and world which appears at first to frustrate the self in relation to that world now raises the possibility that, under the right circumstances, difference can generate resonance and, therefore, harmony.

George Eliot's language of sound and music, then, provides a number of levels of interpretation. At its most abstract, such language relies upon the diction and relationships of acoustics to remind us of our place amidst and perviousness to noise—noise that may or may not announce or call forth harmony. More self-conscious are those metaphors offered by her narrator to explain other, often abstract conditions by means of accepted relationships between sound and ear. Finally, such metaphors seem to generate their own consequences when Eliot makes them of larger fictional significance, formulating scenes and plots that rely on composites of both literal and metaphorical acts of creating and hearing sounds. Although these acts are indeed to be taken literally, their existence "next to" or "on top of" more figurative language gives them their own linguistic resonance.

In writing an extended poem about the figure who first converted sound into music—Jubal—George Eliot provides us with an opportunity to examine this complex of language and meaning in extended fashion. Further, since her poem (unlike Wordsworth's "On the Power of Sound") is not a meditative ode but a narrative, "The Legend of Jubal" provides several insights into the functioning of this musical metaphor in her fiction. In fact, the very structure of the narrative becomes an important aspect of the meaning of the metaphor. Thus, while Eliot agrees with Wordsworth that music is a means to the imaginative reconciliation between mind and world, she emphasizes that the world exists "in time."[3]

The story of "The Legend of Jubal" implies that the invention of music is a part of the self's accommodation to a world that is alive and also capable of dying. As Dinah Morris explains to Lisbeth Bede, "I remember, too, when my dear aunt died, I longed for the sound of her bad cough in the nights, instead of the silence that came when she was gone" (*Adam Bede,* ch. 10, p. 96). The relationship between sound and silence becomes, then, a means of recognizing, not spatial, but temporal annihilation. Indeed, time itself is made known in the poem through sound as a measure of duration:

> Time, vague as air before, new terrors stirred,
> With measured wing now audibly arose
> Throbbing through all things to some unknown close.
>
> (P. 8)

The moment that has separated the "before" of these lines from the anxiety over time is the death of Lamech's son, which first introduces the children of Cain to the reality of God's curse. Cain had hoped to evade death by getting beyond the space ruled by God:

He wandered eastward, seeking some far strand
Ruled by kind gods who asked no offerings
Save pure field-fruits, as aromatic things,
To feed the subtler sense of frames divine
That lived on fragrance for their food and wine:
Wild joyous gods, who winked at faults and folly,
And could be pitiful and melancholy.
He never had a doubt that such gods were;
He looked within, and saw them mirrored there.
(P. 3)

The death of Lamech's "fairest boy" has forced Cain to admit that an angry god has found their "home" and "His most cruel will" shall bind them all (pp. 6, 7). In other words, Cain has not been able to escape the space ruled by another who is emphatically more than a mirror image of his own desires. This awakening to the shock of personal mortality is a major and recurrent moment in George Eliot's fiction, and music is important as a means of transmuting the pulsations of passing time from perpetual reminders of death into expressions of man's immortal power.

George Eliot's narrative offers three possible methods for achieving this transcendence in the stories of Lamech's three remaining sons—Jabal, Tubal-Cain, and Jubal. For each, the anxiety of the "unknown close" to which his life is tending requires that he respond by countering with his own form of closure or ordering. Jabal accepts his condition most calmly, ordering the nature around him into a model of domestic joy: "He began/The pastoral life, and, sire of joys to be,/ Spread the sweet ties that bind the family/O'er dear dumb souls ["the lowing kine"] that thrilled at man's caress" (pp. 12, 11). Jabal, then, has proved his power over Nature (if it is Nature that tells us of our mortality) by binding a part of nature to man's sense of family order.

These efforts to counter Nature's power with man's own are also manifest in the language of a more general passage about the intentions of Lamech's other sons:

Then while the soul its way with sound can cleave,
And while the arm is strong to strike and heave,
Let soul and arm give shape that will abide
And rule above our graves, and power divide
With that great god of day, whose rays must bend
As we shall make the moving shadows tend.
(P. 9)

Tubal-Cain is the man who triumphs through his arm, for he is the plastic artist whose shapes, the outward result of "inspiring vision" (p. 13), provide useful tools to man. He has forced the raw materials of nature to conform to his "will creative" (p. 13) just as man's manipulation of his material environment can force the sun's rays to make shadows as those materials are arranged.[4] But Tubal-Cain's creation, linked as it is to material things, has "mixed-ends"—his apparently "harmless toys" hold the hidden destructive power of the "axe, the club, the spikèd wheel, [and] the chain" as well as "the strong bar, the saw, and deep-curved blade" of "hearth and harvest-home" (p. 14).

The remaining son, Jubal, has a "frame/Fashioned to finer senses" (p. 10), and the various accomplishments of his brothers only make him hungrier to express the emotions generated by those accomplishments. Just as the art of the cloister arouses in Daniel Deronda an awareness of the full implications of the nature that preceded the art, Jubal's response to Tubal-Cain's creativity teaches him simultaneously about the outward world and his own inner life:

Jubal, too, watched the hammer, till his eyes,
No longer following its fall or rise,
Seemed glad with something that they could not see,
But only listened to—some melody,
Wherein dumb longings inward speech had found,
Won from the common store of struggling sound.
Then, as the metal shapes more various grew,
And, hurled upon each other, resonance drew,
Each gave new tones, the revelations dim
Of some external soul that spoke for him:
The hollow vessel's clang, the clash, the boom,
Like light that makes wide spiritual room
And skyey spaces in the spaceless thought,
To Jubal such enlargèd passion brought
That love, hope, rage, and all experience,
Were fused in vaster being, fetching thence
Concords and discords, cadences and cries
That seemed from some world-shrouded soul to rise,
Some rapture more intense, some mightier rage,
Some living sea that burst the bounds of man's brief age.
(Pp. 15-16)

What Jubal awakens to is the power of his imagination's discovering a means for expressing itself in response to external stimuli, and finding eternity in the expression. The blankness of space around him is filled with "tremors" arising from the "giant soul of earth" (p. 18). Indeed, what had been empty space is filled by Jubal and his music (p. 23), and the result not only fills that vacuum with sound but also binds the listeners into a unity of past and future, for the old remember their youth and the young look to the time to come. The completed union in time and space occurs as all arise and begin to dance with "ringèd feet swayed by each close-linked palm" (p. 25).

The passage describing Jubal's intentions and success suggests that Eliot means for music to symbolize mental power of a particular sort. Music brings order or form to brute matter, and the superabundance of artistry itself "informs the sense/With fuller union, finer difference–" (p. 19). This balance of opposing drives toward wholeness and distinctness is echoed in the description of Jubal's first invention, the lyre:

> He made it, and from out its measured frame
> Drew the harmonic soul, whose answers came
> With guidance sweet and lessons of delight
> Teaching to ear and hand the blissful Right,
> Where strictest law is gladness to the sense,
> And all desire bends toward obedience.
>
> (P. 20)

What is crucial for Eliot, both here and in her fiction, is the union of desire and obedience: order in this case is no stern taskmaster who requires the bending of the will away from all that is joyful. Joy itself arises from the perception of an order that pleases both the outward sense and the inward soul. What Jubal has found is a "heart of music in the might of sound" (p. 21)–that is, a center and source of potent feeling within the raw power of outward "noise." Thus Eliot, like Wordsworth, finds in the correlation between sound and music a metaphor for the power of imaginative perception and for the harnessing of that power.

Having had his imaginative insight and his outward proof of its potency in the response of his people, Jubal goes out in confidence to bless the world with harmony and to bring more and more of life's disparate materials under his command. In this regard he is typical of all of George Eliot's "imaginative" characters–characters who expect outward reality to conform to inward vision–from Hetty Sorrel to Mordecai Cohen. Jubal's expectation of ever "higher" personal success, like that of those characters, (and exemplified in the poem by his climbing higher and higher mountains, which will eventually help him to hear the music of the spheres) is doomed to frustration. Instead of one final solid peak to stand upon, Jubal comes to the sea, "this main—/Myriads of maddened horses thundering o'er the plain" (p. 29). Eliot's use of the sea as symbolic of emotion can help explain this section of the poem, for Jubal does seem to believe that a part of his difficulty is internal: "yet no more/Can soul, hand, voice, with interchanging lore/Tell what the earth is saying" (pp. 29–30). Yet this seems to announce a lack rather than an excess of power. Here, then, the sea is associated with the engendering madness of the ocean's "multitudinous roar,/Its plunge and hiss upon the pebbled shore" (p. 29). This shore provides him no "footing," so he wishes to return to the "fair plain" where he was born, hoping to find there the comfort and the energy that seem to have escaped from inside him only to threaten in the sound of the sea.

Jubal finds that energy, although he does not receive the comfort he expects from his family and home. He has been replaced within the familiar landscape, so that even the "buzzing groups" of descendants everywhere about him, "Spread like a murmuring crowd o'er plain and steep," echo the maddened horses that had driven him back from the edge of his stable world (p. 33). The comforting circle of familiar faces dancing in union is no more. Yet there does remain the power that had brought about that earlier, more manageable community; what Jubal meets on his return is not that foregone moment, but his own powers of mind made visible in the stream of singing people—

> Brought like fulfilment of forgotten prayer;
> As if his soul, breathed out upon the air,
> Had held the invisible seeds of harmony
> Quick with the various strains of life to be.
>
> (Pp. 33–34)

The divine word being sung (which corresponds to Wordsworth's concluding praise of God's power as "Logos") is "Jubal," perceived as the "common need, love, joy, that knits them in one whole" as well as the name "for glorious power untouched by that slow death/Which creeps with creeping time" (pp. 34, 37–38). In other words, Jubal's name has come to represent music simultaneously as a power and as an order springing from that power.

Jubal's "little pulse of self" (p. 36) still desires some comfort in its declining age; he has a "burning need" to "claim the deed/That lived away from him" (p. 35). What he wishes is an audience, a recognition of his act and accomplishment: "For no eye saw him, while with living pride/Each voice with each in praise of Jubal vied" (p. 36). Because Jubal's name has been transferred from his single self to the power brought into conscious existence in the world by that self, his attempt at personal recognition is met with scorn and blows. In despair, Jubal asserts that his powerful past is irretrievable; yet a vision comes to him in terms that are pertinent to our understanding of the consolation offered by music itself. Jubal sees that vision as a personification of "great Song," which manages a paradoxical union of light and darkness, past and present:

> The face bent over him like silver night
> In long-remembered summers; that calm light
> Of days which shine in firmaments of thought,
> That past unchangeable, from change still wrought.
> And gentlest tones were with the vision blent:
> He knew not if that gaze the music sent,
> Or music that calm gaze: to hear, to see,
> Was but one undivided ecstasy:
> The raptured senses melted into one,
> And parting life a moment's freedom won
> From in and outer, as a little child
> Sits on a bank and sees blue heavens mild
> Down in the water, and forgets its limbs,
> And knoweth nought save the blue heaven that swims.
> (Pp. 39-40)

As both the voice of his "past" and the personification of the power to which that past is dedicated, the vision reveals its peculiar ability to wrest order from power and power from order (the unchangeable wrought from change). For just as the heavens (whether conceived of as the order of the stars or as the order of God) and the water (conceived of as the depths and power of the self) become one in the passage, so the order of conscious sight and the power of sound conjoin to provide a present that incarnates the reality of Jubal's entire past. The vision wishes Jubal to recognize two apparently contradictory realities: he is both the "out-breathed being" that is the music surrounding him and the poor human remnant about to expire unnoticed in a thicket. Indeed, the hunger he feels now is the very hunger that brought music into being earlier. George Eliot reverts to the metaphor of marriage to express Jubal's doubleness, the "Song" being the Other (the bride) that Jubal wed; yet in the course of the succeeding passage the sexual terms change, and Jubal becomes female, the womb from which the potent seed of music is brought forth. Eliot seems here to be consoling Jubal for his present pain by simultaneously reaching into his past (his bride) and into his future (his child), expecting that the results of his life in both those realms will compensate for his coming dissolution.[5] Whether that is the case or not, what seems certain is that the *felt* consolation for Jubal comes in the union, the "symphony," of his present vision, when at last "he heard more faintly and more faintly knew,/Quitting mortality, a quenched sun-wave,/The All-creating *Presence* for his grave" (pp. 42-43, emphasis mine).

Although Jubal's death may be tragic, George Eliot obviously wishes to derive from it a kind of transcendence which reconciles us to the tragedy; in the face of our powerlessness before the reality of death, she has asserted the twofold power of mind to be moved and to move. Jubal's yearning was awakened by a "resonance" in the world about him which confirmed the difference and the likeness between his inner mind and outward nature. To bring that resonance into full, conscious existence and to express it for others, Jubal had to create music, which is itself a praise of that resonance. Although his capacity to create music cannot negate the power of death, it can negate its effect upon his state of mind by means of his experience—literally felt and metaphorically comprehended—of the opposing power of sound.

George Eliot then, uses the musical term *harmony* to express the orderly relationship between self and world in her fiction. Often, this usage—instead of being an opportunity to explore the implications of metaphoric language—presupposes the acceptance of the analogy by the reader. A few examples will serve to underscore the essential elements of that abstract kind of harmony which "The Legend of Jubal" attempts to "prove."

In Eliot's fiction, admirable characters frequently reveal their imaginative alertness by their ability to delight in nonmelodious sounds that express a harmony in which the mind alone, rather than the ear, can delight. Wordsworth provides a description of this condition through diction that echoes the closing lines of "The Legend of Jubal":

> . . . from the Boy there came
> Feelings and emanations—things which were
> Light to the sun and music to the wind.
> ("Michael," lines 200-202)

Thus, the jocose talk of haymakers in *Adam Bede* can mingle prettily with other joyous natural sounds, for their souls are making merry music (ch. 19, p. 177); Esther Lyon's testifying for Felix Holt in court is a beautiful action from which "came forth music that brought tears" (ch. 46, p. 458); and Daniel Deronda's soul responds not simply to the

"O Patria Mia" but also to the harmonies of an heroic passion expressing itself in unselfish love (ch. 45, p. 420). These "sounds"—even when they have outward grating qualities—express the harmony between man and his world. As such they are like the "service from the lowing mead" and the "hungry barkings" of an eagle in Wordworth's "On the Power of Sound" (lines 197, 201), for "all worlds, all natures, mood and measure keep" (line 206). They imply a perceived order in which all actions and objects have a place. As George Eliot says of Mr. Irwine in *Adam Bede,* "however ill he harmonised with sound theories of the clerical office, he somehow harmonised extremely well with that peaceful landscape" (ch. 5, p. 61). In addition to a harmony with external nature, Eliot also discerns a harmony with the past, as when the "old Florentine" in the proem of *Romola* is asserted to be "duly tinctured with the learning of his age, and judged not altogether with the vulgar, but in harmony with the ancients" ("Proem," vol. 1, p. 7). Yet these usages of the term *harmony* are so clearly intended to be valuative that the speaker has no interest in pausing to consider the possible literal implications of the relationship expressed by the metaphor. More ambiguous are those moments when Eliot asks the reader to focus simultaneously on the literal *and* the metaphorical possibilities of such language. The most obvious examples of such moments involve the presentation of characters as persons susceptible to sound and music.[6]

In general, the most promising characters in George Eliot's fiction are the most sensitive to the possibilities of sound, music, and harmony. Adam Bede, Maggie Tulliver, Romola, Rufus Lyon, Dorothea Brooke, Will Ladislaw, Tertius Lydgate, Daniel Deronda, and Gwendolen Harleth are all susceptible to music, especially musical speech. Even such a narrow figure as Baldassarre in *Romola* retains his capacity to respond to sound despite his loss of reason. In marked contrast are those characters like Casaubon, Celia Brooke, and Henleigh Grandcourt, who are either made nervously irritable by voices or embarrassed by the visual posture of the speaker/singer (*Middlemarch,* ch. 2, p. 13; ch. 3, p. 24; *Daniel Deronda,* ch. 48, p. 442). We can see, then, (as the metaphor of the soul as musical instrument implies) that the capacity to hear and then respond indicates a complex relationship between self and world. Further, as in Eliot's other metaphorical language, the relationship between musical capacity and inner worth is not straightforwardly hierarchical. For instance, the merely superficial ability to create music as a learned talent—a talent that both Rosamond Vincy and Gwendolen Harleth possess—is not necessarily a guarantee of imaginative or moral grandeur. Although triumphant musicians do exist, in the persons of Herr Klesmer and Mirah Cohen (significantly, present only in Eliot's last novel), Eliot's comedy at the expense of those who would simplistically equate music and morality is more frequent. For instance, although she asserts the goodness of Dinah Morris at least partly through the musicality of her voice, she mocks the reader for imagining great things of Joshua Rann just because he can sing well (*Adam Bede,* ch. 18, pp. 170–71). Then there are those characters who possess melodious voices, the sounds of which often comfort others. These characters include Dinah Morris, Dorothea Brooke, Tertius Lydgate, Romola, Daniel Deronda, and Mirah Cohen. There are also figures, like Gwendolen Harleth and Rosamond Vincy, whose tones reveal simultaneously their loveliness and their neutrality or well-bred languor (*Daniel Deronda,* ch. 1, p. 6; *Middlemarch,* ch. 58, p. 434). Felix Holt's powerful voice expresses his powerful personality (*Felix Holt the Radical,* ch. 5, p. 61), while Esther Lyon's silvery tones are a sign of her breeding (ch. 10, p. 129). Comic figures like Lady Arrowpoint of *Daniel Deronda* are cursed with inharmonious voices that bear little relation to their thoughts, although in Lady Arrowpoint's case one can't therefore really assert that a bad voice, like Mary Garth's plainness, will guarantee a good soul (ch. 5, p. 30).

A focal point for such apparent confusion in the use of the language of hearing and harmony to define spiritual worth is the fundamental duality of the metaphor itself. Harmony, whether meant literally or metaphorically, presupposes both a perceiver of that harmony and something or someone that creates or expresses it. George Eliot, at different moments, examines different elements within that process of perception. One example of the shifting nature of her concern—and therefore of the shifting interpretation of such language—is the delineation of the growing love between Rosamond and Lydgate in *Middlemarch.* Whereas Rosamond is the exquisitely correct musician, Lydgate is the "emotional elephant" entranced but unknowing about the techniques of musical production. Rosamond's essentially lifeless accuracy of imitation contrasts with Lydgate's passionate, if unlettered, response to external stimuli. Lydgate's mistake, much like Adam Bede's mistake about Hetty's beauty, is to confuse his own depth of sensibility with the object that calls forth his response. Thus, it is often the hearer, rather than the speaker, who is the focus of admiration in Eliot's fiction.

Further, the impediments to harmony may lodge either in the perceiver/hearer or in the thing perceived (whether the latter is considered to be the sound itself or the creator of that sound). For instance, although we obviously admire Lydgate more than Rosamond in *Middlemarch,* it is easy to recognize that not only the emotional greatness but also the intellectual obtuseness is Lydgate's own; Rosamond *is* musical—but she is not intensely passionate or emotional. Similarly, although Maggie Tulliver is more responsive to music than many of Eliot's other characters, she has perhaps the greatest difficulty in achieving harmony. Her "want" of inward harmony (*The Mill on the Floss,* bk. 5, ch. 5, p. 305) announces a lack, which therefore implies that such harmony must be partly created rather than simply heard or discovered. Yet the blame cannot all be laid at Maggie's psychological door. What has caused Maggie to lose her inward harmony, and thereby her peace with outer things, is at least partly her difficulty with others' passions. Indeed, when the language of sound and harmony is used to express the relationships between persons, rather than simply between a human being and the world in general, the implications of hearing and producing sounds, melodious or otherwise, become fully apparent.

To perceive harmony, of course, one must first be able to hear; George Eliot's complex evaluation of such sensitivity is apparent in *Daniel Deronda.* When Gwendolen Harleth plays Hermione (ch. 6, pp. 41-43), a number of patterns of meaning coalesce, although here our primary interest is in the parable of the statue awakened to life through the striking of a chord.[7] Gwendolen is particularly appropriate for our purposes since she is not immediately recognizable as one of Eliot's admired characters. She has, however, that susceptibility to sounds and cries which, as proof of the power of imagination within her, will be a source of her salvation. But beyond the immediate context of Gwendolen's fate, the symbolic significance of the Hermione myth can illuminate a repeated pattern of response in Eliot's fiction, for it begins to associate the single metaphor with an action. The ability to hear the cry, or, in terms of the parable, the struck chord, and to respond to it (even if only with a cry of fear, as Gwendolen does), affirms one's connection with a palpitating outward life. Appropriately, the chord that brings life also brings death, for the panel opens to reveal to Gwendolen the dead face she fears—much as Eliot had hinted in *Middlemarch* that we could die of too much sensibility. In its broadest terms, to come to life means to come to death, as the sons of Cain learned in their simultaneous awareness of death and of an inner vitality that opposes and fears that death.

An essential step in the pattern of George Eliot's novels is evident in her use of cries. Expressed in *The Mill on the Floss* as "responding to the heart's need," the capacity to hear the cry of another characterizes the relations not only between Maggie and several of the other characters in that novel but also between Esther Lyon and Mrs. Transome, between Lydgate and Dorothea, and between Daniel Deronda and both Mordecai and Gwendolen:

> It was already near midnight, but with these thoughts succeeding and returning in her mind like scenes through which she was living, Esther had a more intense wakefulness than any she had known by day. All had been stillness hitherto, except the fitful wind outside. But her ears now caught a sound within—slight, but sudden. She moved near her door, and heard the sweep of something on the matting outside. . . . She opened her door, and in the dim light of the corridor, where the glass above seemed to make a glimmering sky, she saw Mrs. Transome's tall figure pacing slowly, with her cheek upon her hand. . . . As Esther saw that image of restless misery, it blent itself by a rapid flash with all that Harold had said in the evening. . . . In an instant Mrs. Transome felt Esther's arm round her neck, and a voice saying softly—
>
> "Oh, why didn't you call me before?" (*Felix Holt the Radical,* ch. 49, pp. 475-76; ch. 50, p. 478)

> Lydgate rose, and Dorothea mechanically rose at the same time, unclasping her cloak and throwing it off as if it stifled her. He was bowing and quitting her, when an impulse which if she had been alone would have turned into a prayer, made her say with a sob in her voice— . . .
>
> For years after Lydgate remembered the impression produced in him by this involuntary appeal—this cry from soul to soul, without other consciousness than their moving with kindred natures in the same embroiled medium, the same troublous fitfully-illuminated life. (*Middlemarch,* ch. 30, pp. 213-14)

> The more exquisite quality of Deronda's nature—that keenly perceptive sympathetic emotiveness which ran along with his speculative tendency—was never more thoroughly tested. He felt nothing that could be called belief in the validity of Mordecai's impressions concerning him or in the probability of any greatly effective issue: what he felt was a profound sensibility to a cry from the depths of another soul; and accompanying that, the summons to be receptive instead of superciliously prejudging. (*Daniel Deronda,* ch. 40, p. 373)

> He awaited her coming in the back drawing-room—part of that white and crimson space where they had sat together at the musical

party, where Gwendolen had said for the first time that her lot depended on his not forsaking her, and her appeal had seemed to melt into the melodic cry—*Per pietà non dirmi addio. . . .* If she cried towards him, what then? She cried as the child cries whose little feet have fallen backward—cried to be taken by the hand, lest she should lose herself.

The cry pierced Deronda. (*Daniel Deronda,* ch. 65, pp. 577, 582)

Each of these passages depends upon certain conditions in both the hearer and the speaker of the cry. The figure of the child in the last passage helps explain one important component: the cry is itself often involuntary or unconscious, intended more as an expression of feeling than as directed speech. The relative helplessness of the caller adds a poignancy and urgency to the call, so, for instance, Hetty's denial of her child's cry is an essential part of her failure. The same is true regarding Gwendolen's reaction to the drowning Grandcourt's cry for help. For both Hetty and Gwendolen, the sound of the cry asserts simultaneously their capacity to hear and their failure to respond or, rather, to respond quickly and impulsively enough.

Hearing the cry appears to be an equally involuntary matter. This is clearest regarding Esther prior to her awareness of the pacing figure in the corridor. As her preoccupation with her own troubles subsides, she becomes unconsciously receptive to a reality outside her own thoughts and even her own room. Such a psychological state is admirably described in Wordsworth's portrayal of the Boy of Winander calling the owls: sometimes the boy does not hear the sound he so intently waits for, but the relaxation of his private purpose permits him suddenly to hear the living world going on almost unnoticed all around him (see *The Prelude,* bk. 5, lines 389–422).[8] George Eliot connects this kind of spontaneous awakening with internal as well as external impulses: Mirah remarks about her reaction to the wicked Count of her past that "[s]ome feelings are like our hearing: they come as sounds do, before we know their reason" (*Daniel Deronda,* ch. 20, p. 161).

There are moments when characters in Eliot's fiction experience a sense of oneness as a result of hearing, not just a cry, but harmony of the largest sort. This experience seems reserved for certain particularly susceptible people and reaches its most resonant form in Adam Bede and Daniel Deronda. In chapter 1, I quoted the passage regarding Daniel's response to the Hebrew church service; the ensuing remarks of the narrator may offer further insight about such an experience:

> The Hebrew liturgy, like others, has its translations of litany, lyric, proclamation, dry statement and blessing; but this evening all were one for Deronda: . . . all were blent for him as one expression of a binding history, tragic and yet glorious. He wondered at the strength of his own feeling; it seemed beyond the occasion—what one might imagine to be a divine influx in the darkness, before there was any vision to interpret. The whole scene was a coherent strain, its burthen a passionate regret, which, if he had known the liturgy for the Day of Reconciliation, he might have clad in its antithetic burthen: "Happy the eye which saw all these things; but verily to hear only of them afflicts our soul. Happy the eye that saw our temple and the joy of our congregation; but verily to hear only of them afflicts our soul. Happy the eye that saw the fingers when tuning every kind of song; but verily to hear only of them afflicts our soul." (*Daniel Deronda,* ch. 32, p. 274)

The same sense of oneness that George Eliot stresses in Jubal's first musical performance is emphasized here. Additionally, this sense of union seems the paramount compensation for the "burthen" of the liturgy—for the words speak of the reality of disunion, most particularly a disunion between intangible song and tangible world. This is not unlike Adam Bede's experience in hearing the hymn at his father's funeral service. Here, too, a sense of present oneness is a sense of oneness in suffering:

> But Adam's thoughts of Hetty did not deafen him to the service; they rather blended with all the other deep feelings for which the church service was a channel to him this afternoon, as a certain consciousness of our entire past and our imagined future blends itself with all our moments of keen sensibility. And to Adam the church service was the best channel he could have found for his mingled regret, yearning, and resignation; its interchange of beseeching cries for help, with outbursts of faith and praise—its recurrent responses and the familiar rhythm of its collects, seemed to speak for him as no other form of worship could have done. (*Adam Bede,* ch. 18, p. 170)

Such moments are epoch-making for both men, who are in the midst of complicated crises regarding parent and beloved. The public character of the ritual—indeed, its reality as ritual—connects their private ordeal with a larger social group, allowing each to get beyond self by means of the very intensity of that sense of self. Quite similar to this experience, although significant for selfhood in a different way, is Mirah's description of her vision of her mother:

> I think my life began with waking up and loving my mother's face: it was so near to me, and her arms were round me, and she sang to me. One hymn she sang so often, so often: and then she taught me to sing it with her: it was the first I ever sang. They were always Hebrew hymns she sang; and because I never knew the meaning of the words they seemed full of nothing but our love and happiness. When I lay in my little bed and it was all white above me, she used to bend over me between me and the white, and sing in a sweet low voice. I can dream myself back into that time when I am awake, and often it comes back to me in my sleep. (*Daniel Deronda,* ch. 20, p. 155)

Here, in unadulterated form, is the joy that Jubal believes to be embodied in musical harmony. Mirah experiences it as the first, the fundamental, joy of oneness with the world through oneness with the mother. Certainly, George Eliot is describing here a sense of the fullness of "presence" as the crucial element of such moments.

An alternate kind of hearing which is of recurrent interest to Eliot provides a useful means of examing both the third term of aural perception (the speaker) and those factors that complicate or impede the achievement of harmony between self and world. In this case, instead of hearing the cry for help, the hearer becomes aware of a call to action. A clear example is Romola's first attempt at escape from the imprisonments of her life in Florence: it begins with the language of space and then animates that space with the sudden voice of another:

> When Romola sat down on the stone under the cypress, all things conspired to give her the sense of freedom and solitude: her escape from the accustomed walls and streets; the widening distance from her husband, who was by this time riding towards Siena, while every hour would take her farther on the opposite way; the morning stillness; the great dip of ground on the roadside making a gulf between her and the sombre calm of the mountains. For the first time in her life she felt alone in the presence of the earth and sky, with no human presence interposing and making a law for her.
>
> Suddenly a voice close to her said—
>
> "You are Romola de' Bardi, the wife of Tito Melema." (*Romola,* ch. 40, vol. 2, p. 99)

The voice that breaks in upon Romola's sense of singleness in the world is Savonarola's. He intends not simply to announce his presence or to ask for assistance but to insist that Romola conform to the laws that he perceives derive at least partially from who she is: not just Romola,— but Romola "de' Bardi" and "wife of Tito Melema."

In this situation the speaker, because he self-consciously intends his words, is as important as the listener. Such intentional speeches are frequently delivered by preachers in George Eliot's fiction. Indeed, it is not only her desire to offer moral exhortation which caused Eliot to be preoccupied with the sermonizer but also her conviction that truth is most forceful when it is spoken.[9] As a species of sound, speech combines the sense of life beyond the self with the actual import of the words spoken. Thus, figures like Dinah Morris, Rufus Lyon, and Mordecai exemplify the union of sincerity of tone and fervency of belief in "the good"; yet they often do not engage the reader's sympathies as wholeheartedly as the author seems to expect.[10] Savonarola in *Romola,* on the other hand, provides a more complete example of the degree to which Eliot believes in and expresses the moving power of the human voice.

In many ways, Romola's fate, which provides the plot of a novel otherwise preoccupied with Savonarola,[11] is determined by her hearing certain voices—those of her brother Dino, of Savonarola, and of the child in the village—and responding to them. The real focus in this series of calls for her allegiance or help, however, is upon Savonarola, whose ability to capture the attention of a whole city must have appealed to George Eliot as a real counterpart to the mythical Jubal's success. Romola's first meeting with the Frate brings about her subjection to his personality through the tone of his voice; her retreat from Florence is halted by his voice as it recalls her to faithfulness to the *spoken* word of her marriage; and her wavering faith in subjection to duty is upheld by his voice in the *duomo.*

Savonarola seems most potent in the pulpit. George Eliot characterizes his sense of his mission at its best in words that carry peculiar import for this discussion:

> Sometimes he saw himself taking a glorious part in that revolt [against corruption], sending forth a voice that would be heard through all Christendom, and making the dead body of the Church tremble into new life, as the body of Lazarus trembled when the the Divine voice pierced the sepulchre. (Ch. 52, vol. 2, p. 228)

The awakening of the statue of Hermione in *Daniel Deronda* echoes this passage and suggests the degree to which Eliot links this process of moral awakening with the sound of a voice, even if only the "human voice divine."

Of course, Savonarola's problems as a preacher raise quite new questions about the language of sound as an expression of accommodation, even harmony, between self and world. Savonarola must, in his role as preacher, face the possibility that his own voice is not an extension of the true voice of God but is instead that feeble private voice to which Jubal is reduced at the close of his life. The more educated and subtle of Savonarola's hearers argue directly about the sources of his right and of his potency. The believer Cronaca begins by saying that there "has not been a change since the Quaresima, either in Rome or at Florence, but has put a new seal on the Frate's words." When Cei responds that the Frate's visions are stale and need more poetic imagination, Cronaca answers that great poets "no more think the truth stale which God has given him to utter, than they think the light of the moon is stale." Macchiavelli enters the discussion with a more psychological insight: "The secret of oratory lies, not in saying new things, but in saying things with a certain power that moves the hearers," to which Cennini adds that "part of the secret lies in the prophetic visions. Our people . . . will run after anything in the shape of a prophet, especially if he prophesies terrors and tribulations." Cronaca the believer then asserts that "the chief secret lies in the Frate's pure life and strong faith, which stamp him as a messenger of God." Even this, however, is not allowed to stand without question, for Cei concludes by saying that behind his purity is "the lust of arrogance": "He hears the air filled with his own name—Fra Girolamo Savonarola, of Ferrara; the prophet, the saint, the mighty preacher, who frightens the very babies of Florence into laying down their wicked baubles" (*Romola,* ch. 16, vol. 1, pp. 254–56).

Is it, then, the energy—either of the speaker himself or of the God he believes in—or the orderly relation between speech and reality which confirms Savonarola? Can his speech be considered vivifying, as the analogy with Lazarus implies, or is it a refined form of egoism, sending out sounds that prove his potency and reality only because the air is then filled with the echo of his own name? This dilemma is examined at length by Savonarola himself (and through him by George Eliot and the reader) when Romola pleads with Savonarola to intercede for Bernardo del Nero. The context for this confrontation is revealing: Chapter 59 begins with Romola's traversing one of Florence's many open piazzas, those broad public spaces reached by the narrow labyrinth of streets that are so important to the geography of the town itself. The space is filled with a human sea of gossip eddying about the various handbills, "jutting islets of black capitals" round which were "lakes of smaller characters setting forth arguments less necessary to be read" (vol. 2, p. 297). This crowd is but a preliminary to the throng that awaits the fate of the appeal for mercy at the start of the next chapter:

> Not a hand's-breadth of pavement was to be seen, but only the heads of an eager struggling multitude. And instead of that background of silence in which the pattering footsteps and buzzing voices, the lute-thrumming or rapid scampering of the many night wanderers of Florence stood out in obtrusive distinctness, there was the background of a roar from mingled shouts and imprecations, tramplings and pushings, and accidental clashing of weapons, across which nothing was distinguishable but a darting shriek, or the heavy dropping toll of a bell. (Ch. 60, vol. 2, p. 310)

This crowd becomes the one in front of San Marco for Savonarola's last public speech, as well as the one that views the abortive trial by fire and finally his execution. Indeed, the experience of that crowd during Savonarola's speech offers a fit preliminary to the Frate's private condition, even though it follows chronologically his conversation with Romola. Expectation silences the crowd before San Marco:

> At last there was a *vibration* among the multitude, . . . as when men who have been watching for something in the heavens see the expected *presence* silently disclosing itself. The Frate had risen, turned towards the people, and partly pushed back his cowl. The monotonous wail of psalmody had ceased, and to those who stood near the pulpit, it was as if the sounds which had just been filling their ears had suddenly merged themselves in the force of Savonarola's flashing glance, as he looked round him in the silence. Then he stretched out his hands, which, in their exquisite delicacy, seemed transfigured from an animal organ for grasping into vehicles of sensibility too acute to need any gross contact: hands that came like an appealing speech from that part of his soul which was masked by his strong passionate face. (Ch. 62, vol. 2, pp. 331–32, emphasis mine)

Some people kneel at the stretching out of Savonarola's hands; more kneel when the voice comes, until "it rose to a masculine cry, as if protesting its power to bless under the clutch of a demon that wanted to stifle it: it rang like a trumpet to the extremeties of the Piazza, and under it every head was bowed" (p. 332). When he ceases speaking, and a "stream of brightness" breaks through the clouds to illuminate him, Savonarola feels rapturous confidence in his mission, but the narrator remarks that "it was but a *moment* that expanded itself in that prevision"; for, as the sunlight spreads impartially over all, a "confusion of voices" breaks out, and the "previous silence and universal kneeling" were for some only a "momentary spell" (p. 334, emphasis mine).

When Romola visits Savonarola before this event, she too kneels only momentarily. George Eliot begins here a doubled explanation of Savonarola's fading power, finding changes in both characters which then change their relationship. Nevertheless, Savonarola's mental condition is what concerns us most here, since he is the Jubal-like figure who has wished to confirm absolutely the harmony between his inner visions and the outward world. That this harmony is already absent is apparent since he has "had to quell inner voices that might become loud again when encouraged from without" (ch. 59, vol. 2, p. 300). When Romola insists that he speak now as he had done before, Savonarola approaches the divided nature of his call more directly: "My daughter, I speak as it is given me to speak—I am not master of the times when I may become the vehicle of knowledge beyond the common lights of men. In this case I have no illumination" (p. 302). When Romola begins pleading again, not simply for Bernardo but also for the opportunity to continue to believe in Savonarola, she relies upon the very language and belief that have supported him:

> It is pain to me to have spoken those words—yet I cannot help speaking. I am little and feeble compared with you; you brought me light and strength. But I submitted because I felt the proffered strength—because I saw the light. *Now* I cannot see it. Father, you yourself declare that there comes a moment when the soul must have no guide but the voice within it, to tell whether the consecrated thing has sacred virtue. And therefore I must speak. (P. 306)

George Eliot, continuing the association of light and speech which has been developing in the presentation of Savonarola, points out that the flame of his oratory has that "red" in it which comes from a desire for reflected grandeur from the great ends he seeks. Indeed, the inward tangle of "egoistic demands, false ideas, and difficult outward conditions" makes the "simplicity" of harmony between belief, desire, speech, and act impossible for him (p. 306).

Thus, Romola finally asserts that she "cannot hear the real voice" of Savonarola's "judgment and conscience" (p. 308), whereas Savonarola feels her voice to be "the voice of his enemies" (p. 309). Those enemies he casts out from the space of God's kingdom, whereupon Romola asserts she will stand outside that kingdom with the beings she loves: "The two faces were lit up, each with an opposite emotion, each with an opposite certitude. Further words were impossible. Romola hastily covered her head and went out in silence" (p. 309).

The events of the plot seem to prove both Savonarola and Romola wrong. God does not send a miracle to save his prophet–indeed, Savonarola's last words are that God has withdrawn from him the gift of prophecy (ch. 71, vol. 2, p. 435); and Romola later commemorates Savonarola's martyrdom annually. Romola's returning belief is based upon her own experience: "It was impossible, she said now, that the negative disbelieving thoughts which had made her soul arid of all good, could be founded in the truth of things: impossible that it had not been a *living* spirit, and no *hollow* pretence, which had once breathed in the Frate's *words,* and *kindled* a new life in her" (ch. 71, vol. 2, p. 430, emphasis mine). On the other hand, although Savonarola's grand aim ("the moral welfare of men") was to be achieved "not by vague exhortations, but by striving to turn beliefs into energies that would work in all the details of life" (ch. 71, vol. 2, p. 431), between that belief and the act fell the shadow: "In moments of ecstatic contemplation, doubtless, the sense of self melted in the sense of the Unspeakable, and in that part of his experience lay the elements of genuine self-abasement; but in the presence of his fellow-men for whom he was to act, pre-eminence seemed a necessary condition of his life" (p. 432).

His suffering at the hands of torturers and his failure to withstand them brings Savonarola to a "colloquy with that divine purity with which he sought complete reunion" in a "long cry for inward renovation" (p. 433). In other words, the speaker of commands has become the sufferer who cries out. George Eliot suggests, through the "voice of Sadness," that Savonarola has, "after so many benefits with which God has honored [him], . . . fallen into the depths of the sea" (pp. 433-34). Savonarola, like Jubal, resigns his dream of power and is left with the consolation, when darkness encompasses him, that "the light I saw was the true light" (p. 435).

Savonarola's fate suggests that, although the reality of the experience of presence and union is indisputable, the relationship between that intangible, spiritual reality and the tangible world about us is more problematic (however much George Eliot's language may join the sounds of spiritual truth with visible light). Savonarola's hands may seem to be vehicles for sensibility too acute for gross contact, but they do indeed suffer the pressure of implements of torture, a malign and literal reminder of the limits imposed by brute matter upon human spirit. I believe, however, that Eliot hopes to console us, in the face of Savonarola's inability to renovate the church and the state, by emphasizing the real effect he has had on Romola individually and on various Florentine citizens collectively. As Jubal's confirmation lies in the response of his people, the power of Savonarola's words lies in its ability to move other men and women. When, after all the public celebrations and rituals of the novel, Savonarola's voice receives confirmation only in Romola's home worship, we are probably justified in concluding that Eliot finds support for such belief in experience that is private and individual rather than public and collective; and the lives of her other exhorters in public life, from Edgar Tryan to Dinah Morris, Felix Holt, and Mordecai Cohen, repeat this pattern.

Before departing from this discussion of preachers, we should also look at a recurrent type of episode which treats comically the possible conflict between spiritual voices and the level of command which the minister should have over the harmony engendered within his flock. Eliot uses this kind of interlude in one story from *Scenes of Clerical Life* and in three of her novels; and it is also present in a minor key in *Romola.* In *Adam Bede,* Joshua Rann's complaints about Dinah Morris, whom he sees as a threat to the Reverend Mr. Irwine's spiritual authority, modulate quickly into a complaint about Will Maskery's objections to Joshua's singing, which Will has called "no better nor the cracklin' o' thorns under a pot" (ch. 5, p. 52). Mr. Irwine responds that Will simply has a bad ear for music and will not win any converts to his position as long as Joshua sings as well as he does. The argument over singing returns in *Silas Marner,* this time among the men at the Rainbow Tavern. After Mr. Tookey asserts that "there's people set up their own ears for a standard, and expect the whole choir to follow 'em," he concludes that "there may be two opinions, I hope" (ch. 6, p. 98). Ben Winthrop's response echoes Mr. Irwine's, for he believes that some persons have a gift for music and others are "no better nor a hollow stalk" (p. 98). Mr. Macey has already insinuated that it is simple egoism that sets one man's opinion against the traditional voices of the choir: "There's allays two 'pinions; there's the 'pinion a man has of himsen, and there's the 'pinion other folks have on him. There'd be two 'pinions about a cracked bell, if the bell could hear itself" (p. 98).

When the same sort of difficulty is broached with Rufus Lyon in *Felix Holt the Radical,* George Eliot seems more self-consciously aware of its analogical possibilities for other sorts of disagreements among men. Felix Holt uses the moment as an opportunity to discuss obliquely the relationship between authority and private belief—the terms of Romola's disagreement with Savonarola—so Rufus's response may well have larger fictional implications.

The discussion begins when Mr. Nuttwood complains that the singers "declined to change the tunes in accordance with a change in the selection of hymns" (ch. 13, p. 155). Amos Barton's own parishioners had complained conversely that Amos had insisted on changing the tune for the hymn at a wedding ceremony, in defiance of tradition (ch. 1, p. 47). At first, Rufus Lyon tries to bring Mr. Nuttwood to accept an imperfect state that demands "that there should be a body set apart and called a choir, whose special office it is to lead the singing, not because they are more disposed to the devout uplifting of praise, but because they are endowed with better vocal organs, and have attained more of the musician's art." He then addresses the matter of egoism in familiar language: "For all office, unless it be accompanied by peculiar grace, becomes, as it were, a diseased organ, seeking to make itself too much of a centre" (p. 155). Nuttwood suspects that a good voice like Brother Kemp's may indeed be a snare for the soul through pride and remarks that "the weaker song of the humble may have more power in the ear of God" (p. 156). Felix, who has been listening in, points cogently to the possible vanity of the humble in Nuttwood's remarks and goes on with an anecdote that reminds us, in musical terms, of George Eliot's belief in the fundamental egoism of all people:

> Follow the light of the old-fashioned Presbyterians that I've heard sing at Glasgow. The preacher gives out the psalm, and then everybody sings a different tune, as it happens to turn up in their throats. It's a domineering thing to set a tune and expect everybody else to follow it. It's a denial of private judgment. (P. 156)

Rufus Lyon's response to this "mischief" draws much upon musical language and overtly makes comparisons between musical and spiritual harmony:

> Play not with paradoxes. That caustic which you handle in order to scorch others, may happen to sear your own fingers and make them dead to the quality of things. 'Tis difficult enough to see our way and keep our torch steady in this dim labyrinth: to whirl the torch and dazzle the eyes of our fellow-seekers is a poor daring, and may end in total darkness. You yourself are a lover of freedom, and a bold rebel against usurping authority. But the right to rebellion is the right to seek a higher rule, and not to wander in mere lawlessness. Wherefore, I beseech you, seem not to say that liberty is licence. And I apprehend—though I am not endowed with an ear to seize those earthly harmonies, which to some devout souls have

> seemed, as it were, the broken echoes of the heavenly choir—I apprehend that there is a law in music, disobedience whereunto would bring us in our singing to the level of shrieking maniacs or howling beasts: so that herein we are well instructed how true liberty can be nought but the transfer of obedience from the will of one or of a few men to that will which is the norm or rule for all men. And though the transfer may sometimes be but an erroneous direction of search, yet is the search good and necessary to the ultimate finding. And even as in music, where all obey and concur to one end, so that each has the joy of contributing to a whole whereby he is ravished and lifted up into the courts of heaven, so will it be in that crowning time of the millennial reign, when our daily prayer will be fulfilled, and one law shall be written on all hearts, and be the very structure of all thought, and be the principle of all action. (P. 157)

We never do find out if Rufus, after this exalted speech, was able to "subdue these refractory spirits," but Felix, at least—the one person who hears this speech sympathetically—tells Rufus he is right (p. 158).

The impediments to harmony, then, whether literally or only tangentially vocal, are twofold. First, there is the "iffiness" of speech itself—its possible taint from the egoism of the speaker. As the narrator of *Silas Marner* remarks, "We can send black puddings and pettitoes without giving them a flavour of our own egoism; but language is a stream that is almost sure to smack of a mingled soil" (ch. 10, p. 131). Second, there is the ambiguous state of the audience for that speech. Rufus Lyon thinks vice is "essentially stupid—a deaf and eyeless monster, insusceptible to demonstration: the Spirit might work on it by unseen ways, and the unstudied sallies of sermons were often as the arrows which pierced and awakened the brutified conscience" (ch. 15, p. 173). Thus, although spiritual health seems attainable by means of the experiences George Eliot examines through her language of sound and speech, it is by no means assured.

Another category of episodes involving hearing and creating sounds concerns human relations that are neither religious nor political, but are instead romantic and sexual. Critics have examined the use of musical terms to present such relations in *The Mill on the Floss,* so perhaps this is one of the more accepted aspects of George Eliot's fictional techniques. Some of Maggie's and Stephen's difficulties, however, as well as those of the other singers/lovers of Eliot's novels, may illuminate the recurring dilemmas for people who would speak or sing and thereby achieve harmony.

Some of the ways in which speech between lovers functions as an extension of the language of sound and music can be seen in a passage of a type often found in George Eliot's fiction—a humorous passage that makes fun not only of the characters involved but also of the narrator's own linguistic resources:

> Surely the only courtship unshaken by doubts and fears, must be that in which the lovers can sing together. The sense of mutual fitness that springs from the two deep notes fulfilling expectation just at the right moment between the notes of the silvery soprano, from the perfect accord of descending thirds and fifths, from the preconcerted loving chase of a fugue, is likely enough to supersede any immediate demand for less impassioned forms of agreement. The contralto will not care to catechise the bass; the tenor will foresee no embarrassing dearth of remark in evenings spent with the lovely soprano. (*The Mill on the Floss,* bk. 6, ch. 1, p. 320)

The language of music assures us that Eliot values "mutuality," a fitness that expresses itself not only simultaneously but also consecutively, as the notes "fulfill expectation" at just the right moment as well as at just the right pitch. The irony of the passage is directed at Lucy and Stephen Guest, the lovers who are about to sing and whose love is doomed to massive disharmony in the novel. A hint of the general cause for this lies in forms of speech other than the musical. Whether the lovers at other times speak too much ("catechise") or too little (reveal a "dearth of remark"), the consecutive acts of speaking and hearing may well announce disjuncture rather than agreement.

Indeed, the fates of the various lovers who sing in George Eliot's fiction suggest that their musicality is frequently an ironic commentary on their love. From Tina Sarti, whose songs become a means of expression for all the passion she is unable to manifest otherwise, to Rosamond Vincy or Gwendolen Harleth, whose capacities are intended to impress those who hear them sing, the lovers sing songs that emphasize the difference, in scale or in seriousness, between the feeling embodied in the music and the emotions of the lovers involved. Further, that singing, even though private in the common sense of the term, is frequently not completely so. In *The Mill on the Floss, Middlemarch,* and *Daniel Deronda,* much of the developing romantic and sexual interest is focused in the hearing or overhearing by a third party of the twined voices of two others. Philip must listen as Stephen sings to

Maggie (bk. 6, ch, 7, pp. 365-67); Dorothea overhears Will and Rosamond (ch. 43, p. 315); and Daniel Deronda becomes conscious of Gwendolen's need as Mirah sings (ch. 45, p. 424). Such situations have long been a staple of the drama, and perhaps their dynamics are best explained as dependent on conceptions of audience (see chapter 6, below). A quotation from Philip Wakem summarizes indirectly what is announced to the self as it hears but does not participate in the harmony of love:

> There is no feeling, perhaps, except the extremes of fear and grief, that does not find relief in music—that does not make a man sing or play the better; and Philip had an abundance of pent-up feeling at this moment, as complex as any trio or quartet that was ever meant to express love and jealousy, and resignation and fierce suspicion, all at the same time.
>
> "Oh yes," he said, seating himself at the piano, "it is a way of eking out one's imperfect life and being three people at once—to sing and make the piano sing, and hear them both all the while—or else to sing and paint." (Bk. 6, ch. 7, p. 363)

Too often, a variety of factors force people like Philip, who wish to be at one with someone, to be separate, so the human (or social), spatial and temporal oneness in a present joy—which Jubal's music first represented—is an experience often longed for or remembered by lovers but rarely sustained. George Eliot praises its achievement in language deriving from time, space, and sound:

> If [you have been in love], you will no more think the slight words, the timid looks, the tremulous touches, by which two human souls approach each other gradually . . . trivial than you will think the first-detected signs of coming spring trivial, though they be but a faint indescribable something in the air and in the song of the birds. . . . Those slight words and looks and touches are part of the soul's language; and the finest language, I believe, is chiefly made up of unimposing words, such as "light," "sound," "stars," "music," —words really not worth looking at, or hearing, in themselves, any more than "chips" or "sawdust:" it is only that they happen to be the signs of something unspeakably great and beautiful. I am of the opinion that love is a great and beautiful thing too; and if you agree with me, the smallest signs of it will not be chips and sawdust to you: they will rather be like those little words, "light" and "music," stirring the long-winding fibres of

> your memory, and enriching your present with your most precious past. (*Adam Bede,* ch. 50, pp. 411-12)

There are several elements in music—a species of sound—which make it representative of the great and the beautiful. The importance of tone, the fundamental quality of a single note, is evident when George Eliot speaks of the "ground tones" of Tina Sarti's nature ("Mr. Gilfil's Love-Story," ch. 2, p. 145) or the ground notes of Mr. Jerome's character ("Janet's Repentance," ch. 8, p. 304). Such tones seem to carry the valency of primary emotion or energy, much as the inflection of Rosamond's "What can *I* do" reveals her soul's fundamental quality (*Middlemarch,* ch. 58, p. 434). Added to tone must be rhythm, a word that for Eliot announces stable, predictable movement; the dominant characteristic of rhythm is order, as Eliot has emphasized in her definition of poetic form: "emotion, by its tendency to repetition, i.e. *rhythmic persistence* in proportion as diversifying thought is absent, creates a form by the recurrence of its elements" (emphasis mine, see chapter 1, above).

Jointly, these elements—tone and rhythm—produce melody, a pattern of different tones which evokes that sense of progressing time so important to George Eliot because it incorporates past, present, and future. The appeal of a melody is dependent upon hearing it in the present, although our sense of it as melody can only come from our remembrance of the notes that have come before and our expectation of the notes that will come after. Similarly, the conception of harmony, the hearing not of single notes but of chords, provides that union in space which melody provides in time; within chords, notes that are distinct nevertheless accommodate one another in such a way that, in the words of Robert Browning, they form, "not a fourth sound, but a star" ("Abt Vogler," line 52).

Last, George Eliot relies increasingly in her later novels upon the specific and individual pieces of music which make up man's cultural heritage. Such music often carries with it not only the import of the words of the song but also the implications of narrative—Eliot being particularly fond of referring either to ballads or to songs from opera. By this means her characters, as well as the narrator, are able to communicate indirectly those complex meanings for which mere consecutive speech is inadequate. One typical example of such communication is Philip's first song in *The Mill on the Floss:*

> "Don't you know that?" said Philip, bringing out the tune more definitely. "It's from the *Sonnambula*. . . . I don't know the opera,

> but it appears the tenor is telling the heroine that he shall always love her though she may forsake him. You've heard me sing it to the English words, 'I love thee still.'"
>
> It was not quite unintentionally that Philip had wandered into this song, which might be an indirect expression to Maggie of what he could not prevail on himself to say to her directly. Her ears had been open to what he was saying, and when he began to sing, she understood the plaintive passion of the music. (Bk. 6, ch. 7, p. 365)

The failure of love between these two people who so appreciate the emotional and intellectual possibilities of music indicates that although the language of sound and music can permit George Eliot to embody much of the relationship between the single ego and the world in which he wishes to find order, its capacity to embody the relationship between the ego and its progenitors or successors requires extensive examination through other linguistic means.

5

THE LANGUAGE OF GENERATION AND THE GENERATION OF PLOT

INSOFAR AS METAPHORS of eating and of building rely upon an assumption that consciousness is single—that there is one devourer or builder to whom all things are raw material—they reveal the possible perversity of human behavior in a world where consciousness is indeed not single. This is perhaps the most important point to be derived from metaphors of sound and music: they insist upon another voice and thus upon another self. In this way, the language of sound moves George Eliot toward a recognition of, if not a satisfactory solution to, the primary dilemma of the doubled world of self and others; at the same time, it provides a situation or rudimentary plot for her fiction. That is, the sequence of events—the quest pattern—which is generated by the power of hearing and producing sounds in "The Legend of Jubal" can be found to inhere in any number of human situations and thus in any number of possible fictional plots, although here again the necessarily metaphorical relationship between such a pattern and other quests that do not pertain to the literal creation of music may limit the implications of such fictions. Indeed, the truth to be discovered in hearing and creating sounds and music is most potent in George Eliot's novels when it is literally as well as metaphorically significant. Another, equally potent "creative" energy that can help us understand how her more complicated plots and more complex meanings are generated is that of sexual desire or the power of procreative love. As we have already seen, desire is frequently spoken of through the language of animal appetite and of the loss of self through infinite expansion in space. Sexual desire, however, constitutes a new pattern that is not single or even double but is in a sense triadic, for the ultimate proof of such energy (as well as the order created by it) must lie in a relationship with another which can be seen outside both the self and the other; that is, in the child of that union.

The language of George Eliot's fiction provides several significant definitions of sexual desire. First, of course, such desire is a fundamental form of energy, identifiable with the very foundations of life itself. As such, it is a mystery that lies impenetrable (and perhaps unspeakable) behind all others; as Adam Bede thinks,

> We're like enough to find life a tough job—hard work inside and out. It's a strange thing to think of a man as can lift a chair with his teeth, and walk fifty mile on end, trembling and turning hot and cold at only a look from one woman out of all the rest i' the world. It's a mystery we can give no account of; but no more we can of the sprouting o' the seed, for that matter. (*Adam Bede,* ch. 11, p. 105)

Thus, attempts to explain this mystery can only be themselves mysterious or, in other words, metaphorical.

Second, there is the description of such desire as sexual "appetite," as an urge to reproduce the species. When George Eliot speaks of sexual energy in such terms she is, as we have seen in chapter 2, frequently being ironic:

> "I'm no friend to young fellows a-marrying afore they know the difference atween a crab an' a apple; but they may wait o'er long[,]" [said Mr. Poyser.]
>
> "To be sure," said Mrs. Poyser; "if you go past your dinnertime, there'll be little relish o' your meat. You turn it o'er an' o'er wi' your fork, an' don't eat it after all. You find faut wi' your meat, an' the faut's all i' your own stomach." (*Adam Bede,* ch. 14, p. 126)

Third, descriptions of passion which rely upon the language of space and expansion generate problems for the self:

> But for the last few weeks a new influence had come over Hetty—vague, atmospheric, shaping itself into no self-confessed hopes or prospects, but producing a pleasant narcotic effect, making her tread the ground and go about her work in a sort of dream, unconscious of weight or effort, and showing her all things through a soft, liquid veil, as if she were living not in this solid world of brick and stone, but in a beautified world, such as the sun lights up for us in the waters. (*Adam Bede,* ch. 9, p. 86)

Finally, when George Eliot wishes to paint desire at its most exalted, she draws upon the language of music and harmony:

> Is it any weakness, pray, to be wrought on by exquisite music?—to feel its wondrous harmonies searching the subtlest windings of your soul, the delicate fibres of life where no memory can penetrate, and binding together your whole being past and present in one unspeakable vibration: melting you in one moment with all the tenderness, all the love that has been scattered through the toilsome years, concentrating in one emotion of heroic courage or resignation all the hard-learnt lessons of self-renouncing sympathy, blending your present joy with past sorrow, and your present sorrow with all your past joy? If not, then neither is it a weakness to be so wrought upon by the exquisite curves of a woman's cheek and neck and arms, by the liquid depths of her beseeching eyes, or the sweet childish pout of her lips. (*Adam Bede,* ch. 33, pp. 297-98)

On the basis of my earlier discussion of these metaphors and their attendant "realities," certain aspects of desire may be fairly easily delineated. As an appetite, sexual love is the expression of a need that must be "filled" by some means external to the self; thus, it is potentially a devouring. Equally, the power of that love may be the power of receptivity, the emptiness within the self being exactly that space which some exterior sound may fill with harmony or waken to resonance. Of course, in pragmatic ways sexual love expresses a crucial "fact of life" unlike either of these two metaphoric conditions, for it propagates a world and inhabitants of that world much more readily, both in fiction and in fact, than does the power of hunger or the power of music. Further, it generates relationships that are not simply double but triadic. In addition to the lover and the beloved there is the child of that union, a third term which does indeed express a relationship but which has a reality that complicates and tests the language that George Eliot's fiction relies upon to explain the world. Finally, like the power of mind, this power of body must be neither exalted nor negated, but rather accommodated or "domesticated" in Eliot's world.

In simplest terms, George Eliot examines the conflict between the sexual appetite and human and social order on both the personal and public levels. Of course, sexual desire is most similar in its terms and conditions to her other accommodations of personal need to the realities of the world—accommodations of desire to law. Thus, although there are several collateral issues, the crucial moment for her characters as sexual creatures usually comes when they must realize that the sexual act (virtual or accomplished) has transformed the self in a unique way; he (or she) who had been someone's child has become a parent. The acceptance of the future fact of the child thus becomes the acceptance of the reality of one's own past sexual act. Stated another way, such acceptance is an assertion of the reality of one's self which simultaneously alters that self.

As energy or power, sexual desire seems at first to be amply elucidated through the contraries that define gustatory appetite. However, sexuality can itself frequently become a metaphor for something else in George Eliot's fiction. For instance, while Arthur Donnithorne's presence has a great effect upon Hetty Sorrel, she herself is aware of her own effect upon Adam Bede, which she considers in an entirely different light:

> [Hetty] liked to feel that this strong, skilful, keen-eyed man was in her power, and would have been indignant if he had shown the least sign of slipping from under the yoke of her coquettish tyranny, and attaching himself to the gentle Mary Burge. (*Adam Bede,* ch. 9, pp. 85-86)

Her attitude mirrors that of one of the persons in many other couples in Eliot's fiction: Anthony Wybrow's toward Tina Sarti, Bertha's toward the narrator of "The Lifted Veil," Harold Transome's toward Esther Lyon, Rosamond Vincy's toward Tertius Lydgate, Gwendolen Harleth's toward Henleigh Grandcourt. In each case, desire seems to be less a power within the self than the means to power. That is, gratification of the self has become an intangible rather than a physical matter. Such "desire" as this is really no more than the assertion of will.[1]

True desire, although it may itself be a part of a power struggle, is also partially a more primitive (i.e., bodily) response. Thus, although Gwendolen Harleth is presented as a woman eminently *not* driven by such desires, she does indeed participate in a struggle for dominance with Henleigh Grandcourt—a struggle in which her most potent weapon is her attractiveness. That attractiveness is made apparent in her manifold relationships to the men in the novel and even sets the keynote for its beginning:

> Was she beautiful or not beautiful? and what was the secret of form or expression which gave the dynamic quality to her glance? . . . Why was the wish to look again felt as coercion and not as a longing in which the whole being consents? (*Daniel Deronda,* ch. 1, p. 1)

There is, as Daniel Deronda recognizes, an energy about Gwendolen (she is "dynamic"), but the effect of that energy on him is at least partially repressive or coercive, because there is something else about Gwendolen which violates other orders than the "natural" one of "boy desires girl." That order we quickly discover or infer to be a moral one, although its precise terms are never fully explained. There is, however, a later, more complete discussion of the drawbacks to any action based upon the desire that Gwendolen awakens:

> But in the movement which had led [Deronda] to redeem Gwendolen's necklace for her, and which was at work in him still, there was something beyond his habitual compassionate fervour—something due to the fascination of her womanhood. He was very open to that sort of charm, and mingled it with the consciously Utopian pictures of his own future; yet any one able to trace the folds of his character might have conceived that he would be more likely than many less passionate men to love a woman without telling her of it. Sprinkle food before a delicate-eared bird: there is nothing he would more willingly take, yet he keeps aloof, because of his sensibility to checks which to you are imperceptible. . . . It seemed to foreshadow that capability of reticence in Deronda that his imagination was much occupied with two women, to neither of whom would he have held it possible that he should ever make love. Hans Meyrick had laughed at him for having something of the knight-errant in his disposition. (*Daniel Deronda,* ch. 28, pp. 240–41)

Although there are certainly more delicate motivations for Deronda's reticence in this matter, the most obvious cause is that he does not believe that he can conclude his love-making to either woman with a proposal of marriage. Two of the most important reasons for that impossibility are the truly indisputable fact that Gwendolen is now married to another man, and the apparently—although not truly—indisputable one that Deronda is not Jewish and the reputation of the unprotected Mirah is too vulnerable at this point in the novel. In other words, certain public and social constraints operate to limit the gratification of any desires on his part.

This conflict between desire and social law provides one basis for plot even in George Eliot's earliest fiction. Whether such an order is seen as purely social (i.e., created by a class system) or as also ethical and spiritual, the focus of attention is upon the accommodating of one's primal desires to the hierarchies of reality which supposedly determine affinities. Although these difficulties are present in *Scenes of Clerical Life,* they receive their most direct and extensive treatment first in *Adam Bede.* In that novel, Arthur Donnithorne is unable to pursue Hetty publicly because of differences in social rank, and Seth Bede is unable to approach Dinah Morris because of differences in spiritual condition. The conflict reappears with predictable regularity throughout the course of Eliot's fiction—many couples face it: Stephen Guest and Maggie Tulliver, Godfrey Cass and Eppie's mother; Tito and Tessa; Esther and Felix (at least from Harold Transome's point of view); Dorothea and Ladislaw; Mary Garth and Fred Vincy; and Daniel Deronda and Mirah Cohen. The ambiguities of such hierarchies are, of course, easily apparent. For instance, Stephen Guest, although superior socially to Maggie, is inferior emotionally and spiritually, and the same inversion is true regarding Esther and Felix as well as Mary and Fred. The implied suitability of the unions between Dorothea and Will and Daniel and Mirah depends upon their discovering in each other an equality that is both social and spiritual. For such lucky people desire has satisfied more than just itself, for it has been validated by (and has validated) the outward order of things.

Such simple, if important, conflicts and quests—summed up in the plot "boy meets girl and boy marries girl"—do not undergo the alterations and permutations suffered by another aspect of physical desire. Although the larger social order (and perhaps even the spiritual one) may ultimately derive from an order engendered by procreation, it is sufficiently large and static to appear to have its own ground of being. The order more intimately connected with the energy of sexual desire is a temporal one of generation, one which I associated in Chapter 2 with the organic metaphor and, tentatively, with the organic plot. Yet even here direction is not straightforward, as a quotation from *Daniel Deronda* reveals:

> The moment wrought strongly on Deronda's imaginative susceptibility: in the presence of one linked still in zealous friendship with the grandfather whose hope had yearned towards him when he was unborn, and who though dead was yet to speak with him in those written memorials which, says Milton, "contain a potency of life in them to be as active as that soul whose progeny they are," he seemed to himself to be touching the electric chain of his own ancestry; and he bore the scrutinising look of Kalonymos with a delighted awe, something like what one feels in the solemn commemoration of acts done long ago but still telling markedly on the life of to-day. (*Daniel Deronda,* ch. 60, p. 542)

The phrase "electric chain" is an apt one for my purposes, since it underscores the doubleness of desire itself. Although sexual generation is "electric," i.e., a form of energy, it also creates its own order by its capacity to bind or "chain" us to our ancestors and successors. Thus, it transfers vitality as it delimits obligation. And yet, that chain stretches not only forward in time but also backward. In the case quoted above, the focus of both plot and point of view is upon the child discovering the reality of the parent rather than the parent discovering the reality of the coming child. The reality Deronda is about to discover has been created not simply by the sexual act (a thing momentary in itself and certainly long completed) but also by word or by name. The potency that Deronda is most interested in seems transmitted through the written memorials. This is of a piece with George Eliot's other resolutions of the ultimate dilemma created by desire, insofar as that dilemma concerns the needs and identity of the individual self. If that desire is actually procreative, then the child born of that desire becomes an extension of self which nevertheless asserts otherness; and outward acceptance of that child becomes a validation of both selfhood and otherness. In this sense, Eliot's fiction reveals a continuing preoccupation with birth: in virtually every plot there is a quasi-illegitimate birth; in many there is the adoption of a child or the adoption of a parent (which is not quite the same thing), as well as the related matter of one sibling's recognition of parental sexuality, based on the presence of siblings.[2] Here again, Eliot confronts the fact that apparently outward effort brings an unexpected recoil that obligates the self to achieve an accommodation, and that accommodation has important connections with the use and presence of language itself.

In recent years, the idea of plot has been elaborated beyond simple temporality. Although the naive definition of plot as "a sequence of events over time which implies a kind of causality in those events" has certainly not been abandoned, some refinements of that conception are particularly relevant to George Eliot's fiction—in fact, her works are often useful in helping discover those refinements.

The study of earlier, "non-novelistic" narratives offers the best insight into the other possibilities for the form of plot. Angus Fletcher, in examining allegory, suggests that there are essentially two kinds of plot: the battle and the progress, or quest.[3] Even more suggestive for George Eliot's work is Charles Altman's implicit expansion of these plot conceptions into two different forms of narrative—"single-focus" and "dual-focus." In the former, "the narrator focuses on a single character, following him throughout, and organizing the entire text around his development." In the latter, the narrator "instead alternates regularly between two groups whose conflict provides the plot."[4] The single-focus narrative is most familiar in the novel and appears to be the basis for our naive definition of plot. Thus, Altman's elaboration of the dual-focus narrative is useful for revealing the essential qualities of another kind of plot that is not so absolutely tied to temporality—a plot in which the matter of space is crucial.

Altman expresses the importance of space in two different ways, the first linguistic and the second geographical:

> Whereas single-focus narrative is built on predicate transformation and the passage of time ($S_1 P_1 \longrightarrow S_1 P_2$, where the two terms represent separate moments), the dual-focus form gains its meaning from subject transformation and the division of space ($S_1 P_1 \longrightarrow S_2 P_1$, where the two terms take place in clearly opposed spaces). . . .
>
> Each new pair of following-units is related to the previous pair not by psychological motivation or any other type of causality but by the principle of replacement. . . .
>
> To describe that basic story is in fact not a difficult task: two *different* groups claim and try to occupy the *same* space. That space may be a country, a city, or a weapon; in the hands of an allegorist . . . it may be man's soul, or in later fiction the right to a woman's hand.[5]

Since Altman's primary interest in his essay is narrative in a Christian era, the resolution of the dual-focus plot derives from the choice God makes as judge between the "us" and the "not-us" in the conflict. The real shift from one form to the other, then, occurs when the story "places responsibility for the discovery of values squarely in the hands of the central character." When the static conflict between world views is replaced by a "psychology of increasing perfection, of choice, and of education," "time is essential; along with order, history is created."[6]

George Eliot's use of multiple perspectives and multiple plots, especially in her later fiction, might be considered a return to the dual-focus narrative of conflict, but without the comforting presence of a God who will reward those on the right side. This, roughly, is Peter Garrett's assertion in his study of "dialogical form" in Eliot's fiction.[7] But if we look at the possibilities for these two kinds of plot within the focus of family relations (the "space" in which virtually all of Eliot's stories take place), new possibilities present themselves.

This focus on the battlefield (or simply the field for individual endeavor and choice) within the family receives ample justification in

Tony Tanner's introductory remarks about adultery in the novel.[8] As he explains, the family and society are so mutually interdependent in the bourgeois nineteenth-century novel that the failure of the former precipitates the failure of the latter. Further, Tanner introduces into his discussion of plot terms that are essential to my argument:

> It is such an obvious and legible phenomenon that many of those nineteenth-century novels that have been canonized as "great" . . . center on adultery. . . .
>
> Adultery as a phenomenon is in evidence in literature from the earliest times, as in Homer (and indeed we might suggest that it is the unstable triangularity of adultery, rather than the static symmetry of marriage, that is the *generative* form of Western literature as we know it). [Emphasis mine]
>
> Since desire, which is always involved in some way with the sense of incompletion, is an essential source of action in any social structure, which by its very nature tends toward a self-perpetuating stasis, it is necessarily a central topic of all literature. Desire in action reveals itself as energy, and energy encountering structure is the paradigmatic tension of much of our literature.[9]

Tony Tanner's terms, then, support my earlier generalization that George Eliot's fictions explore the conflict between the energy of passion and the social structure, especially as that structure is mirrored in its marital forms and restrictions. Thus, she tells of sexual energy in conflict either with the social order, with a perceived higher, spiritual order, or with a single rival or lover. But when that energy itself creates an order (the genealogical one), a new form of conflict emerges. This conflict becomes increasingly important in Eliot's works, for it embodies that paradox she confronts in the other aspects of her fiction.

Jonathan Arac puts this well with regard to *The Mill on the Floss* (using language that echoes Altman's description of a dual-focus conflict over place). In quoting Mr. Tulliver about educating Tom so that "he may make a nest for himself, an' not want to push me out o' mine" (bk. 1, ch. 3, p. 15), Arac remarks that "the principle of generational continuity is split at its center; the 'nest' has no place for two and therefore demands displacement."[10] Indeed, whether the order generated by procreation is static or dynamic, more than one difficulty arises for both parent and child; further, all these difficulties focus upon the acceptance or rejection of that fact of procreativeness. In some cases in Eliot's novels, it is the parent who can or cannot accept the consequences of "blind rut."[11] Equally often, however, a conflict derives from the child's difficulty in accepting the "generational" reality of the parent. This latter difficulty can be twofold: on the one hand, there is the obvious issue of the authority and responsibility of the parent as creator of this child; on the other, there is the issue of the parent's continuing procreativity, which results, in the terms of Eliot's spoiled child Gwendolen Harleth, in "superfluous" siblings (*Daniel Deronda,* ch. 3, p. 20).

The most revelatory situation is that wherein all of these issues conjoin: the "illegitimate" child and his relation to his parents, real and/or adopted, as well as to his possibly more "legitimate" siblings. The "illegitimate" child appears repeatedly in George Eliot's novels as a crucial trigger for the plot—sometimes centrally, as in *Felix Holt the Radical,* sometimes more peripherally; even such an apparently minor character as Joshua Rigg-Featherstone is nevertheless essential to the generation and resolution of Eliot's narratives.

In George Eliot's first story, "Amos Barton," the conflict between desire and society is a matter of comic mistake. The Shepperton community believes in the illicit relationship between the Countess Czerlaski and her brother Mr. Bridmain and between the Countess and Amos himself. Ironically, both the Countess and Amos are more morally inclined than the community that chooses to judge them—so much so that the possibility of their status being misunderstood does not occur to them. Yet, as Steven Marcus has pointed out, there is in the story another kind of passion, often unrecognized by the reader himself, and perhaps only partly acceded to by the author: the passion that begets child after child for Millie Barton.[12] The implications of his real sexual acts could very well be another of those realities that Amos Barton so often misapprehends or fails to recognize, and in that sense he might be considered the first of Eliot's ambiguous parents. It is also true that his eldest daughter must in the end "mother" him and replace the wife he has lost. Finally, there is the other "real" sexual attraction that disrupts the apparent relations between the Countess and her brother: Bridmain does indeed act "promiscuously," violating the social orders of his world by falling in love with his sister's maid. Thus, by a series of mistaken perceptions and unexplained impulses related to sexuality, Amos Barton's life is first complicated and then completed—at least as far as its worth as a narrative is concerned.

In George Eliot's later works, the choice of the maid rather than a more socially accepted mate receives tragic rather than comic treatment. The list of such unsanctioned unions includes couples from all of George Eliot's novels: Tina Sarti and Anthony Wybrow ("Mr. Gilfil's Love-Story"), Arthur Donnithorne and Hetty Sorrel (*Adam Bede*), Maggie Tulliver and Stephen Guest (*The Mill on the Floss*), Godfrey Cass and Molly Farren (*Silas Marner*), Tito Melema and Tessa (*Romola*), Mrs. Transome and Lawyer Jermyn (*Felix Holt the Radical*), Dorothea Brooke and Will Ladislaw (*Middlemarch*), and Henleigh Grandcourt and Lydia Glasher (*Daniel Deronda*). Some of these partake of the "conventional" situation of the servant girl debauched by the gentleman (Tina, Hetty, Molly, Tessa).[13] Others fall into the category that Tony Tanner considers: the wife who engages in an adulterous affair (Mrs. Transome, Lydia Glasher).

Maggie and Stephen and Dorothea and Will may seem to be anomalies in this list. Society opposes both of these couples' unions, however, seeing, among other things, a discrepancy in caste between the partners. More thought-provoking are two other complications they reveal. Maggie's and Dorothea's difficulties derive in large measure from their relations to other members of the familial group, most specifically to brother and to father. For Maggie it is her brother who appears to be the predominant consideration, although, of course, the novel explores extensively the degree to which Tom is an extension of his father's "will." In Dorothea's case, the "brother" is her brother-in-law, Sir James Chettam, and the "father" is that father-figure she marries, Mr. Casaubon. Indeed, what operates in each of these situations or plots is the entanglement of the woman's kinship roles: her attitudes toward and relationships with father and brother have a significant impact on her relationships of affinity and love.

This brief sketch does not exhaust the societal aspects of George Eliot's plot conflicts. More true to their complexity might be a schematization along the lines that have been so useful in examining Sir Walter Scott's fiction, fiction Eliot admired. That is, the pattern of choice by a protagonist between possible spouses, one "light" and the other "dark," can make sense of a large segment of Eliot's fiction.[14] This pattern constitutes a kind of triangularity which is not the same as the triangularity of desire which Mr. Girard speaks of (see note 1 above) and does not always correspond to the triangularity of adultery which Mr. Tanner defines. A list of such triangles is sufficiently extensive that a chart will be useful.

"Light Figure"	*S/He who Chooses*	*"Dark Figure"*
Millie Barton	Amos Barton	Countess Czerlaski
Maynard Gilfil	Tina Sarti	Anthony Wybrow
Mr. Tryan	Janet Dempster	Lawyer Dempster
Adam Bede	Hetty Sorrel	Arthur Donnithorne
Dinah Morris	Adam Bede	Hetty Sorrel
Latimer	Bertha	Latimer's brother
Philip Wakem	Maggie Tulliver	Stephen Guest
Lucy Dean	Stephen Guest	Maggie Tulliver
Nancy Lammeter	Godfrey Cass	Molly Farren
Silas Marner	Sarah	William Dane
Romola	Tito	Tessa
Mr. Transome	Mrs. Transome	Lawyer Jermyn
Felix Holt	Esther	Harold Transome
Dorothea Brooke	Tertius Lydgate	Rosamond Vincy
Edward Casaubon	Dorothea Brooke	Sir James Chettam
Edward Casaubon	Dorothea Brooke	Will Ladislaw
Mr. Farebrother	Mary Garth	Fred Vincy
Daniel Deronda	Gwendolen Harleth	Henleigh Grandcourt
Gwendolen Harleth	Henleigh Grandcourt	Lydia Glasher
Mirah Cohen	Daniel Deronda	Gwendolen Harleth

Several matters are revealed in this chart. In the first place, the proper choice is clearly not always the "light" figure over the "dark." For instance, although Tina Sarti should have loved Maynard Gilfil, Dorothea was by no means right in choosing Mr. Casaubon. One could well object, however, that the men for Dorothea's choosing should be reversed, since society, in the form of Mrs. Cadwallader, would have applauded Dorothea's marriage to Sir James, whereas it is offended by her marriage to Edward. Equally ironic (given the archetypal situation of *Ivanhoe*) is the reversal of the Jewish and the Anglo-Saxon heroine in *Daniel Deronda,* another indication of the degree to which George Eliot's beliefs are not straightforwardly conservative. After all, as Maggie Tulliver remarks, one can have a kind of sympathy for the dark unhappy ones (*The Mill on the Floss,* bk. 5, ch. 4, p. 291). A comic version of this sympathy is perhaps what justifies Mary Garth's choice of Fred Vincy.

As a step in examining George Eliot's plots, this chart permits us to see her methods on two levels. On the first level, the chart implies that the structure of her fictions might be the battle or conflict incarnated in the opposition between one kind of spouse, or beloved, and another. Of course, the real determinant in each case is the choice that the central figure makes between the two opposed characters, such a choice really defining the values that the chooser wishes to "quest after" or affirm in the world. Indeed, despite assertions that Eliot turns away from the romance plot to other more public matters[15]—matters that are indeed amply present in her fiction—the reader is forced to recognize that none of those other subjects is what it is except insofar as it influences or is influenced by the choice of spouse. Even *Middlemarch*'s supposed extraneous plot—Bulstrode's story, which is apparently not about marrying—is not really extraneous; the catastrophe of Bulstrode's life has been prepared because he chose to marry the pawnbroker's widow rather than the church.

This emphasis on marriage is probably appropriate for this important reason: the choice is simultaneously public and private, physical and spiritual. It is the nodus at which one's nonconscious urges seek domestication in a world inhabited by others whose existence matters. The choice, to be made public, must be uttered and thereby made more than simply selfish.

This chart also expresses a second level of structure. In several novels, the triangle is multiplied, so that, for instance, Adam is one-half of a choice for Hetty, and he himself must choose between Hetty and Dinah. Obviously, this is consistent with George Eliot's recognition that marital choice expresses mutuality; i.e., the world is made up of more than one ego capable of choice. Further, one must recognize that in the first case the matter of choosing is real—that is, Adam and Arthur are present as possibilities for Hetty at the same time; Adam, on the other hand, is presented with his two choices in temporal succession, although Dinah does exist as an unrecognized possibility during his infatuation with Hetty. (This is essentially the situation that justifies my inclusion in the chart of Lydgate's subliminal choice between Dorothea and Rosamund.) To a large degree, this complicates the chart, so that it looks somewhat like this:

Dinah Morris	Adam Bede	Hetty Sorrel	
	Adam Bede	Hetty Sorrel	Arthur Donnithorne

One might even add Seth Bede's name as another choice for Dinah.

The extended chart for *Daniel Deronda* is similar:

Mirah	Daniel Deronda	Gwendolen		
	Daniel Deronda	Gwendolen	Grandcourt	
		Gwendolen	Grandcourt	Lydia Glasher

Both of these charts, of course, announce themselves as hierarchies, turning the multiple conflicts of the plot into spatial replicas of one another. What remains important, however, is that such systems show "possibilities" about which a story may be written.[16]

George Eliot's novels are not, of course, replicas of each other, each one posing and then resolving the same tensions. Indeed, beginning with "Mr. Gilfil's Love-Story," Eliot introduces into the choice of beloved a new factor that thereafter never disappears from her work, for a large segment of that story narrates events unconnected with Anthony Wybrow; there is in addition the tale of Tina's adoption by the Cheverels in Italy. She is thus the first of many figures in Eliot's novels who have more than one parental figure to contend with. Indeed, this list of such triangularities is almost as extensive as the previous one.

"Natural Parent"	*Child*	*"Adopted Parent"*
Mr. Sarti	Tina Sarti	Sir Anthony Cheverel
Mr. Tulliver	Maggie Tulliver	The Dodsons
Mr./Mrs. Faux	David Faux	The Freelys
Godfrey Cass	Eppie	Silas Marner
Bardo	Romola	Savonarola
Bycliffe	Esther Lyon	Rufus Lyon
Lawyer Jermyn	Harold Transome	Mr. Transome
Aunt Julia	Will Ladislaw	Edward Casaubon
Sarah Dunkirk	Will Ladislaw	Mr. Bulstrode
Alcharisi	Daniel Deronda	Sir Hugo Mallinger
Mrs. Cohen	Mirah	Lapidoth

Again, it is not always clear which choice is proper for the protagonist. In some cases, most archetypally Eppie's, it is the one who chooses to father, rather than the one who begets (the Jermyn/germinator) who deserves allegiance. Yet, with both Will Ladislaw and Daniel Deronda (and probably with Maggie Tulliver, too), the discovery of the true significance of a hidden heredity predominates.

When the two kinds of charts are conjoined, an obvious conclusion presents itself: the relationship to the father figure has a large impact on the choice of a beloved. Stated more provocatively, by choosing a father, one chooses a spouse. Thus, we have the first of a series of paradoxically disruptive situations in George Eliot's fiction: Tina's role as child to Sir Anthony Cheverel provides her with both the fear of his displeasure with her attachment to Anthony Wybrow (which forces her into repression and then guilt) and the conditions for the development of that attachment. The fact that she lives apparently as both Anthony's and Maynard's sister raises a problem of affinity/consanguinity which receives fuller, if not more lucid, treatment in *The Mill on the Floss.* For Maggie, of course, questions of affinity and consanguinity seem hopelessly complicated. The incestuous possibilities of her relations with her own brother (who is so different from her) have often been pointed out;[17] further, she tries to define her relationship to Philip in brotherly terms rather than sexual ones, and Lucy, who is a rival, is nevertheless the closest she comes to a sister. Here indeed, choosing to be a Tulliver or a Dodson (and to love accordingly) seems by no means to be under the protagonist's command. Matters are strikingly similar for Romola, who sees Tito simultaneously as a son for her father—who will replace her lost brother—and a passionate husband. For her, too, the bonds of daughter and sister do not generate adequate relations of affinity.

A closer look at sibling relationships in Eliot's novels, some of which are more closely tied to sexual matters than others, indicates three sorts of situation. First, and rarest, is the pairing (à la *Wuthering Heights*) in which boy- and girl-child attempt a kind of oneness of affinity and affection. This oneness is tragically aspired to by Maggie and Tom (he actually wishing for their unity on matters of value as much as she) and rather idealistically achieved by Mirah and Mordecai. Indeed, Mirah's choice of a beloved (like Tina's, Maggie's, and Romola's) looks strikingly like the choice of a brother, for Daniel appears first for Mirah as brother to her own brother (although even this role is predated by his role as savior).

Second, there are those pairs of same-sex siblings who undergo varieties of affection and conflict, sometimes apparent and sometimes latent. From Adam and Seth Bede, to Nancy and Priscilla Lammeter, to Dorothea and Celia Brooke, we see kinships that tolerate distinctions, and often the less complex sibling is able to offer an ironic commentary on the "spots of commonness" of the not-so-common brother or sister. For Latimer and his brother, for David and Jacob Faux, for Godfrey and Dunsey Cass, and for Harold Transome and his elder brother, the hostility and rivalry is more apparent. Here, one child more or less blames the parent for presenting him with an unwanted brother. Often such revulsion from the brother is of a piece with the egoist's refusal to share the world with another. Thus, such siblings most frequently fight over inheritance of land, money or affection. The converse of this theme arises from another sibling situation, for Eliot provides single characters who recognize and even thrive in a condition of "superfluous siblings." These include Mr. Irwine with his invalid sisters, Mary Garth and the other Garths, and the Meyrick girls. Gwendolen Harleth stands out strikingly here as one whose ego has not survived her mother's remarriage and subsequent childbirths. When she asks, "'Haven't children reason to be angry with their parents? How can they help their parents marrying or not marrying'" she suddenly realizes that this is what she has felt in the past—a reproach of her mother for that second marriage of hers (*Daniel Deronda,* ch. 29, p. 248). Gwendolen is both an only child and a sister (the other girls being the children of Mr. Davilow), which epitomizes the psychological difficulties of the ego in a world of others whose claims for brotherhood are bound up with one's own origins of being.

If the foregoing conflicts define certain recurrent tensions within George Eliot's narratives, successive stages within those oppositions—desire, union, childbirth—should delineate the relationship between their apparently static confrontations and the dynamics of plot sequence. In other words, how do these contraries—of kinds of lovers, kinds of parents, and kinds of siblings—become embedded in (work themselves out through) time? This question can best be answered by an examination of each of Eliot's plots.

George Eliot's earlier fictions pay close attention to the awakening of sexual desire and the difficulties attendant upon its appearance outside the accepted structures and sanctions of the community. Here we have the long-recognized conflict in her work between the demands of the single ego and the ways of the world. Thus, Tina Sarti desires Anthony, the reverend Mr. Tryan desires Lucy, Arthur desires Hetty, Maggie desires Stephen, and Godfrey desires Molly Farren. In none of those cases does George Eliot seem to condemn passion per se. Rather, she laments either the inability of the character so moved to accept the reality of that passion in its relation to other social, and especially familial, obligations or, more profoundly, the inability of the character to recognize the absolute reality of actions derived from that passion. Such inability to recognize is expressed, significantly, in various misuses of and failures to use language—failures to name the thing one does.[18] Although it is one of Eliot's most melodramatic, Tina Sarti's narrative examines the difficulties of such passion more extensively than any of Eliot's other narratives (with the possible exception of Mrs. Transome's, whose story is told from the perspective of the end rather than from the present).

Tina, aware that Anthony Wybrow is returning to Cheverel Manor with his betrothed, must sit with "cold lips and palpitating heart," a condition only to be counteracted by the coming of "night and solitude" ("Mr. Gilfil's Love-Story," ch. 5, pp. 166–67). Her agony is the direct result of a perception that her own desires are in conflict with those of her foster father, who exults in a marraige that fulfills his own will—"Cheverel Manor would be inherited by a grand-nephew, whom he might even yet live to see a fine young fellow with at least the down on his chin" (p. 167). Tina is first angry at Anthony because he can speak with such "nonchalance," although she quickly recognizes that the illicitness of their feelings requires subterfuge (p. 169). Her first defense against the presence of Beatrice Assher is the tendency not to reply to remarks whose meaning she cannot assent to; thus, she sits "aloof and dumb" (pp. 172-73). Her only vocal outlet is singing, a kind of displaced speech which permits her expression without exposing the reality of her feelings. Nevertheless, when Anthony makes actual gestures of affection to Miss Assher in her presence, Tina's only refuge is the locked room within which she can at last burst out aloud, "I cannot bear it" (pp. 174-75). The difficulties between her and Anthony are only exacerbated by speech. When he wishes to speak to her, his tone and his meaning are offensive; when she does respond to Miss Assher, her impatience is too revealing. Most irritating as a new wrong is his willingness "to snatch a caress when she justly claimed an *expression* of penitence, of regret, of sympathy" (ch. 7, p. 185, emphasis mine). Anthony uses his lips for kisses rather than for words, or, rather, his kisses belie his words.

Unfortunately for Anthony, both women demand speech of him. As Miss Assher says, "An honourable man will not be placed in circumstances which he cannot explain to the woman he seeks to make his wife" (ch. 8, p. 187). Anthony's means of removing himself from such a doubled difficulty is to *speak* to his uncle about *speaking* to Maynard about *speaking* a proposal of marriage to Tina; he finally perceives that a spoken proposal is the way out of the dilemma of desire. It is, of course, too late to mend things in this way, for Miss Assher's speech to Tina continues to be tainted by her egoistic cruelty, and Anthony's is poisoned by its failure to make an unbroken chain of past and present acts: "To make her love him so—*to speak such tender words*—to give her such caresses, and then to behave as if such things had never been. He had given her the poison that seemed so sweet while she was drinking it, and now it was in her blood, and she was helpless" (ch. 10, p. 194, emphasis mine).

The final blow for Tina's love and sanity comes when, having first imagined the worst—that Anthony has told Miss Assher that Tina has fallen in love with Anthony without cause—and then dared to utter this possibility to Anthony (ch. 11, p. 198), she discovers it to be actually true when Miss Assher speaks to her of it ("'He told you that, did he?'" ch. 13, p. 211). Finally, both Anthony and Tina believe that their salvation lies in speech—she to tell him she hates him (ch. 12, p. 205), he to have a long quiet talk with her (ch. 13, p. 208). Their conversation, prepared for by the agreement of all parties concerned that they should go off alone, takes place in the exterior wildness of the rookery. There Tina, intending to kill "the man whose very voice unnerves her," cries unavailingly, "Speak to me" (ch. 13, p. 212).

This final, massive disjuncture of world, act, and speech brings Tina to silence. Only after she is able both to speak her confession and to respond to music by singing again is she able to achieve a much diminished relation to the world through marriage to Maynard Gilfil. Her recovery is insufficient, however, for her to survive the full implications of that marriage, and she dies as a result of pregnancy.

The portion of this short story devoted to Tina's agony is so large that its significance for George Eliot cannot be only as an attempt to prove the romance behind Mr. Gilfil's prosaic exterior. Although this kind of dilemma of passion is not always central to Eliot's later plots, the outlines of that dilemma remain strikingly similar. There are permutations–in Mr. Tryan's case, the girl dies, and the man survives to lead a better life; in Arthur's the inescapability of time is present through the conception and birth of the illegitimate child; in Godfrey's, interestingly, the passion is sanctified by marriage, but its secrecy makes it virtually null (although its reality makes of Godfrey's love for Nancy a kind of sanctioned adultery); and in Stephen's case, the passion is never consummated, so it is the idea of passion alone which is damned in the world of St. Ogg's. Yet, for all of these couples, passion breeds in a world of silences, and salvation or damnation derives from speech of the proper sort: Tryan must finally confess his crime to another man, Hetty must be brought to speak of her child while Arthur provides the written words of pardon, and Godfrey must say whether or not the child in Silas's cottage is his own. For Maggie and Stephen alone the problem is less clearly paradigmatic.

Although the reasons for the nature and relative success of the finale of *The Mill on the Floss* are many and varied, it becomes apparent in the light of the foregoing cases that one significant difference between those plots of passion and this one is the sequence of its events. For each of the other characters, the revelations of passion and its aftermath are the primary awakening. It is this awakening that teaches about desire and about time. Such is clearly not the case for Maggie Tulliver. Her experiences with Stephen Guest do not make a conscience for her, for her mental life has already been bifurcated by the discrepancies between what one wants and the negative consequences of those wants. Ironically, her earlier relationship with Philip Wakem corresponds in virtually every particular to the pattern of unsanctioned love except for the absence of that very passion we are discussing. Her "dress rehearsal" in the Red Deeps, then, prepares her for elopement with Stephen and guarantees that her awakening to conscience will be quick and absolute.[19] In other words, the order of the plot in this story makes the advent of passion, not the first, but the last event in Maggie's development. This may in part explain why in this alone of George Eliot's novels no marriages take place among the younger generation within the main time scheme of the novel. As it is in the world of Hamlet, time is out of joint, so there can be no more marriages.

Marriage conventionally follows passion, and its significance as word and act for George Eliot is great.

> 'The Omnipresent,' said a Rabbi, 'is occupied in making marriages.' The levity of the saying lies in the ear of him who hears it; for by marriages the speaker meant all the wondrous combinations of the universe whose issue makes our good and evil. (*Daniel Deronda,* ch. 62, p. 560)

Eliot clearly believes in the metaphoric possibilities of the term *marriage* as much as William Blake does. Frequently, as in this passage, the term is used to express metaphorically some larger abstract truth about the doubleness of the world—and the progeny ("issue") of that doubleness. Equally, metaphors themselves are used in order to explain the nature of marriage. These metaphors are of particular concern since they often link two tangibilities, permitting Eliot that fruitful ground of a world made up at once of real things and potent words for them.

Lisbeth Bede speaks several times about the loss of her husband, offering several revealing metaphors in the process:

> When one end o' th' bridge tumbles down, where's th' use o' th' other stannin'? I may's well die, an' foller my old man. There's no knowin' but he'll want me. . . .
> But if thy feyther had lived, he'd ne'er ha' wanted me to go to make room for another, for he could no more ha' done wi'out me nor one side o' the scissars can do wi'out th' other. . . .
> An' if thee'st set thy heart on a lass as'll bring thee nought and waste all, when thee mightst ha' them as 'ud make a man on thee, I'll say nought, now thy feyther's dead an' drownded, for I'm no better nor an old haft when the blade's gone. (*Adam Bede,* ch. 10, pp. 91, 93).

Lisbeth, like the Wife of Bath, uses terms from her own domestic world—bridges, scissors, knives—to present a picture of marriage as a relationship formed for use. Further, the analogies begin in mutuality and move to difference, for the ends of the bridge and the halves of the scissors are identical but contrary, whereas the haft and blade of the knife are complementary. Equally significant for our purposes, Lisbeth sees the great disadvantage of Thias's death to be its effect on her son's marrying. Her own marriage provided her with a function (one she thinks she had perhaps better pursue beyond the grave, as Thias will undoubtedly need her help there, too) and a potency for determining the future—a potency that she feels she now loses.

Whatever marriage represents in the abstract or by analogy, its fundamental condition is expressed by George Eliot's narrator in *Romola* as one of either sympathy or conquest (ch. 48, vol. 2, p. 188). Couples whose marriages become contests of will, attempts of one character to assert power over another, are prominent enough in Eliot's fiction: Janet and Dempster, Latimer and Bertha, Romola and Tito, Lydgate and Rosamond (perhaps), and, most extensively, Gwendolen and Grandcourt. For all of these marriages, the matter of children is either irrelevant to the plot (Janet and Latimer), displaced to another relationship (Romola), denied viability (Lydgate—the one pregnancy that occurs during the time scheme of the novel ends in miscarriage), or feared as a possibility (Gwendolen). Eliot sums up the "mutuality" of such marriages in the brief tale of Madonna Pia and her husband in *Daniel Deronda:*

> [Madonna Pia's] husband, feeling himself injured by her, took her to his castle amid the swampy flats of the Maremma and got rid of her there. . . . We know little about the grounds of mutual discontent between the Siennese couple, but we may infer with some confidence that the husband had never been a very delightful companion, and that on the flats of the Maremma his disagreeable manners had a background which threw them out remarkably; whence in his desire to punish his wife to the uttermost, the nature of things was so far against him that in relieving himself of her he could not avoid making the relief mutual. (Ch. 54, p. 502)

Between the mutual hatred engendered by such struggles for power over another and the mutual sympathy that George Eliot offers as an ideal for marriage lie certain unions in her fiction which show a comic or pathetic kind of inequality of spiritual condition, although that inequality is accommodated through a combination of sympathy and the obverse of conquest—submission. Her treatment of these sorts of marriages reveals Eliot at her most insightful about human relationships, although these marriages do not provide a very clear outline of the order that marriage should establish.

The couples who enact such marriages include Amos and Millie Barton, Tina and Maynard Gilfil, Annette and Rufus Lyon, Dorothea and Casaubon, and even, perhaps, Fred Vincy and Mary Garth. In each case, of course, the more sensitive or imaginative character is apparently at the mercy of the more unconscious, so conquest is not directly proportional to the development of one's own conscious will. George Eliot explains this sort of inversion of power directly when she analyzes Mr. Lyon's love for the delicately bovine Annette:

> The stronger will always rule, say some. . . . But what is strength? Is it blind wilfulness that sees no terrors, no many-linked consequences, no bruises and wounds of those whose cord it tightens? Is it the narrowness of a brain that conceives no needs differing from its own? . . . There is a sort of subjection which is the peculiar heritage of largeness and of love; and strength is often only another name for willing bondage to irremediable weakness. (*Felix Holt the Radical,* ch. 6, pp. 80–81)

Lyon's marriage to Annette acts out the conditions that Eliot asserts early in that novel to be necessary to long-lived love ("much suppression of self, and power of living in the experience of another," ch. 1, p. 23): "Those three years were to Mr. Lyon a period of such self-suppression and life in another as few men know" (ch. 6, p. 93).

George Eliot reserves for a few of her couples a special state that is the result of mutual sympathies and capacities. We are obviously meant to view the marriages of Adam and Dinah, of Felix and Esther, of Dorothea and Will Ladislaw, and of Mirah and Daniel Deronda in this light—although a residue of the master/pupil relationship remains between Felix and Deronda and their willing wives. Eliot's most direct definition of the "ideal" marriage emerges, however, in the more peripheral, and perhaps therefore more concise, discussion of the match between Catherine Arrowpoint and Herr Klesmer.

Chapter 22 of *Daniel Deronda* offers in miniature the plot of an entire novel of romance, in the recognition of love between the plain heiress and the temperamental artist. The context or frame of George Eliot's comedy here consists in the incomprehension of Catherine's parents (who can conceive of marriages only within the range of their own social and political tastes) combined with the irony that their pride in those tastes has provided the very conditions that have presented Catherine with a choice and made her capable of making that choice. In this case, Eliot's opinion about "monotonous attraction"—i.e., animal passion—is satiric:

> That Klesmer, though very susceptible to [obvious beauty], should have a passionate attachment to Miss Arrowpoint, was no more a paradox than any other triumph of a manifold sympathy over a monotonous attraction. We object less to be taxed with the enslaving excess of our passions than with our deficiency in wider passion; but if the truth were known, our reputed intensity is often the dulness of not knowing what else to do with ourselves. Tannhäuser, one suspects, was a knight of ill-furnished imagination, hardly of larger discourse than a heavy Guardsman; Merlin had certainly seen his best days, and was merely repeating himself, when he fell into that hopeless captivity; and we know that Ulysses felt so manifest an *ennui* under similar circumstances that Calypso herself furthered his departure. (P. 177)

Instead, Klesmer and Catherine enjoy a mutuality in difference which is perhaps George Eliot's best description of love, a description that does not rely on the language of religion or of renunciation:

> Klesmer was as versatile and fascinating as a young Ulysses on a sufficient acquaintance. . . . His foibles of arrogance and vanity did not exceed such as may be found in the best English families; and Catherine Arrowpoint had no corresponding restlessness to clash with his: notwithstanding her native kindliness she was perhaps too coolly firm and self-sustained. But she was one of those satisfactory creatures whose intercourse has the charm of discovery; whose integrity of faculty and expression begets a wish to know what they will say on all subjects, or how they will perform whatever they undertake; so that they end by raising not only a continual expectation but a continual sense of fulfilment—the systole and diastole of blissful companionship. (P. 178)

Even for this well-matched pair, however, there are difficulties that make for a plot, difficulties that again depend upon the potential conflict between generations and the concomitant problem of bringing passion into speech. What generates the fateful conversation between Klesmer and Catherine is Klesmer's extravagant speech to Mr. Bult—a speech that ends with Klesmer's assertion that "a man who speaks effectively through music is compelled to something more difficult than parliamentary eloquence" (p. 180). The conversation with Catherine returns repeatedly to matters of speech and hearing, for Klesmer complains of having to hear his gods blasphemed, Catherine fails to answer his assertion that he must leave, he has recourse to echoing his feelings through a melody at the piano, and then he taxes her with her earlier remarks on the motives of men who love heiresses (pp. 180–81). When Catherine finally does speak her mind ("Why should I not marry the man who loves me, if I love him?"), "the effort was something like the leap of a woman from the deck into the lifeboat" (p. 182). Here at last "the decisive word had been spoken" (p. 182). The tragi-comic response of Catherine's mother provides a final indirect comment on the importance of that word: "It is hard for us to live up to our own eloquence, and keep pace with our winged words, while we are treading the solid earth and are liable to heavy dining" (p. 182).

The interview that Catherine's parents have with Klesmer pays equal attention to language, as Mrs. Arrowpoint unsuccessfully tries to leave the speaking to her husband, and Klesmer is reduced to silent irony or a refusal to violate the code of a gentleman by retorting to a lady's insults. The scene ends, importantly, with Mr. Arrowpoint's cogent rejoinder to his wife's threat to disinherit Catherine if she marries Klesmer: "It's all very fine, . . . but what the deuce are we to do with the property?" (p. 185).

George Eliot approaches the chief dilemma in marriage—adultery—by means of a discussion of marrying in *Silas Marner.* It is doubly important for me to examine this discussion since it is frequently offered as a proof of George Eliot's preference for deed over word,[20] which appears to contradict my own assertions about passion and language.

Mr. Macey's long speech in the Rainbow Tavern manages to touch upon many of George Eliot's favorite topics before centering on marriage. It begins after a disagreement between the farrier and the butcher over cows, moves on to the rights and wrongs of church singing, and then turns to the arrival of Nancy Lammeter's grandfather in the region surrounding Raveloe. The climax of the narrative of the Lammeters is the problem of the present Mr. Lammeter's marriage to Miss Osgood. The initiating difficulty is the time of the wedding: "And young Mr. Lammeter, he'd have no way but he must be married in Janiwary, which, to be sure, 's a unreasonable time to be married in, for it isn't like a christening or a burying, as you can't help; and so Mr. Drumlow . . . when he come to put the questions, he put 'em by the rule o' contrairy, like, and he says, 'Wilt thou have this man to thy wedded wife?'" (ch. 6, pp. 100–101). That is, the first important difference between birth or death and marriage is the control exerted over time by one's choice of a mate within a social and public context. It is an act of foresight, not of impulse. Mr. Macey indirectly attributes the resulting difficulties about the legal validity of the Lammeter ceremony itself to the unceremonious time of the wedding.

Mr. Drumlow resolves Mr. Macey's dilemma about whether the meaning or the words determines the legal validity by an assertion that at first appears to belittle the importance of the vows at the altar. He says that "it's neither the meaning nor the words"—neither the inner reality nor the individual speech act; instead it's "the re*ges*ter does it"—the public and written proof of union in the setting down of names (p. 102). This assertion echoes George Eliot's words about the reality of Daniel Deronda's parentage; the most important, the finally real, presence of that parentage is not in Deronda's inner conceptions, nor even in the fact of his own, private, circumcised penis,[21] but in the written memorials of his grandfather's intentions and hopes.

Even adultery finally resolves itself to this particular issue, since, for each of George Eliot's adulterers, the fundamental problem is less the discovery of an illicit passion that violates their marriage vows than the need to provide the child of that adultery with an inheritance reserved for legitimate offspring. Mrs. Transome, Mr. Featherstone, and Mrs. Glasher all know what they wish to "do with the property." They realize the consequences of their passions in the difficulties they face in providing a socially acceptable situation for their children, a situation they were once willing enough to abandon themselves.

Early in her fiction, then, George Eliot discovered the necessary dependency of any understanding of individual passion upon the conditions of time past or time future which are made present through the family relationship—a dependency she exploited in the construction of all her later plots. Passion as energy commits one to the order of generation. The sequence of passion, union (premarital and adulterous), and procreation "generates" Eliot's plots.

As George Eliot well knows, however, the pattern of generation is cyclical, so the choice of any beginning is arbitrary. In her own first story, "Amos Barton," she starts in the middle—if something that appears to be without a plot can be said to have a middle, a beginning, or an end. Amos's courtship and marriage to Millie have long been accomplished, and the actual sequence of events in the narrative is a double one of apparent and real sexual engagement. That is, Amos's story achieves its denouement by the conjoining of public belief in his adultery with his private acts of procreation; that denouement is the death of his wife, thereby of his marriage, and thus of his tale.

"Mr. Gilfil's Love-Story" begins earlier, although it appears, because of its frame story, to begin later. Here, the adoption of the child by the happily married couple is followed by the story of the child's own growth to passion as a result of that adoption. The climax is Tina's recognition, through the death of her beloved and her "parents'" heir, of the extent of her disjuncture from the norms of her family. The marriage that is to compensate for this death achieves little of the power necessary for compensation, and this fact is mirrored in the death of Tina's unborn child.

"Janet's Repentance" is apparently set entirely in the time of adulthood, although the relationships between Janet and Dempster and their respective mothers are significant for the psychology of each. The story begins, like "Amos Barton," with comic misinterpretations of the relationship between a minister and the female members of his flock; here, however, the amorous undercurrent to the attentions paid to Mr. Tryan is not hypothetical but real. Yet Janet, the main focus of the plot, moves from a passionate union to a spiritual one, although Mr. Tryan's death may imply a comment on the ultimate vitality of such a development. Her awakening to the higher life, which is brought about by her own sufferings and her discovery of the sufferings of another, is usually considered to be the moral paradigm of George Eliot's fiction; and it is true that the series of conscious attitudes Janet adopts (described as the awakening to the cry of another in chapter 4) is reenacted in large and small versions throughout Eliot's novels. That is, this awakening of the soul is sufficiently a given that it does not require her to devise later narratives in order to examine or eliminate the paradoxes inherent in its structure. Rather, "problems" arise from such a plot because, in the achievement of an adequate stance before the world, passion must be either exploded or sublimated, not really accommodated in the narrative.

To be more specific, Janet's and Lawyer Dempster's marriage appears to have been a love-match; yet their inability to achieve the stability I have ascribed to Klesmer and Catherine Arrowpoint seems to be a product of their failure to encompass any human relationships beyond the sexual. Perhaps their "intoxication" and the physical rages and physical stupor they jointly display are a comment on pure sexuality, valid at least for this stage in George Eliot's development. Eliot explicitly points out that when Dempster's mother dies, all other forms of affection seem to die with her. His attachment to Janet then becomes a blind and sometimes silent assertion of his will and a denial of her separate selfhood.

Janet herself seems to vacillate between an equally passionate willfulness and an infantile inability either to understand or to take command of her situation. The distinctive character of her response to Mr. Tryan is not the growth of a distinctly Christian faith—others, like Mr. Jerome and Mrs. Raynor, have shown even more piety than he has without infecting her with a similar resignation. Instead, it is the growth of a maternal attitude toward both Tryan and Dempster which provides Janet with a stance whereby to confront and survive in her world. That is, although she cannot comprehend the nature of her own sexual identity and its attendant responsibilities when faced with her husband's brutal animality (an animality she tries in a variety of ways to deny) or when faced with her own mother's solicitude toward her as an only child, she does manage to accommodate love for a man within a motherly solicitude when she provides a home for Tryan during his last illness. Of course, many readers would find the transference of the maternal relation from the child to the "spiritual spouse" to be, although metaphorically comprehensible, psychologically suspect. Eliot, through the characters in her plots, must eventually come to terms with the literal child.

In *Adam Bede,* George Eliot uses for the first time a sufficient cast of characters to permit a somewhat simultaneous investigation of events along the line (or around the circle) of generation. The story begins with two men in love with the same woman, but almost immediately Eliot focuses on Adam's relationship to his father. Indeed, that relationship is explicitly seen to be a precursor of his relationship to Hetty—a first lesson prior to his discoveries about her. Equally, Arthur's behavior is placed in the light of his relationships to his grandfather—a man who displays "unloving love" (ch. 22, p. 218)—and to his godmother. The act of procreation performed and then denied by Hetty (a child without parents in the novel) is intended to be the climax of the novel's plot. By recognizing the reality of that child, Hetty (maybe), Arthur, and Adam achieve a recognition about themselves and what they are. Only Adam, of course, manages thereafter to consciously plan a marriage, the result of a newly awakened passion for Dinah Morris. Their passionate (Dinah experiences telltale blushes of sexual consciousness early in the novel) and public commitment is rewarded in the novel with children—and the first happy ending in Eliot's fiction.

"The Lifted Veil" is usually seen as an anomaly among George Eliot's works, although several critics have indicated its manifold connections to preoccupations worked out in her novels.[22] Most cogent of the analyses of this story are those that see in the special consciousness of Latimer an image of Eliot face to face with the possible horrors of artistic insight into other subjectivities.[23] My examination is not meant to deny such an interpretation, but it is certainly true that, except for the unusual quality of Latimer's extrasensory perceptions, the entire content of the story is focused upon familial jealousy and hatred, ungoverned passion, and the failure of love and marriage. That is, the plot continues to concern generation.

Here, as in "Mr. Gilfil's Love-Story," we begin in childhood—leaving out of account for the moment the not insignificant premonition of Latimer's death, which in effect begins the story at its end. It is clear early on that the determining factor for Latimer's development is an unlikeness between himself and his father, echoed in the unlikeness between him and his brother. Many things prepare Latimer for that incapacitated susceptibility which reveals itself as prevision and telepathy: the lack of "loving eyes" following the death of his mother, his father's choice of Latimer's half-brother to be his "representative and successor"—and so to receive the very education for which Latimer longs—and his father's unloving fulfillment of every outward duty toward him (p. 291). Even his first vision of Prague draws upon the failure of benevolent energy between generations:

> And the blackened statues, as I passed under their blank gaze, along the unending bridge, with their ancient garments and their saintly crowns, seemed to me the real inhabitants and owners of this place, while the busy, trivial men and women, hurrying to and fro, were a swarm of ephemeral visitants infesting it for a day. It is such grim, stony beings as these, I thought, who are the fathers of ancient faded children, in those tanned, time-fretted dwellings that crowd the steep before me. (P. 293)

Equally significantly, his second vision centers on the appearance of Bertha, a willowy figure with "luxuriant blonde hair" (p. 294) who reminds Latimer of water-nixies and sirens. He himself repeatedly refers to his infatuation with her as a passion—"Doubtless there was another sort of fascination at work—that subtle physical attraction which delights in cheating our psychological predictions, and in compelling the men who paint sylphs to fall in love with some *bonne et brave femme,* heavy-heeled and freckled" (p. 296). Even before this self-revelation, however, Latimer has made clear that much of the impetus of his interest in Bertha derives from his envy of his brother Alfred in general and of Alfred's projected marriage to Bertha in particular. That envy reveals itself outwardly only twice: when Latimer tries to take over his brother's role by speaking Alfred's own words before he can speak them himself (p. 297) and when he utters a remark about his marrying his brother's betrothed wife (p. 301).

One event of the plot works against the usual interpretation, that Latimer's story points up the virtues of ignorance over prevision: Bertha's inner character is not completely unknown to Latimer prior to their marriage; he does have a vision of her in which, wearing the serpent brooch, she reveals to him the depth of their mutual hatred. But even this vision is insufficient to stem his passion to possess Bertha and thereby displace his brother. When he gets his wish, however, when the hated brother is dead, he begins to develop a sensitivity that will finally free him from his infatuation with Bertha. That sensitivity is the growth of actual affection for his father—"My softened feeling toward my father made this the happiest time I had known since childhood" (p. 302).

Like the other passionate conflicts, the growing one between Bertha and Latimer reveals itself through speech disfunctions. Because he cannot (will not?) read Bertha's thoughts, Latimer has to rely upon her words, which are, of course, false; and when both characters discover that their marriage will not fulfill their intentions (Latimer's for sympathy and Bertha's for conquest), their alienation is silent, inaudible (p. 304).

The two crucial events that lead to Latimer's despairing demise—the preliminary arrival of Mrs. Archer and the providential absence of his servants on 20 September, 1850—are each the result of more conventional loving and marrying within the servant world—Bertha must hire a new maid because Fletcher is to be married (p. 305), and Latimer's housekeeper has rushed from the house after a lover's quarrel (p. 290). Latimer increasingly loses touch with this world as his insights, combined with his morbid inability to sympathize with those less sensitive than he, grow keener. Eventually that lack of sympathy catches up with his power of vision and brings about a kind of atrophy. The true revelation of his position in life is then provided to him, not by prevision or even by conventional statement or act, but through an event that seems quite unprepared for: the resuscitation of Mrs. Archer is, even in this story, so out of the ordinary for its artistic function that even explanations of her rebirth as a frightening vision of life's never-ending hatefulness are inadequate. In the context of our discussion, the word *rebirth* is the possible key to the necessary presence of Mrs. Archer's resuscitation.

The normal result of passion and marriage is children; the lack of children announces the sterility of the relationship between Bertha and Latimer. Certain issues become clearer, however, when one realizes the echo of the childbirth bed in this deathbed scene. As George Eliot says elsewhere of evil, Latimer discovers in the "new life" brought forth in this bed that the fruits of his marriage are not merely negative, but horribly positive. In his own life, Latimer has violated most ties of family affection, and his singleminded pursuit of his own happiness has denied the very meaning of passion and marriage. His marriage is brought to bed of only death, in Mrs. Archer's announcement of Bertha's murderous intentions. Further, it is not insignificant that even the ability to grasp and accept this insight is dependent, proximately, on Latimer's late feelings for his father and, directly, on his affection for the orphaned Doctor Meunier (testified to by Meunier's presence).

Thus, although "The Lifted Veil," like "Janet's Repentance," is indeed a story about the movement of consciousness to recognition of itself, its plot is passionate and perversely procreative. Such an interpretation equally justifies beginning the story with the narrator's death.

As we move from the earlier novels and stories to the later, we discover a growing interest in the period of time prior to the awakening of passion. Childhood and the child's relation to parental figures become increasingly important to George Eliot's conception of the human dilemma. *The Mill on the Floss* provides the most extensive examination of this period of time, as well as the first direct consideration of the sibling relationship. Yet, because the siblings are of the opposite sex, several issues complicate their situation. Indeed, although Maggie and Tom are obviously in competition with each other for the affection and regard of their parents, they are also aware of their differences as boy and girl—each knows, finally, that he or she cannot be a full replacement for the other. Eliot also examines the degree to which being a boy or a girl creates certain conditions *vis-à-vis* the parent.[24] Certainly, early childhood difficulties clearly account for both Maggie's and Tom's later failures of love. Tom's unspoken love for Lucy is not emphasized, but it is as essential to that entanglement of relationships that prevent fruitful marriage as are Maggie's feelings for both Philip and Stephen. Baldly stated, the society of St. Ogg's and the mill has not adequately defined its rules of matrimony, or, perhaps, has simply defined them in such a way that no satisfactory "giving in marriage" to an outsider is possible or desirable. For Maggie's relatives, Philip Wakem is too far without the bounds of affinity, whereas Stephen Guest, as her cousin/sister's fiancé, is too far within. Finally, the ending of the novel makes the uncomfortable assertion that the only inescapable union in such a world is created by the blood bond, which Tom recognizes and seals when he speaks Maggie's childhood name just prior to their joint drowning.

Tony Tanner's remarks about the potential disruptiveness of marriage are relevant here. In speaking of marriage as a fundamental means to mediate between the patterns and demands of nature, family, society, and even religion, he notes the possible tensions it must transcend:

> One may immediately discern a potential tension between differing time schemes here. For if nature works seasonally while God works through eternity, the family works by generational changes (*each particular family has to disintegrate to make sure the family continues with different members*), while society . . . tends to believe in what Sartre calls the myth of its own "perenniality," or permanence and stasis. (Emphasis mine)[25]

In other words, as critics of the novel have repeatedly indicated, the world of *The Mill on the Floss* is finally so "family oriented" that the necessary disintegration and reintegration through marriage to an outsider is impossible. Incest and death are the only alternatives.

In the short story "Brother Jacob," George Eliot reduces the ambiguities of familial relationships to sharp and satiric dichotomies. The protagonist, David Faux, feels no affection for parent, brother, or even betrothed. He is without passion and impervious to maternal tenderness. Indeed, in this narrative the gustatory appetite replaces all other motivations and explanations of human behavior, driving out even the sexual. Nevertheless, the point of the plot is clear: one cannot choose to do without parents and siblings. Their existence is an inescapable fact for David, and even his attempt to replace them with more attractive relations in order to hoodwink the people of Grimworth is insufficient protection against consanguinity. Yet, this issue of alternative parents, first broached in "Mr. Gilfil's Love-Story," receives far different treatment in the succeeding novel, *Silas Marner,* perhaps because there the parent first chooses the child.

Although *Adam Bede* and *The Mill on the Floss* each have multiple focuses of interest and in many ways tell the same story twice, *Silas Marner* is the first of George Eliot's novels to have a real double plot. Yet, in its abstract form, if not in its all-important particulars, this doubleness is really very much like the story of Tina Sarti's childhood and young adulthood told simultaneously rather than consecutively. This may be Eliot's way of determining the degree to which the stories of parent and child are really separate, their only unavoidable connection being the moment of generation.

Both triadic love relationships and sibling relationships are important in *Silas Marner.* If we focus first on Godfrey and then on Silas, the pervasiveness of such relations becomes apparent. Godfrey's character is clearly presented to be the result of parental presence and absence—his father being what he is and his mother not being at all. His life is further complicated by his connections with and yet differences from his brother Dunsey, who is a kind of David Faux in that he robs Godfrey of his peace of mind, of his horse, and could, if he chooses to tell their father about Molly, rob him of his very patrimony. Godfrey's passionate involvement with Molly is of that socially disruptive kind which he himself is ashamed to recognize yet too weak to avoid. Thus, Godfrey is the social transgressor in that relationship, whereas Silas is the figure transgressed against, betrayed by his brotherly friend William Dane as well as by his sweetheart. Moreover, in his role as Godfrey's replacement Silas is even betrayed by his "brother" Dunsey's theft of his gold. He overcomes these betrayals through his affection for his departed sister, an affection that is the latent energy within him that permits him to become a nurturing father in the novel.

George Eliot must, in this plot, provide some sort of rationale for the resolution it achieves; that resolution itself conforms to the pattern of generation we have been examining. That is, each character—Godfrey, Silas, Eppie—speaks his or her feeling and by so doing affirms who he or she is or has been. For Eppie, this also means affirming whom she will marry; and for the fathers, it means asserting the reality of an act in time—a single moment of creation in Godfrey's case, and fifteen years of protection in Silas's. Yet even this is not completely accurate, for Silas's first commitment to Eppie was as momentary and impulsive as Godfrey's propagation of her: "The proposition to take the child from him had come to Silas quite unexpectedly, and his speech, uttered under a strong sudden impulse, was almost like a revelation to himself: a minute before, he had no distinct intention about the child" (ch. 13, p. 172). What makes Silas one of Eliot's lucky ones is his steadfastness to the letter and spirit of this impulsive commitment to the child, "confirming by distinct successive impressions the first instinctive bias" (*The Mill on the Floss,* bk. 6, ch. 7, p. 359). This union of momentary impulse and successive time makes Silas a proper father.

As the obverse of this fathering, Godfrey's later childlessness is usually examined. There is another person, however, whose involvement in that childlessness is unavoidable—Nancy—and her role in that condition is not usually considered. Nancy has qualities that echo the family-bound Dodsons of *The Mill on the Floss.* Her behavior regarding dress, her refusal to permit unlikeness between siblings, and her denial of the possibility of adoption (a possibility the novel emphatically affirms in Silas) suggest an orderliness that finally stifles passion and energy and the life-giving differences they generate. We do know that Godfrey is capable of passion and thereby of procreation—he has a child, although he loses her. Nancy never has a child at all.

What, then, has George Eliot achieved in *Silas Marner* by telling the stories of passion and of nurture separately? In the first place, because those stories insist nevertheless on implicating each other, she shows that they cannot be told separately. Second, by providing as a climax for each of those stories the moment of recognition of child by parent and of parent by child, she focuses the reader's attention on that moment, which, although it has certainly been prepared for by fifteen years of negation and of affirmation, achieves its status as a moment because the characters each speak who they are. Here, then, she also achieves an accommodation between time as momentary present and time as orderly succession, each drawing energy and significance from the other.

In *Romola,* even more clearly than in *Adam Bede,* the behavior of the lovers is entangled with their relationships to their fathers. Romola almost seems to suffer from an excess of fathers, beginning with blind Bardo, replacing him with Savonarola, and finally choosing to be loyal to her godfather Bernardo. Tito, on the other hand, keeps being forsaken by his fathers, in that he is first orphaned of his natural father and then of his adoptive one. Of course, Tito becomes willing to help this process along and confirms this willingness when he denies any obligation to his dead father-in-law. Such an absence of the sense of generational obligation also manifests itself in his nonchalant fathering of Tessa's children, who must, in the end, be cared for by Romola, his legal and social representative. Even more clearly, Tito's behavior toward Baldassarre is symbolic of his crime, which is to wish to retain his patrimony without speaking the name and thus the reality of Baldassarre, his father. By keeping silent about him when he himself arrives in Florence and then when he sees Baldassarre as a prisoner, Tito (like David Faux) attempts to hold to the privileges of a social and familial position without the obligations and connections of kinship. Further, the rage awakened in Baldassarre by Tito's behavior is equally destructive, so that he too loses his power over a language that has always before determined his identity. That language may return to him fitfully in private, but he cannot make himself heard in a public gathering. Yet his final assertion of connection to his son is as unanswerable and final as Maggie's and Tom's, for he clutches Tito's throat until both of them are dead, saying only, "You see me—you know me!" (ch. 67, vol. 2, p. 394).

The plot of *Felix Holt the Radical* is one of George Eliot's most complex and, as a result, one of her most implausible. Here, more overtly than in any of the previous novels, the questions of marriage, of the inheritance of property and position, and of the recognition of the true parent are multiplied for each of the three young people who are the central characters within the principle time frame of the novel. The novel begins with Harold as an unknown quantity, a result of Mrs. Transome's long-buried adultery. Thus, our interest seems at first to be primarily in the consequences of that adultery for her and only secondarily in its effect upon her child. Conversely, Esther is presented as an anomaly in Rufus Lyon's world before we are introduced to the hidden romance of his past. Between Mrs. Transome's tragic tale and Rufus's melodramatic one lies the comic disagreement between Felix Holt and his parents—dead and alive—over the virtues and social benefits of their patent medicine patrimony. Like Eppie's before her, Esther's choice of a husband is finally determined by her choice of her adopted father, although in both cases one might argue that the choice of the father was influenced by the choice passionate love had already made.

Much of the conflict and resolution in this plot depends upon the status of names and of language. Esther's identity as Bycliffe's daughter has been confused because Bycliffe chose to change names with Christian and to give away the written testimonials of his own marital relations. The slippage of language in such a world is manifested in a variety of other ways as well. For instance, the retaliation that Scales performs in cutting off Christian's coattail is called for by Christian's punning of the night before. Yet the action has good consequences in providing Rufus with tangible and legible clues to the hidden connections between his daughter and others. Further, Tommy Trounsem's family name is a debased form of Transome which only hints at his more respectable ancestry. His job as a sign hanger is perversely appropriate, for his own name is the sign of the legal right of the Durfey-Transomes to the estate. That right depends, as all rights in George Eliot's novels seem to, upon the true fact of kinship. That is, as long as a true relative of the original Transome remains living, and generates a new Transome who too will live, the Durfeys may maintain possession of the estate. The failure to generate means the end of their right to determine the possessors of the property. In a sense, then, Harold's right to his estate is threatened in two ways. His familial claims are at the mercy of Trounsem's mortality, and his personal ones are at the mercy of his mother's errant passions—passions that have violated both the words of her marriage vows and the ties of blood between mother and son and between brother and brother. This last violation is mirrored in the hatred of and the reflexive degeneracy displayed by Durfey, the older brother and true heir.

Felix's place in this appears suddenly to be peripheral. He seems unhampered by the family ties that so determine Harold's, and even

Esther's, fate. Yet I think we are meant to see in Felix's behavior certain analogies to these primal tensions. Felix hopes to reach the working men of Sproxton by "lay[ing] hold of them by their fatherhood": "I'll take one of their little fellows and set him in the midst" (ch. 11, p. 136). His intentions as a Radical, then, are less political than educational, for "if he could move these men to save something from their drink and pay a schoolmaster for their boys, a greater service would be done them than if Mr. Garstin and his company were persuaded to establish a school" (p. 136). Felix's means to this, of course, is through words and not property, and his words are often singularly effective, although his actions bring about catastrophe. His mistakes and subsequent arrest might even be necessary simply to provide Esther with the opportunity to speak her belief in Felix, and thereby indirectly her love for him, in a public place. It is certainly true that their "plot" makes more sense as a love story than a political story.

If we look at Felix directly, we see that his personal difficulties are the familiar ones of language and passion. The excesses of his language are apparent first, and Rufus Lyon warns him in words that show his own recognition of the doubleness of hearing and listening between fathers and sons:

> It is good that you should use plainness of speech, and I am not of those who would enforce a submissive silence on the young, that they themselves, being elders, may be heard at large. . . . I have to keep a special watch over myself in this matter, inasmuch as I have a need of utterance which makes the thought within me seem as a pent-up fire, until I have shot it forth, as it were, in arrowy words, each one hitting its mark. Therefore I pray for a listening spirit, which is a great mark of grace. (Ch. 5, p. 68)

Felix is enamored of metaphor, of language, which asserts its "thingness" in violent and obtrusive ways, so he is quick to say to Rufus that "truth-vendors and medicine-vendors usually recommend swallowing. When a man sees his livelihood in a pill or a proposition, he likes to have orders for the dose, and not curious inquiries" (p. 70). His first conflict with Esther builds on this discussion of language as a gauge of reality, for he rebukes her for her interest in the niceties of words in general and in the words of Byron in particular.

Felix's remarks about swallowing truth and medicines are echoed in the conclusion of this chapter, where they become the language of passion and marriage; he thinks, "I'll never marry, though I should have to live on raw turnips to subdue my flesh." Even more revealing are his next thoughts:

> I'll never look back and say, "I had a fine purpose once—I meant to keep my hands clean and my soul upright, and to look truth in the face; but pray excuse me, I have a wife and children—I must lie and simper a little, else they'll starve;" or "My wife is nice, she must have her bread well buttered, and her feelings will be hurt if she is not thought genteel." (P. 77)

He is a stage ahead of Lydgate in understanding what sort of woman not to marry, but Felix is clearly ignorant of the impossibility of keeping one's hands clean and one's soul upright while being an avowed member of the family of man. This of a piece with his belief that he may be fatherly without coming to terms with the passion within him; he tells his mother "pray don't use that limping argument again—that a man should marry because he's fond of children. That's a reason for not marrying. A bachelor's children are always young: they're immortal children—always lisping, waddling, helpless, and with a chance of turning out good" (ch. 22, pp. 232-33). In other words, he wishes to divorce children from generation and from time.

Felix is, then, one of several characters who recognize the power and significance of passion as a force, both positive and negative, which "embeds" them in time and reality. In this he joins Dinah Morris, Tom Tulliver, Romola, Dorothea Brooke, and even Daniel Deronda. Indeed, his likeness to Dorothea is striking; like her he begins with high social intentions and little understanding of his own emotions and "dwindles" in the course of the novel into a spouse. Given the lack of fictional representation of that Eastern landscape toward which he journeys, it is possible that Daniel Deronda really does the same.

Between *Felix Holt the Radical* and *Middlemarch* lie George Eliot's poems, including "The Legend of Jubal" and the tragedy of *The Spanish Gypsy*. Because it presents the titular heroine with a conflict between father and lover, the latter poem is related to the family plots we have been examining. In many ways, however, we have already seen the outlines of this conflict in the lives of such earlier characters as Eppie, Maggie, and Esther. Ironically, given Eliot's respect for roots, the daughters who choose their adopted fathers achieve happy endings, whereas the daughters who remain faithful to biological ties undergo tragedy. The cultural worlds that both Maggie and Fedalma inhabit are much to blame. Furthermore, their choices in some ways have less to do with loyalties to specific individuals than to conceptions of higher and lower lives—Zarca's most potent appeals remind Fedalma that in choosing the Duke she would be choosing luxury and inactivity; she would be property rather than a person.

The Duke's situation is somewhat more intriguing, for he finds the dissociation of passion from the social order more extensively catastrophic. After her first provocative dance in the plaça, Fedalma is conspicuously rigid and immobile, revealing her condition primarily by those she stands near or between; the Duke, on the other hand, is impulsively, compulsively, moved to action and to speech acts by the dilemma of his situation. For him, especially, the divorce of passion from vows of loyalty, and of words from their habitual realities, creates a nightmare world in which he must defend the "father" (Father Isador), who seeks the death of his beloved by killing her father (Zarca). Both acts achieve their significance not simply from the deaths that result but also from the lingering reality of the words that have preceded them. Among these words are Zarca's vow to end Father Isador's "inquisition" and the Duke's vow to serve Zarca (because of his earlier vow to marry Fedalma). The Duke's real suffering comes from his realization that he is mentally and emotionally bound by mutually exclusive vows: he cannot be loyal both to Spain and to the Zincali. His only hope for peace at the close of the play is dependent upon the spoken forgiveness of the "Holy Father" in Rome.

So extensive and direct a consideration of the loyalty owed to father rather than to beloved in *The Spanish Gypsy* seems to have freed George Eliot from considering this conflict directly in *Middlemarch.* Although in three of the four plots in that novel—the love plots—the situations of the young people are placed within the context of their parent's behavior, none of these characters directly perceives his or her choice to be dependent upon forces unleashed by the earlier generation. It is quite true, as U. C. Knoepflmacher has explained, that father figures are central to the novel,[26] primarily by reason of their absence. The young people are permitted to work out the relations between their passionate attachments and their positions in the world without the complications of ancestral loyalties.

Yet the story of Peter Featherstone contains a residue of the dilemma of procreation. Here is a man who chooses to defy and ridicule his blood relations—relations who reincarnate the Dodson characteristics—while carrying on an inconsistently friendly intercourse with his relatives by marriage. He appears to have adopted Fred Vincy as his son, believing that the tie that binds Fred to him is a monetary one. The promise of inheritance is the key to his sense of fatherhood; and if it weren't for Fred's love for Mary Garth, Peter's influence on him would have been decisive.

In the end, however, Peter asserts potency of a very different sort, although it is true that just before his death he wishes to favor the adopted son over the natural one. But by drafting a will in favor of Joshua Rigg at all, Peter reminds his society of his singular and personal identity through his power to make love to whomever he privately chooses. The limits of that power are soon apparent. He does cause Joshua Rigg to take the Featherstone name, but Joshua shows that he also has his own identity when he sells the property to which that name entitles him in order to be a money-changer. Further, Joshua rids himself of his adopted father as well when he insists that he will have nothing to do with Raffles. Since Raffles displays a selfishness and cruelty equal to Featherstone's (his only significant difference being the wealth he possesses), Joshua is really only denying the same sort of absent father twice.

These acts of acceptance and then denial on Joshua's part reverberate through the plot of the novel. Featherstone's two acts as father—begetting and willing[27]—first bring Joshua to Stone Court and then send him from it. Because Joshua comes, Raffles does; because he goes, Bulstrode arrives. By that sequence of events, Joshua's impact on the lives of the novel's characters is extended to Lydgate and Will Ladislaw as well, for Bulstrode's fear of Raffles makes him try to act as a father figure to both these men, one of whom (as George Eliot remarks) is sensible enough to deny his patronage/patrimony.

In the acts of both Peter Featherstone and Joshua Rigg-Featherstone there is affirmation of both kinship and difference. In a somewhat different way, Will Ladislaw chooses both to affirm and deny his ancestry. On both his mother's and his father's sides, his female progenitors defied family and society by deserting their families and then marrying an ambiguously foreign figure. In choosing to remain true to those choices, Will affirms his own parental figures, who nevertheless define the limits of parental authority and control. His remarks upon learning that Bulstrode wishes to reinvest him with the money his mother had abandoned are revealing.

> It is eminently [my business] to ask such questions, when I have to decide whether I will have transactions with you and accept your money. My unblemished honour is important to me. It is important to me to have no stain on my birth and connections. And now I find there is a stain which I can't help. My mother felt it, and tried to keep as clear of it as she could, and so will I. . . . If I had any fortune of my own, I would willingly pay it to any one who could disprove what you have told me. What I have to thank you for is that you kept the money till now, when I can

refuse it. It ought to lie with a man's self that he is a gentleman. (Ch. 61, p. 457)

Will is particularly embittered because of the bearing this revelation has upon his love for Dorothea; indeed, one thought he has at this time is that if he did take the money, he would never be able to tell Dorothea that he had done so. Unlike Fred Vincy, then, Will refuses to identify himself with a base act by a relative in order to receive a gift of money. He cannot deny the fact of his inheritance, although he can, and does, refuse to affirm and perpetuate it by word or deed.

I should briefly remark, before turning to *Daniel Deronda,* that Dorothea's proposal to Will at the close of the novel echoes Catherine Arrowpoint's to Klesmer, as Dorothea's feelings too become a flood that forces her to make the leap of speech after the pent-up frustrations of silence (ch. 83, p. 594). Further, in this speech she renounces the "will" of the "father" Casaubon, as well as the social role defined for her by that will (and by the acquiescence of her relatives and friends), choosing, like Ladislaw, to do without the money, which would require a sacrifice of personal choice.

All of the issues we have examined are central to *Daniel Deronda,* George Eliot's last novel, and many critics have already discussed their significance, especially insofar as they explain Deronda's place in the novel.[28] Certain distinctive features of that narrative, however, should be explored in the light of George Eliot's career-long examination of the dilemma of being a son and a lover. The crucial sexual acts in this novel have all taken place in the past—Daniel's conception, Mrs. Davilow's second marriage, and Grandcourt's adultery. The novel, then, is preoccupied with the extent to which those acts have committed the future to a particular course. And nearly everyone agrees, finally, that these acts cannot be negated or denied: Alcharisi must finally confess to the reality of her motherhood; Gwendolen must suffer the consequences of Mr. Davilow's brutality and death, especially their final economic consequences;[29] and Gwendolen (and through her, Grandcourt) must acquiesce in the reality of Grandcourt's children. Even for Mordecai and Mirah, the fact of their father is inescapable, although his authority is not.

In this novel, as in *Silas Marner,* George Eliot has again chosen to separate the story of the adopted child from the story of dangerous passion—Daniel is preoccupied with his relations to Sir Hugo and his unknown parents, while Gwendolen is caught within a world of passion, power, marriage, and adultery. Gwendolen's triumph in this role is the fascinating result of Eliot's combining qualities she generally kept separate in her other women. That is, Gwendolen is as preoccupied with her own singularity (disliking siblings, dominating those around her) as is Rosamond Vincy, and yet she is reachable through susceptibilities like Dorothea's, which finally appear to be the repressed offshoots of her own unrecognized passions. This may seem to be an odd interpretation of the virginal girl who so fiercely dislikes being made love to, but in many ways Gwendolen's virginity has that exaggerated recoil which suggests not the absence of passion but excessive fear of its presence. Her enjoyment of riding has distinct echoes of Dorothea's, and her physical repulsion from Lush has sexual overtones. Her tendency to desire those appurtenances of power and position which society seems to reserve for people who acquiesce in the orderly connections of property and legitimate inheritance is combined with an emotional and psychic energy that is at variance with such systems of order; this odd conjunction makes Gwendolen's tragedy. Had she been either less selfish or less at the mercy of the energies of that self, she would not have come to possess a husband and an estate which she knows are entangled by other obligations engendered by Grandcourt's own sexual identity.

George Eliot had revealed her convictions about the necessity to recognize passion and its implications in earlier plots. Deronda's story, however, appears to present certain new narrative difficulties. Here, as Peter Garrett has cogently explained, the orders of time which we have seen in Eliot's earlier fiction are reversed, for Deronda's story focuses on a process of discovery, prophecy, and fulfillment, "where meaning is determined by a remote, mysterious origin and a remote, beckoning goal."[30] Leon Gottfried calls this the world of romance, a world without society or psychology, containing instead the omens, mysteries, recurrences, and rituals of myth.[31] Although all of this may be true, there is nevertheless a real attempt on Eliot's part to keep Daniel Deronda imbedded in the here and now, and the psychological reality that one can discern in his behavior has similarities to the conditions and choices others of her characters have experienced, although here the situation is presented in more grandiose form.

Will Ladislaw's remark to his step-grandfather, Bulstrode, may help to clarify the meaning of Daniel's discovery of identity: "What I have to thank you for is that you kept the money till now, when I can refuse it." In Daniel's case, Alcharisi has kept Daniel's heritage until now, when he can accept it. Although Cynthia Chase asserts that George Eliot's message is confusing because the story makes becoming a Jew a speech act rather than a genealogical act (so that either his empathy or his actual heritage become redundant),[32] it is this very redundancy we have been pursuing in Eliot's fiction. Eliot permits both father (or mother) *and* son to determine identity, although for both that determination is not only a silent and momentary act but an audible and durational one. It is not merely that the sexual act of his parents created Daniel, nor that he chooses to recognize them verbally and socially as his parents, but also that those parents (that is, his grandfather) choose to recognize that they are implicated in the life and reality of that child. This is the real double focus, the doubled center, of Eliot's plots. It may be said in a variety of ways: in the metaphorical image of parent and child walking hand in hand from "Janet's Repentance"; in the simultaneous yearning of progenitor and progeny to which the written memorials in Daniel Charisi's trunk testify; in the repeated necessity in Eliot's novels that the parent both act and speak his procreation—so that the creation may live in word and deed.

Thus, Daniel Deronda's story has striking similarities to the paradigm that J. Hillis Miller finds in the fiction of Charles Dickens.[33] Daniel's temporary adoption by Sir Hugo has provided him with that special opportunity to step outside his genealogical identity so that, after having surveyed it from such a position, he may recognize its reality for himself and resume it. Thus, while he does not escape the authority of his heritage, by making his choice of that heritage important, he subtly alters his relationship to it: it becomes both more and less important in determining his identity and his mode of living in the world. He too has confirmed "by distinct successive [behavior] the first instinctive [genealogical act]."

Each of three related issues—mothers, recognitions and reversals, and the transformative relation between passion and speech— presents us with a revealing view of the dilemma of generation (the "problem" that George Eliot's plots explore).

Much has been said about Eliot's attitude toward mothers[34] and about the degree to which Eliot suffers, as all nineteenth-century bourgeois novelists do, from an enslavement to the patriarchal plot.[35] Without attempting either to refute or to complement those assertions, I would like to remark that Eliot's most provocative mothers (in conjunction with some motherlike lovers) provide an insight into the maternal role which is, although sex-linked, not merely a repetition of sexual stereotypes.

A great singer and actress is a queen, but she gives no royalty to her son" [said the Princess Halm-Eberstein]. (*Daniel Deronda,* ch. 51, p. 477)

The mother's love is at first an absorbing delight, blunting all other sensibilities; it is an expansion of the animal existence; it enlarges the imagined range for self to move in: but in after years it can only continue to be joy on the same terms as other long-lived love—that is, by much suppression of self, and power of living in the experience of another. (*Felix Holt the Radical,* ch. 1, p. 23)

For Eliot, mothering is neither the momentary procreative act nor the determination of the child's future through inheritance—monetary or spiritual; rather, it is an existence in the present which creates conditions affecting the child's sense of reality. Since Alcharisi knows that she cannot "will" her identity (or, better, her social position) to her son, and since she chooses not to provide a "maternal ambience," she is undoubtedly right to give Daniel to a man who displays certain of the avuncular qualities that Knoepflmacher has noted as significant for nurturing.[36] Those mothers in Eliot's fiction who do choose to fulfill that role repeatedly emphasize its creation of a present that unifies space and time; and whenever any love (human or divine) partakes of this quality, it is associated with mothering:

In the love of a brave and faithful man there is always a strain of maternal tenderness; he gives out again those beams of protecting fondness which were shed on him as he lay on his mother's knee. ("Mr. Gilfil's Love-Story," ch. 19, p. 230)

[Maynard] had not lost the object of a few months' passion; he had lost the being who was bound up with his power of loving, as the brook we played by or the flowers we gathered in childhood are bound up with our sense of beauty. . . . For years, the thought of her had been present in everything, like the air and the light; and now she was gone, it seemed as if all pleasure had lost its vehicle." ("Mr. Gilfil's Love-Story," ch. 19, pp. 227-28)

[Christ] neither condemns nor reproaches you for the past, he only bids you come to him that you may have life: he bids you stretch out your hands, and take of the fulness of his love. You have only to rest on him as a child rests on its mother's arms, and you will be upborne by his divine strength [said Mr. Tryan]. ("Janet's Repentance," ch. 18, p. 361)

But the mother's yearning, that completest type of the life in another life which is the essence of real human love, feels the presence of the cherished child even in the debased, degraded man; and to Adam, this pale hard-looking culprit was the Hetty who had smiled at him in the garden under the apple-tree boughs. (*Adam Bede,* ch. 43, p. 361)

[Mordecai's intense life in an invisible past and future] was something more than a grandiose transfiguration of the parental love that toils, renounces, endures, resists the suicidal promptings of despair—all because of the little ones, whose future becomes present to the yearning gaze of anxiety. (*Daniel Deronda,* ch. 42, p. 401)

If paternity presents in George Eliot's novels the necessity for bringing a moment of blind rut into conformity with one's own genealogical future, then maternity (rightly conceived) becomes a means not unlike music for consciously accepting the reality of the past and the future in the present (as the mother is conscious of the presence of the child over the nine months of gestation). This is, at least, the case from the point of view of the properly nurtured child. Of course, as the earlier quotation from *Felix Holt the Radical* makes clear, mothers have an identity larger than maternity, whose demands raise again the dilemma of living as a "self" in a world composed of related others.

That dilemma reappears in a slightly altered form during a crucial moment in George Eliot's plots: the moment of recognition, or anagnorisis. Although this chapter has not focused directly on the degree to which Eliot's plots conform to the pattern described by Aristotle, Eliot was certainly aware of the centrality of the concept of recognition in the *Poetics.* When she uses terms from Aristotle, however, her tone is in general ironic, implying a kind of revision of his concepts for the different world of the novel. Indeed, she refers to the "fine peripateia [sic]" in "Brother Jacob," her most "low" work of fiction (p. 317), and she comments on the lack of that "ti megethos" necessary to tragedy in Maggie's shoving Lucy in the mud (*The Mill on the Floss,* bk. 1, ch. 10, p. 90).[37] Nevertheless, the pivotal point in the development and resolution of her family or generational plots tends to be that moment of recognition which reverses one's gaze, if it does not always reverse one's sense of identity. Such a moment either transforms the sense of the self or the sense of the world (especially the past of that world), from Adam's sight of Arthur and Hetty alone in the woods (*Adam Bede,* ch. 27, p. 250) to Harold's vision of his own and his father's face in the mirror (*Felix Holt the Radical,* ch. 47, p. 466). Moments like these frequently crystallize a sexual or a parental reality; further they make recognition of the sexual act an essential aspect of its reality. Eliot's plots revolve around this moment of recognition and around what it implies for future and past.[38]

Last, I do not wish to underemphasize the importance of language to this moment of recognition. The perception of the act (almost always the act of generation) cannot but work a transformation of one kind or another. That transformation may simply be of what was unconscious to what is conscious or of what was momentary to what is durational, but at its most potent it is of what was physical to what is verbal. Even if the recognition is denied by the perceiver, a kind of transformation of that perceiver still takes place. Irving Massey, in examining metamorphosis per se, provides an admirable explanation of this kind of change. He finds in the transformation of the human into another bodily form (often that of an animal) an implied critique of language that is frequently an expression of decline and decay.

This critique has significant connections with a writer's attempt to deny the patriarchal plot, for it is an attempt to flee into the animal form in order to escape the clutches of public language, "the forces of linguistic impersonality, whether as structuralist code or as public dogma; in other words, to remain, at whatever cost, in [one's] own story."[39] Characters who refuse to recognize in language the reality of their parent or their child (or, in Mrs. Transome's case, the parent of her child)—who refuse to be a character in another's story—become prisoners of their own selves by trying to avoid being prisoners of the family's and society's demands on that self. Since the metamorphic pole (i.e., the thing into which one may be transformed) of human identity is often associated with human sexuality, the refusal to speak one's procreative acts can become a reduction of the human self to a bestial "rutting" self. Thus, in Eliot's fictional universe, it is better to sing than simply to eat—or to procreate.

6

THE LANGUAGE OF THE DRAMA: FROM PLOT TO POINT OF VIEW

THE LANGUAGE OF SOUND and sexuality generates many of the largest elements of George Eliot's fiction, often determining the entire direction of her narratives. Yet one aspect of Eliot's novels is not directly implicated in that language. It is true that a shifting perspective that argues for a shifting point of view is implicit in all of the systems of metaphor as I have analyzed them. Indeed, in the contraries of the prolific and the devouring, the concept of speakers and hearers, and the discussions of parents and children, Eliot has exposed the doubled nature of perspective itself. But because point of view implicates the author (and reader) more fundamentally than any of the other elements of narrative, it is not surprising that Eliot pursues that topic in its own right, not at first as an aspect of the world of art, but as an aspect of the world of ordinary living. Thus, the language that is the means of that exploration derives from acting rather than from writing; the dichotomy generated by such language is that of actor and spectator. In other words, the drama, in a theatrical sense, reveals Eliot's developing attitude toward the actors in her plots as well as their watchers—ourselves included.

The conclusions I have reached regarding sound and sexuality have relevance for the drama as well. For instance, speakers like Savonarola might well be considered as orators, performers, actors. Adam Bede's and Daniel Deronda's association of harmony with church liturgy is made provocative by the close connection between such ritual and the drama. The archetypal Hermione episode in *Daniel Deronda* is, of course, a pantomime from *The Winter's Tale*. More importantly, the human dilemma expressed through the doubleness both of hearing and speaking and of being a child and a parent, can be examined anew in the doubleness of acting and watching. For example, the musical Jubal must recognize that his aging has converted him from an actor into a spectator, and Adam Bede in the woods must realize that he is not the hero of Hetty's romance, but the viewer of the drama of two others.

Thus, a full discussion of "dramatic" matters in Eliot's fiction requires that we examine not only single words and metaphors but also the scenes, actions, performers, and, especially, audiences in her novels. Some of these passages may be trivial and cliché-ridden, whereas others form part of a major and self-conscious system of explanation. From a preliminary examination of all of their possibilities, however, we can begin to determine Eliot's evolving "point of view" regarding the relationship between art and life. Included in that point of view are convictions about the relationship between the self as actor and the world as audience (and vice versa) as well as about the morality of art as an element in living.

The words *drama* and *dramatic* come up frequently in George Eliot's fiction. Her first use is revelatory: "And the singing was no mechanical affair of official routine; it had a drama" ("Amos Barton," ch. 1, p. 42). The term is usually intended to convey the qualities of conflict, of uncertainty, of suspense—to relate to plot.[1] The closest Eliot comes to assigning a particular structure to that suspense is embodied in a cliché she uses throughout her career.

> I, at least, hardly ever look at a bent old man . . . but I see also . . . that Past of which [he is]the shrunken remnant, and the unfinished romance of rosy cheeks and bright eyes seems sometimes of feeble interest and significance, compared with that *drama of hope and love* which has long ago reached its catastrophe, and left the poor soul, like a dim and dusty stage, with all its sweet garden-scenes and fair perspectives overturned and thrust out of sight. ("Mr. Gilfil's Love-Story," ch. 1, p. 128, emphasis mine)

> [Writes Hans Meyrick to Daniel Deronda,] "But you, with your supreme reasonableness, and self-nullification, and preparation for the worst—you know nothing about the *drama of Hope,* that immortal delicious maiden, for ever courted, for ever propitious, whom fools have called deceitful, as if it were Hope that carried the cup of disappointment, whereas it is her deadly enemy Certainty, whom she only escapes by transformation." (*Daniel Deronda,* ch. 52, p. 483, emphasis mine)

For Hans, as for Mr. Gilfil, the primary drama is amorous, and the future happiness of both characters is, for much of each story, uncertain indeed. It is this uncertainty (and the possible conflict of desire and fact) that links such dramas to similar ones, like the "rustic drama" of Hetty's life (*Adam Bede,* ch. 16, p. 148), or the "dramas" of Savonarola (*Romola,* ch. 25, vol. 1, p. 359), Latimer ("The Lifted Veil," p. 305), or Rex Gascoigne (*Daniel Deronda,* ch. 7, p. 46). In addition, as the extended simile quoted above from "Mr. Gilfil's Love-Story" indicates, the most intense drama is often internal, so George Eliot frequently uses the word *drama* to define the conflicts and uncertainties within the human soul, much as the scenery of the stage has been internalized in that passage. Thus, for example, we have Mr. Tulliver's inner drama (*The Mill on the Floss,* bk. 3, ch. 9, p. 234), Nancy Lammeter's (*Silas Marner,* ch. 11, p. 151), and Edward Casaubon's (*Middlemarch,* ch. 42, p. 307).

The use of drama to define life's structure in this way is a philosophical convention, and George Eliot's lifelong familiarity with Shakespeare's plays makes them likely to be her literary source for this comparison.[2] Her situating of the action "inside" has also come to be conventional, at least among critics of her fiction. Somewhat more intriguing is her presentation of such dramas in a manner that begins to implicate the psychology of the characters involved. When Hans speaks jokingly about the perpetuation of uncertainty by transformation, he is making an oblique commentary upon his own mental acts, acts intended to keep alive the possibility of his having a relationship with Mirah. Will Ladislaw, a figure much like Hans in important ways, has similar tendencies, which are spoken of in similar terms, although this time through the voice of the narrator.

> There are characters which are continually creating collisions and nodes for themselves in dramas which nobody is prepared to act with them. Their susceptibilities will clash against objects that remain innocently quiet. (*Middlemarch,* ch. 19, p. 142)

> To a creature of Will's susceptible temperament—without any neutral region of indifference in his nature, ready to turn everything that befell him into the collisions of a passionate drama—the revelation that Rosamond had made her happiness in any way dependent on him was a difficulty which his outburst of rage towards her had immeasurably increased for him. (*Middlemarch,* ch. 82, pp. 587–88)

Here is a hint of the delusion, or the self-aggrandizement, that constitutes the negative pole of any comparison between life and the drama which focuses upon the actors in that drama. Gwendolen Harleth seems to be George Eliot's most extended portrait of such self-dramatizing susceptibilities. Further, Eliot's recourse to the language of drama in examining Gwendolen's psychology suggests a second complication in the metaphor. Although she had begun her marriage day wondering about the fulfillment of her girlish dreams to be "the heroine of an admired play without the pains of art," Gwendolen's mood shifts when the scenery of that dream becomes real, and she speculates about whether "her hurrying life of the last three months [was] a show, in which her consciousness was a wondering spectator" (*Daniel Deronda,* ch. 31, p. 266). Thus, despite the usual evaluation of references to dramatizing or acting as derogatory,[3] it appears that there are equivalent (contrary), at least potential, dangers in being too much a "spectator" of one's own drama.

There are also possibilities in the verb and adjective forms of the word *drama,* for George Eliot's use of *dramatize* and *dramatic* reveals too an ambiguity of response. Further, whereas the noun form frequently embodies the sense of the temporal—of a plot defined by conflict or by uncertain quest—the verb and the adjective most often define the spatializing of certain invisible but present conditions. Thus, Esther "dramatizes" Felix Holt's objections to her possible inheritance by imagining a speech by him (*Felix Holt the Radical,* ch. 38, p. 368); Dorothea exclaims over Celia's interest in jewels with "an air of astonished discovery animating her whole person with a *dramatic* action which she had caught from that very Madame Poinçon who wore the ornaments" (*Middlemarch,* ch. 1, p. 9, emphasis mine); and Daniel Deronda, upon seeing Gwendolen in the gambling hall at Leubronn, suddenly "felt the moment become dramatic" (*Daniel Deronda,* ch. 1, p. 3).

These usages, then, associate the dramatic with the embodied or the gestural. Insofar as we have already confirmed George Eliot's convictions about the importance of the body—in gastronomic, tactile, or sexual terms—as the medium of human existence, such references to dramatic (i.e., bodily) presence must carry a weight of seriousness for her.[4] This seriousness is also artistically important, given the frequent reference among critics to her desire to "clothe," or "costume," her ideas in such a way that her fiction does not lapse from the picture to the diagram.[5]

Initially, then, George Eliot's reliance upon the language of drama appears to be connected to her preoccupations with space, speech, and act. That is, such usage raises questions about the relationship between inner and outer realities, about speech as rhetoric or as dialogue, and about acting (and stage-managing) as opposed to watching (or being part of an audience). This last pair of contraries has the potential for a further reflexivity of two sorts: first, there is the reversal of seeing the drama in others' lives to seeing the drama in one's own life; and second, drama in others' lives to seeing the drama in one's own life; and second, there is the movement from unconscious to conscious dramatic gesture. This movement may embody "self-consciousness" in either a negative or a positive sense and may also point to an "artfulness" beyond both conscious and unconscious gesture—an "artfulness" that was undoubtedly one of Eliot's chief concerns in *Daniel Deronda,* her last novel. In all her novels, however, the "stage," the "actors," and the "plays" have important implications.

> In this artificial life of ours, it is not often we see a human face with all a heart's agony in it, uncontrolled by self-consciousness; when we do see it, it startles us as if we had suddenly waked into the real world of which this everyday one is but a puppet-show copy. ("Janet's Repentance," ch. 18, p. 357)

> I am not concerned to tell of the food that was eaten in that green refectory [Cardell Chase on the day of the Archery Meet], or even to dwell on the glories of the forest scenery that spread themselves out beyond the level front of the hollow; being just now bound to tell a story of life at a stage when the blissful beauty of earth and sky entered only by narrow and oblique inlets into the consciousness, which was busy with a small social drama almost as little penetrated by a feeling of wider relations as if it had been a puppet-show. (*Daniel Deronda,* ch. 14, p. 109)

These two passages, one written at the beginning of George Eliot's career and the other at the end, rely upon the contrast between two worlds, a "real" world and a "puppet-show" world—this latter term suggesting the mechanical, artificial, and trivial. Yet the first passage posits reality within the human being, whereas the second posits it in the surrounding natural world. Indeed, the disputed territory is consciousness itself, for it is pain that makes of the human face a mask of truth, whereas social preoccupations close off the human interior from wider beauties (although one might argue that "blissful" as well as "beauties" points to the ideal rather than the real). Further behind the apparent lack of symmetry between these similar metaphors is Eliot's supposed intent, in her fiction, to elevate the significance of the everyday world of social drama, here nevertheless referred to as a "puppet-show."

There are then, three arenas, or "stages," upon which George Eliot's dramas may be enacted: the interior, the social, and the natural or cosmic. On the most intimate stage, that of the interior, the conflict concerns incompatible impulses with the human soul. Mirah describes such conflict upon meeting her father in London: "Is there any pain like seeing what ought to be the best things in life turned into the worst? All those opposite feelings were meeting and pressing against each other, and took up all my strength. No one could act that. Acting is slow and poor to what we go through within" (*Daniel Deronda,* ch. 52, p. 489). Thus, the discrepancy between inner and outer drama is one of magnitude and complexity. This contrast is ironically underscored by Mordecai later in *Daniel Deronda* when he contradicts Mirah's analysis of the psychology of king and maiden:

> "My sister, thou hast read too many plays, where the writers delight in showing the human passions as indwelling demons, unmixed with the relenting and devout elements of the soul. Thou judgest by the plays, and not by thy own heart, which is like our mother's."
>
> Mirah made no answer. (Ch. 61, p. 554)

Part of the point of this dialogue is that, although Mirah's heart is indeed like her mother's, it also contains a mixture of other elements, elements that underscore the truth of the very plays that Mordecai (and Mirah, earlier) finds too passionate and melodramatic.

Thus, George Eliot's fiction alternates between two levels: the falsity of acted dramas when compared to real human suffering and the truth and significance of such dramas. This alternation is possible because of the intensity with which drama can invest human expression. For some people, of course, such intensity is excessive; the restrained Lady Cheverel rebukes Caterina when she enacts her feelings by throwing herself about Sir Christopher's knees: "Caterina, that is foolish. . . . I wish you would leave off those stage-players' antics" ("Mr. Gilfil's Love-Story," ch. 2, p. 143). In *Felix Holt the Radical,* such disdain for the unreality of the stage is characteristic of a cynical public, dismissed by the narrator somewhat contemptuously for its prudent evaluation of Harold Transome's scruples over his right to possess the estate: "Nobody off the stage could be sentimental about these things, or pretend to shed tears of joy because an estate was handed over from a gentleman to a mendicant sailor with a wooden leg" (ch. 36, p. 343).

In *Daniel Deronda,* of course, the correlation between the stage and inner reality is much more profound. When Daniel questions the realism of Hans's Berenice series, Hans asserts that art must intensify (ch. 37, p. 344); yet, when Mirah must dress herself to sing, it is Hans who objects to her choice of dress ("as fastidious and conventional on this occasion as he had thought Deronda was, apropos of the Berenice-pictures"); he declares that a plain dress "looks a little too theatrical." Mirah's response makes the final reversal from the stage as illusion to the stage as reality: "It is all real, you know, . . . even if it seemed theatrical. Poor Berenice sitting on the ruins—any one might say that was theatrical, but I know that is just what she would do" (ch. 39, pp. 367-68).

Several passages from her other novels reveal a further reason for George Eliot's association of drama with the inner mind. She presents thought and recollection as kinds of interior play-watching in which the conscious self views its own past, present, or future:

> The drowning man, urged by the supreme agony, lives in an instant through all his happy and unhappy past: when the dark flood has fallen like a curtain, memory, in a single moment, sees the drama acted over again. ("Janet's Repentance," ch. 15, p. 343)

> Bodily haste and exertion usually leave our thoughts very much at the mercy of our feelings and imagination; and it was so to-night with Adam. While his muscles were working lustily, his mind seemed as passive as a spectator at a diorama: scenes of the sad past, and probably sad future, floating before him, and giving place one to the other in swift succession. (*Adam Bede,* ch. 4, p. 42)

> The memory has as many moods as the temper, and shifts its scenery like a diorama. (*Middlemarch,* ch. 53, p. 383)

> As [Dorothea] sat waiting in the library, she could do nothing but live through again all the past scenes which had brought Lydgate into her memories. . . . These thoughts were like a drama to her. (*Middlemarch,* ch. 76, p. 557)

Such similes are sufficiently consistent that they probably constitute a cliché, although they remain a major element in George Eliot's convictions about the nature and development of moral action. They are significant because they combine the actions of memory and imagination as a means, not simply to see, but to comprehend the world. Thus, drama may be valuable for the training that it provides in discovering and exercising such imaginative capacities in one's own life (as Dorothea does in the passage above) as well as in the lives of others.

The second "stage" on which George Eliot's dramas are enacted is that of the natural world. Eliot's examinations through the language of drama, like her other linguistic explorations into the human interior, show a striking similarity between what is discovered within the soul and what is outside it in the largest sense. Much as Lockwood's penetration deeper and deeper into the enclosures of Wuthering Heights during his night's stay there finally brings him in contact with the ghost outside the window, Eliot's language of scenes, curtains, and dramas becomes descriptive of natural (i.e., external) as well as psychological realities. Early in *Adam Bede,* for instance, Eliot stages a "natural" drama that may also be seen as an ironic commentary on the unrecognized "glories of the forest scenery" noted in the passage about Cardell Chase quoted above:

> the picture we are apt to make of Methodism in our imagination is not an *amphitheatre of green hills,* or the deep shade of broad-leaved sycamores, where a crowd of rough men and weary-hearted women drank in a faith which was a rudimentary culture, which linked their thoughts with the past, lifted their imagination above the sordid details of their own narrow lives, and suffused their souls with the sense of a pitying, loving, infinite Presence, sweet as summer to the houseless needy. (*Adam Bede,* ch. 3, p. 33, emphasis mine)

In the reference to the "amphitheatre," the physical structure of the drama provides the largest metaphoric element in a system that includes references to ingesting ("drank in a faith"), residing ("narrow lives" and "houseless needy"), and achieving "presence" through sound (the sermon "suffuse[s] their souls with . . . Presence"). Although the village does provide a literal outdoor theater here, the sense of the passage makes it likely that we must see the whole world as a stage if we are to understand the full scale of the drama. This, of course, makes all of life into a play, and Eliot does speak of "the tragedy of life" in *Adam Bede* (ch. 5, p. 58) and of the "mighty drama" of history in the 1860s in *Daniel Deronda* (ch. 11, p. 90). Yet, to make all of life into a drama raises immediate questions about the identity and status of the principal figures for that drama: the actor, the spectator, and the dramatist.

George Eliot may intend us to perceive the elemental drama of nature itself, a drama that, even when small in scale, provides an opportunity for people to observe and profit: "The fact was that this Sunday walk through the fields was fraught with great excitement to Marty and Tommy [Poyser], who saw a perpetual drama going on in the hedgerows, and could no more refrain from stopping and peeping than if they had been a couple of spaniels or terriers" (*Adam Bede,* ch. 18, p. 163). Here, the human spectators are not particularly exalted figures either intellectually or morally—they are children quickly become spaniel or terrier. Yet a certain naive enthusiasm and a quickness of perception make these children seem more in harmony with the intentions of the dramatist who creates this little hedgerow play than are the unpenetrating archers of Cardell Chase. The creating dramatist is, of course, Eliot's Nature, that mythic figure embodying things as they must be, whose very reality is here made somewhat suspect by its presentation in the language of the theater. Such dramatic language is also used for Nature at other times in Eliot's fiction:

> Perhaps [the stranger on horseback] was one of those who think that nature has theatrical properties, and, with a considerate view of facilitating art and psychology, "makes up" her characters, so that there may be no mistake about them. (*Adam Bede,* ch. 2, p. 21)

> But any one watching keenly the stealthy convergence of human lots, sees a slow preparation of effects from one life on another, which tells like a calculated irony on the indifference or the frozen stare with which we look at our unintroduced neighbour. Destiny stands by sarcastic with our *dramatis personae* folded in her hand. (*Middlemarch,* ch. 11, p. 70)

Whereas the first passage seems to dismiss the possibility that Nature is an extrahuman dramatist consciously molding events, the second asserts this to be the case. Because George Eliot's accepted philosophical beliefs preclude assigning much reality to the conscious control of human events by a godlike figure, her attitude toward such a personification is less important than the peculiar position that is forced upon an individual by this configuration. In the passage from *Adam Bede,* the stranger on horseback is clearly a spectator of the drama unfolding before him, potentially as naive about the language of the dramatist as Marty and Tommy Poyser are. Yet, if the true vantage point for viewing the human drama is extrahuman, as the second passage asserts, then even the stranger on horseback is not simply a spectator, but an actor, ignorant of the fact that he is on stage. In *Adam Bede,* of course, the stranger does indeed become an actor later, during Hetty's trial.

Here, then, we have the same doubleness of role which is a crucial aspect of George Eliot's presentation of man's sexual identity: each person is potentially both spectator of the actions of others and actor himself in the "great drama of human existence" (*Romola,* ch. 44, vol. 2, p. 148). Further, in order to achieve any degree of insight into the drama going on before them, people must place themselves, as spectators, in a position like that of Destiny, beyond the normal human position; and both of these passages imply that such a position is the aesthetic one. In other words, the figure of the artist, as watcher and as actor/creator, is crucial.

The third stage upon which such plays may take place is the social one, where the mental and the world stages intersect in a theatrical sense. It is here that several further ambiguities within the drama metaphor appear. Three separate issues are generated by the metaphor; the first concerns spectators:

> It is doubtful whether our soldiers would be maintained if there were not pacific people at home who like to fancy themselves soldiers. War, like other dramatic spectacles, might possibly cease for want of a "public." (*The Mill on the Floss,* bk. 2, ch. 4, p. 156)

George Eliot's sarcasm about war as spectacle plays upon a series of reversals in reality which constitute the relationship between individuals and larger social groups. At first, she ascribes reality to the soldiers, who are tolerated only because those people who sit on the other side of the footlights like the illusion that they themselves are soldierlike "on the inside." Yet, the second sentence returns to a reality that remains because of such illusions: war is an unavoidable action demanded by a public willing to deny the flesh-and-blood reality of individual soldiers, much as the "enlisting sergeant . . . never troubles himself with the drama that brings him the needful recruits" (*Daniel Deronda,* ch. 40, p. 370). Eliot's most famous soldier, Arthur Donnithorne, provides her with an opportunity to ascribe reality to the actors, while those who watch for their own amusement lose much of their humanity: "When they had entered the hall . . . the folding-doors of the drawing-room were thrown open, and Arthur entered in his regimentals, leading Mrs. Irwine to a carpet-covered dais ornamented with hot-house plants, where she and Miss Anne were to be seated with old Mr. Donnithorne, that they might look on at the dancing, like the kings and queens in the plays" (*Adam Bede,* ch. 26, p. 239). During the birthday festivities, the interior of the manor house functions like a theater, although suddenly, in the last phrase, those who really "live" there are indeed no more real than "kings and queens in the plays."

A second kind of ambiguity, sometimes also amounting to a reversal of reality, is apparent in another passage from *The Mill on the Floss*:

> Fear is almost always haunted by terrible dramatic scenes, which recur in spite of the best-argued probabilities against them; and

during a year that Maggie had had the burthen of concealment on her mind, the possibility of discovery had continually presented itself under the form of a sudden meeting with her father or Tom when she was walking with Philip in the Red Deeps. She was aware that this was not one of the most likely events; but it was the scene that most completely symbolised her inward dread. Those slight indirect suggestions which are dependent on apparently trivial coincidences and incalculable states of mind, are the favourite machinery of Fact, but are not the stuff in which imagination is apt to work. (Bk. 5, ch. 5, p. 295)

Here George Eliot begins with mental activity, which asserts its reality through its intensity and its capacity to compel consequences. Yet there appears to be a discrepancy between the drama that Maggie imagines for herself and the real elements that will affect her life's action. In other words, although her mental scenes of discovery are real enough psychologically, they are not factually true as predictors of the future. The logic of the novel belies this, however, for Maggie does indeed undergo the obligatory discovery scene, which appears to fulfill all the requirements of her fearful prevision of it. This is, of course, of a piece with other justifications of an aesthetic "falsity" that nevertheless becomes, on another level, unavoidable truth. Even more immediately important for Eliot's attitude toward the actor figure in her drama metaphor is the implicit sense here that Maggie's conception of herself as an actor in her own drama is not a cause for moral derision, as it seems to be with someone like Rosamond Vincy, but an opportunity for moral growth.[6]

The third ambiguity generated by the drama metaphor concerns self-styled dramatists of social comedies. This is also exemplified in *The Mill on the Floss,* when Lucy says to Maggie:

"There is something romantic in it—out of the common way—just what everything that happens to you ought to be. . . . O, I shall puzzle my small brain to contrive some plot that will bring everybody into the right mind, so that you may marry Philip, when I marry—somebody else." (Bk. 6, ch. 3, p. 338)

This passage begins with an ironic evaluation of the application of dramatic techniques to life, for such plotting not only turns real people into actors to be manipulated but often backfires, because of the very large and supposedly extraneous reality that must be ignored if such plotting is to be as neat in life as it is on the stage. George Eliot's attitude toward the plotter or planner is not always so mocking, however. The effects of Tito's plots are real enough in *Romola,* even if he, like Lucy, loses the end of his own story in the process. And Mordecai Cohen, who moves from being the actor in his own drama (as Maggie is) to being the architect of another's (as Lucy is), appears to be triumphantly successful on both the personal and public levels. Of course, in order to make these comparisons, we must leap from the image of the dramatist as plotter to the image of the egotist as plotter, assuming that the one will illuminate the other. This leap is undoubtedly important for the analysis of Eliot's fiction, because it raises the issue of the moral status of the artist.

Certain implications of George Eliot's attitude toward the artist as dramatist need to be mentioned. Most important is the similarity between the configuration of actor/audience/dramatist and that of novel/reader/narrator. In *Middlemarch,* Eliot deliberately relies upon stage language to explain this last configuration: "[Fielding] glories in his copious remarks and digressions as the least imitable part of his work, and especially in those initial chapters to the successive books of his history, where he seems to bring his arm-chair to the proscenium and chat with us in all the lusty ease of his fine English" (ch. 15, p. 105). If the novel is a history that here becomes a stage drama, which is nevertheless nothing more than a fireside chat between living individuals, then from what does the validity and the reality of the novel derive? Should we congratulate ourselves most on being actors, spectators, or plotters?

The second dramatic element revolves around the actor. In order for that figure to be theatrical rather than simply existential, there must be some sense of an audience for his acting. In other words, the actor must be aware to a degree that his actions are observed, and he must consciously present his person in such a way as to have an effect upon that audience. Such an image of humanity is an advance upon the most absolute of egoisms, which does not recognize the watchful gaze of another. This relationship of performance and audience has both negative and positive manifestations in George Eliot's fiction. First, there are those actors whose very sense of reality is dependent upon the gaze of others, with the important proviso that the gaze be in some way admiring:

> And Hetty looked at herself to-night with quite a different sensation from what she had ever felt before; there was an invisible spectator whose eye rested on her like morning on the flowers. . . .

> For Hetty could conceive no other existence for herself in future than a hidden one, and a hidden life, even with love, would have had no delights for her. (*Adam Bede,* ch. 15, p. 129; ch. 36, p. 311)

> Meanwhile Tom . . . had returned to the carriage-house, where he found Mr. Poulter, with a fixed and earnest eye, wasting the perfections of his sword-exercise on probably observant but inappreciative rats. But Mr. Poulter was a host in himself; that is to say, he admired himself more than a whole army of spectators could have admired him. (*The Mill on the Floss,* bk. 2, ch. 4, p. 155)

> It is true that Grandcourt went about with the sense that he did not care a languid curse for any one's admiration; but this state of not-caring, just as much as desire, required its related object—namely, a world of admiring or envying spectators. (*Daniel Deronda,* ch. 48, p. 440)

Less negative is the reference in "The Lifted Veil" to the gaze of Latimer's mother watching his early performances. After his mother dies, Latimer recalls this gaze poignantly: "I rode my little white pony with the groom by my side as before, but there were no loving eyes looking at me as I mounted, no glad arms open to me when I came back" (p. 291). Such loving eyes become more complex in their effect as the child grows older, so that the relationship of a young man like Fred Vincy to the woman he loves combines affection with possible criticism:

> In fact, it is probable that but for Mary's existence and Fred's love for her, his conscience would have been much less active both in previously urging the debt on his thought and in impelling him not to spare himself after his usual fashion by deferring an unpleasant task, but *to act* as directly and simply as he could. Even much stronger mortals than Fred Vincy hold half their rectitude in the mind of the being they love best. "The *theatre* of all my actions is fallen," said an antique personage when his chief friend was dead; and they are fortunate who get a *theatre* where the *audience* demands their best. (*Middlemarch,* ch. 24, pp. 177–78, emphasis mine)

Here we see that the naive awareness of audience gives rise to changes within the self as that self conceives of the possibility that what its audience sees and hears is different from what the self desires. The conscience then becomes capable of taking part against the self, which generates an inward difference:

> Mr. Brooke got down at a farmyard-gate, and Dorothea drove on. It is wonderful how much uglier things will look when we only suspect that we are blamed for them. Even our own persons in the glass are apt to change their aspect for us after we have heard some frank remark on their less admirable points. (*Middlemarch,* ch. 39, p. 288)

Like Destiny in the earlier passage from *Middlemarch,* Nemesis, in the form of conscience, begins to take on qualities derived from this relationship between the self and its audience of others:

> Nemesis can seldom forge a sword for herself out of our consciences —out of the suffering we feel in the suffering we may have caused: there is rarely metal enough there to make an effective weapon. Our moral sense learns the manners of good society, and smiles when others smile; but when some rude person gives rough names to our actions, she is apt to take part against us. (*Adam Bede,* ch. 29, p. 263)

There is, then, a virtue to be derived from the actor's role; conversely, there is a danger inherent in the spectator's role. I noted earlier in this chapter the insensitivity apparent in the attitudes of the Irwines and Donnithornes toward the lower orders present at the dance on Arthur's birthday. Ironically, an audience's denial of the actors' reality, such that the actors become objects of amusement, diminishes the humanity of the audience as well.

A different kind of danger lies in the attitude of the spectator who wishes to understand in order to manipulate. Even relatively minor characters such as Mrs. Cadwallader and Christian reveal this capacity:

> Mrs. Cadwallader's eyes, diverted from the churchyard, saw a good deal of dumb show which was not so intelligible to her as she could have desired, and could not repress the question, "Who is Mr. Ladislaw?" (*Middlemarch,* ch. 34, p. 240)

> When Christian quitted the Free School . . . he felt very much like an uninitiated chess-player who sees that the pieces are in a peculiar position on the board, and might open the way for him to give checkmate, if he only knew how. Ever since his interview with Jermyn, his mind had been occupied with the charade it offered to his ingenuity. (*Felix Holt the Radical,* ch. 25, p. 252)

It might be asserted that the danger for these spectators derives not from their watching, but from their desire to make of their watching an opportunity for acting or directing the actions of others, so the role of spectator is made subservient to egoistic demands. Certainly, George Eliot's presentation of the spectator as a positive figure focuses repeatedly, not on the desire to untangle or to dominate by knowing, but instead on the receptivity that permits a change within the self who is watching (rather than a change in the events being watched). Thus, when Tina Sarti's father dies, "even Mrs. Sharp had been so smitten with pity by the scene she had witnessed when she was summoned upstairs to fetch Caterina, as to shed a small tear, though she was not at all subject to that weakness; indeed, she abstained from it on principle, because, as she often said, it was known to be the worst thing in the world for the eyes" ("Mr. Gilfil's Love-Story," ch. 3, p. 151).

The treatment of Mrs. Sharp is clearly comic, and her moment of pity is not more than that. But more major characters, like Lydgate and Dorothea, show that the role of spectator at the drama of another can generate inner energies that then have their own effects. For Lydgate, Dorothea's actions regarding Casaubon, "the unaffected signs of intense anxiety in her face and voice about whatever touched his mind or health, made a drama which [he] was inclined to watch" (*Middlemarch,* ch. 30, p. 212). This watching makes him receptive to Dorothea's appeal for aid—her "cry from soul to soul." Equally, Dorothea's conscious attempt to draw upon the reserves of pity and sympathy which have been a part of her attitude toward both Rosamond and Will during her all-night vigil in chapter 80 is the result of theaterlike perceptions. Further, the change within—the return of her sympathetic experience as a power that will not let her see in ignorance (p. 577)—results in a conscious and specific activity on her part. The ultimate danger behind the role of spectator is not the likelihood of becoming an actor, but the unlikelihood:

> Said Philip, rather sadly[,] "but I think of too many things—sow all sorts of seeds, and get no great harvest from any one of them. I'm cursed with susceptibility in every direction, and effective faculty in none." (*The Mill on the Floss,* bk. 5, ch. 3, p. 286)

Mordecai Cohen, also relying on the seed image, makes much the same point by asserting the virtues of the actor over the onlooker:

> I say that the strongest principle of growth lies in human choice. . . . The Nile overflowed and rushed onward: the Egyptian could not choose the overflow, but he chose to work and make channels for the fructifying waters, and Egypt became the land of corn. Shall

man, whose soul is set in the royalty of discernment and resolve, deny his rank and say, I am an onlooker, ask no choice or purpose of me? That is the blasphemy of this time. The divine principle of our race is action, choice, resolved memory. (*Daniel Deronda,* ch. 42, p. 404)

In this context, several of George Eliot's characters reveal their limitations. From Seth Bede and Bartle Massey to Latimer, Dr. Kenn, and Piero di Cosimo, perceptive and susceptible men betray a distancing from life which reveals a fatal passivity. In Seth and Dr. Kenn, the difficulty seems to be a kind of weakness of character; in Bartle, Piero, and Latimer, the fault lies in the bitterness engendered by their very perceptual capacities. Piero's answer to life's black comedy, of course, is to stuff his ears with cotton and retreat into a belief in the abstract passion of form and color alone (*Romola,* ch. 8, vol. 1, pp. 130, 134). Yet, one might say that, with the exception of Latimer, none of these figures is central to the plots of Eliot's novels; each is a partial, and perhaps partially distorting, mirror for the narrator's own perceptions about the actors in the drama. That cannot be said of Philip Wakem, however. In *The Mill on the Floss,* Eliot consciously explores the results of casting such a personality as an actor in a love drama.

Chapter 9 of Book 6 of *The Mill on the Floss* makes use of the structure of the dramatic stage to embody the roles of and relationships between Philip, Maggie, and Stephen. George Eliot's language, as well as her construction of the scene, reveals how much the ground of reality shifts as she examines the relationships between action and perception and between self and appearance. The chapter begins with the description of the timeless and theatrical white muslin dress Maggie wears to the St. Ogg's bazaar—ironically, a dress that makes those people who are dressed for the social realities appear artificial (p. 376). The bazaar itself, with its connotations of vanity fair and its accompanying entertainments, is housed in an old hall that possesses a stage at one end:

> A grand arch, cut in the upper wall at one end, surmounted an oaken orchestra, with an open room behind it, where hothouse plants and stalls for refreshments were disposed: an agreeable resort for gentlemen, disposed to loiter, and yet to exchange the occasional crush down below for a more commodious point of view. . . . Near the great arch over the orchestra was the stone oriel with painted glass, which was one of the venerable inconsistencies of the old hall; and

> it was close by this that Lucy had her stall. . . . Maggie had begged to sit at the open end of the stall, and to have the sale of [certain large plain articles]. (Pp. 376–77)

For the bazaar, the relationship of stage and pit has been reversed, so that the somewhat artificial loungers watch humanity carrying on its business below. Yet Maggie, too, is framed by a kind of proscenium at her open-ended stall, and she is clearly the object of observation by the ladies of St. Ogg's even as the various gentlemen play their parts with her. These gentlemen include Lawyer Wakem and Stephen Guest. Conversations with both men are fraught with tension and reality for Maggie, but crucial to her self-consciousness in each is her awareness that she is being watched.

> "Pray, go away," said Maggie, looking at him helplessly, her eyes glancing immediately from him to the opposite corner of the orchestra, which was half hidden by the folds of the old faded green curtain. . . . Stephen turned away at once, and, following her upward glance, he saw Philip Wakem seated in the half-hidden corner, so that he could command little more than that angle of the hall in which Maggie sat. (P. 379)

Stephen is shocked to discover that Philip is not simply an onlooker but potentially an actor in a triangle involving himself and Maggie. The cause within Philip that makes his role in this triangle so unsuccessful is more significant than Stephen's shock. More than his physical deformity per se, Philip's attitude toward the deformity makes him as bitter and defensive as Bartle Massey or Piero di Cosimo. He chooses to suffer rather than to act, to be embarrassed by the physical nature of his body, to internalize the disdain of an active man like Tom Tulliver for his own physical slightness. Most telling, he insists upon indirection in his wooing of Maggie, indirection that is matched in Eliot's fiction only by Henleigh Grandcourt's; and his reasons for such circuity are alarmingly similar to Grandcourt's:

> Philip had not spoken to her himself about the removal of obstacles between them on his father's side—he shrank from that; but he had told everything to Lucy, with the hope that Maggie, being informed through her, might give him some encouraging sign that their being brought thus much nearer to each other was a happiness to her. (P. 382)

It is true that his hesitancy expresses delicacy and modesty, but it also expresses a fear of rejection and humiliation. Finally, helpless to save Maggie by any act, he can only watch her progress and comment upon it. In this he clearly adumbrates Henry James's aesthetic observers, Ralph Touchett in particular. Given the lesson Philip provides, it is not suprising that George Eliot is at pains to transform her other susceptible men—Will Ladislaw and Daniel Deronda, specifically—into capable actors.[7]

In George Eliot's fiction, then, there is an unstable relationship between people who might be classified as members of the audience and people who are "on stage." In this, Eliot's construction of events shows a growing awareness of the degree to which kinds of consciousness, on the part of actor and audience alike, affect speech and event. These multiple kinds of consciousness are, in fact, a part of the history of the stage in England. A brief summary of such history will reveal a great deal about the possibilities in Eliot's own use of the drama metaphor.

Ann Righter, in explaining Shakespeare's attitude toward the reality and significance of the theater, begins with the very different attitude toward plays apparent in medieval drama.[8] At that time, the significance of the play as an extension of church ritual, not to mention as an enactment of timelessly true biblical events, made the play itself the important focus of reality, although the audience, for whose eternal benefit these events first occurred and then were reenacted, was equally important. Thus, the play was both ultimately real and specifically rhetorical. With the secularization of the stage and the increasing emphasis upon the inner dynamics of the more human actions portrayed thereon, plays gained psychological realism and at the same time lost the capacity directly to recognize the presence of the audience. Luckily, loss of the ability to speak to the audience did not mean loss of the ability to move the audience, for the pity and fear evoked by the internal reality of the play was powerful enough.[9] Indeed, the significance of the play as a metaphor for life is increased by the distinction in level between watcher and player, for that separation permits the fruitful tension of unlikeness and yet likeness, which would be dissipated by their equivalence.

Just as Shakespeare uses the play and actor metaphor to explore the relationship between illusion and real life, George Eliot examines the meaning of watching versus doing through similar linguistic means. In certain crucial situations in each of George Eliot's fictions, there is a moment when the roles of spectator and actor suddenly shift—or at least the awareness of these roles suddenly shifts—resulting in clear consequences for the plots. Further, the structure of such moments, like the structures of Eliot's sexual plots, is usually triadic. Of course, these moments may begin with two persons, one of whom wishes to act out certain attitudes with the rhetorical and strategic intention of affecting a particular listener. In order for such a moment (the sort examined as speech in Chapter 4) to be dramatic rather than merely rhetorical, either the speaker must in some way be aware of the discrepancy between his intentions and his behavior or between the limited intentions of this moment and the total reality of his identity; or the spectator must be conscious that he or she is watching an enactment of something, that the speech or gesture is not simply to be recorded but interpreted. That is, it must be classified as art.[10] Savonarola's ordeal is the best example of the former:

> Our naked feelings make haste to clothe themselves in propositions which lie at hand among our store of opinions, and to give a true account of what passes within us something else is necessary besides sincerity, even when sincerity is unmixed. In these very moments, when Savonarola was kneeling in audible prayer, he had ceased to hear the words on his lips. They were drowned by argumentative voices within him *that shaped their reasons more and more for an outward audience.* (*Romola,* ch. 64, vol. 2, pp. 358–59, emphasis mine)

This leads, of course, to Savonarola's playing of a part during the proposed ordeal by fire, when Savonarola has become more concerned about the effect upon his spectators than upon his true relationship with God.

Examples of the second sort of actor/spectator relationship are more common in George Eliot's fiction, forming the staple of her presentation of society, individually and collectively, as the audience for the actions of the principals in her plots; Mrs. Cadwallader in *Middlemarch,* and Christian in *Felix Holt the Radical,* exemplify this kind of relationship. For other characters, the diadic quality of the relationship is altered. For instance, whereas Dorothea is faced only with Ladislaw relating the history of his mother, to which she at first responds by "looking with serious intentness before her, like a child seeing a drama for the first time" (*Middlemarch,* ch. 37, p. 269), most of the other watchers have viewed actions between two others, or overheard a dialogue. Thus, as Shakespeare's audiences are affected, not only by the actor's speeches aimed rhetorically at them but also by interactions between actors which, although not directed at the audience overhearing them, nevertheless do affect that audience,[11] George Eliot's listeners are also affected by what does not, apparently, directly concern them. Because they are concerned, these listeners frequently transform the triadic relationship of two actors and a spectator by choosing to write themselves into the play.

Although the relationship between Nanny and her betters in "Amos Barton" is not consciously that of audience and actors, the difference in social levels permits the creation of a situation similar to later, more consciously theatrical constructions. The basis for the "dialogue" between Nanny and Mr. Tomms is the "fine stories" being told about the Countess in the village (ch. 7, p. 101); as an insider, Nanny is aware of the true situation despite the appearances of wrongdoing. The climax of the action (p. 100) is unexpected, however, since the Countess—one of the principals—does not expect any true dialogue with the servant. Nanny, of course, is well aware not only that her sympathies (as audience) have been violated by the Countess's playing of the great lady but also that her duties (as actor) have been increased. Her insolence forces the Countess "to see her position at the Vicarage in an entirely new light" (p. 103) and to act quickly to depart the scene. Thus, in a way more explicitly intrusive than Nelly Dean's in *Wuthering Heights,* a servant supposedly outside the range of the main plot becomes an essential actor in its denouement.[12]

The presence of the drama metaphor in this triadic form is more apparent in "Mr. Gilfil's Love-Story": Miss Assher asks Captain Wybrow, "What is likely to be the next scene in the drama between you and Miss Sarti?" (ch. 12, p. 199). She, of course, believes that the principal drama should include Anthony and herself; meanwhile, Maynard Gilfil is forced to watch the three of them while his own heart is intimately concerned in the action. He fails to act, however, thereby expressing the same dilemma and suffering much the same fate as Philip Wakem. What we discover in this proliferation of watchers and listeners is a particularly intense drama of egoisms. Each character's heightened awareness of the presence of a watching other is matched by a heightened awareness of self and an increased effort to bring himself or herself to center stage. Here, too, part of the separation of levels of reality in George Eliot's work is achieved through disparity of social class rather than through the physical separation of stage from pit: Miss Assher, Anthony, and even Tina wish to deny a part to people they consider beneath them.

Gilfil's particular difficulty in entering the drama of passion acted out in "Mr. Gilfil's Love-Story" derives largely from Tina's unwillingness to see him as a significant actor, to turn her gaze in his direction. In "Janet's Repentance," the Reverend Mr. Tryan is successful with Janet because of this redirection of gaze. Further, the moment at which this redirection is achieved reveals the same triadic, potentially dramatic structure. In chapter 12, Janet goes to see an ailing Sally Martin in order to bring her nourishing food—something she believes is much better for the girl than Mr. Tryan's fine words (p. 330). When she enters the house she sees no one but, hearing voices from the next room, knows immediately that Mr. Tryan is with Sally. Instead of leaving "she stood still, and was obliged to hear what Mr. Tryan was saying" (p. 331). Her surprise over Mr. Tryan's tone and remarks—"none of the self-satisfied unction of the teacher, quoting, or exhorting, or expounding, for the benefit of the hearer" (*not* rhetorical)—inclines Janet's good will toward him. Further, she is sympathetic because she believes suddenly in his human reality: "Mr. Tryan, too, like herself, knew what it was to tremble at a foreseen trial" (p. 331). When Mr. Tryan then appears, their transformation of roles is complete: "The sight of Janet standing there with the entire absence of self-consciousness which belongs to a new and vivid impression, made him start and pause a little" (p. 331). In the direct meeting of their eyes more is achieved for each, both spiritually and practically, than would have been accomplished by "the fullest exposition of Mr. Tryan's doctrine"; a directly rhetorical appeal, in other words, would instead have convinced Janet that Tryan had "an odious self-complacency in believing himself a peculiar child of God" (pp. 331–32).

Frequently, then, the relationship between the watcher and the performance is one of two sorts: either it is like that of Nanny and Gilfil, in which an individual's perceptions and emotions lead him to involve himself in the drama; or it is like Janet's, in which a person observes a scene that influences his state of mind and, later, his actions. Examples of the former include Adam Bede vis-à-vis Arthur and Hetty; Farebrother vis-à-vis Fred Vincy and Mary Garth; Dorothea vis-à-vis Ladislaw and Casaubon (concerning the inheritance), as well as Dorothea vis-à-vis Lydgate and Rosamond; and Daniel Deronda vis-à-vis Gwendolen as well as Mirah. Examples of the latter include Romola watching both the public and private events in Florence, Esther watching Mrs. Transome's fate unfold, and Fred Vincy watching Lydgate gamble.

In *Silas Marner,* one last type of shifting relationship occurs: Godfrey Cass presents himself as a spectator at Molly's death, even though he is in reality deeply involved in her story. This is acting of a new sort, in that Godfrey is attempting to deny himself significance in the plot by denying the reality of his own actions. This abdication, the obverse of the transformation of the spectator into an actor, is one of the clearest examples of George Eliot's complex evaluation of the relative moral importance of these roles.

Despite the significance of the spectator's shifting roles, the most ambiguous element from the theater remains the actor or the actor/stage-manager. Although George Eliot presents clearly unsympathetic characters who appear to be so primarily because of their theatrical propensities, there are, equally clearly, distinctions to be made among this group. The most useful means of distinguishing is to rely upon the original discrepancy between internal and external reality, or between the ganglia of emotion and sensation within and the roles and gestures that clothe and thus perhaps inaccurately portray those internal facts to spectators without. For some, the role covers an inner vacuity, so that the self portrayed is all illusion. As a kind of advance in complexity upon such actors, Eliot also presents characters who "play a part" in order to hide intensity, whether that intensity be merely internal or externalized in past but hidden acts. Among these are characters whose parts, whether they derive from absence or intensity, require them to manipulate the other actors about them. For such characters, theatrical deception has farther-reaching consequences, both for themselves and for those who must become entangled with them. Finally, there are characters whose consciousness of the shifting boundaries of reality and the stage enables them to achieve a revelation of reality through the very means of theatrical illusion. These last characters only appear in Eliot's last novels—perhaps in *Daniel Deronda* alone.

The least attractive of George Eliot's actors are primarily female; their playing at illusion derives from the emptiness of their social lives, wherein outward social position and beautiful appearance are all.[13] Miss Assher of "Mr. Gilfil's Love-Story" is the first such figure, and the conventionality of her presentation suggests that this type has not yet engaged Eliot's imagination; indeed, Beatrice seems to derive from the world of *Jane Eyre,* a world in which the parlor also becomes a social stage complete with curtains, dramas, and unnoticed watchers.[14] From Beatrice the line of development is clear: Hetty Sorrel in *Adam Bede,* Esther Lyon in *Felix Holt the Radical,* Rosamond Vincy in *Middlemarch,* and Gwendolen Harleth in *Daniel Deronda* are all similar characters. Each of these later actresses undergoes a trial that breaks down, if it does not transform, her role. Hetty learns the awful truth of the social roles she imagined were manipulable visions; Esther is forced to watch the drama of another lady and to profit emotionally and morally from it;[15] Rosamond Vincy, the "charming stage Ariadne left behind with all her boxes full of costumes and no hope of a coach" (ch. 31, p. 221), shows the frightening degree to which a firm belief in the dramatic illusion can compel reality (like Iago's, Rosamond's strength in her role undoes the stronger and better man); and Gwendolen manages, in ways more subtle than those either Hetty or Esther displayed, to grow through and beyond her social role to a truly tragic one.

The actresses just mentioned wish to, and often do, believe in the truth of the role they play—in its rightness as an expression of their being and importance. Other, more ambiguous actors, aware of the discrepancy between the part they must play and the emotional truths within, are able to express for the reader, if they cannot always achieve for themselves, an awareness that can only come by distinguishing the actor from the role. Much as Shakespeare's portrayal of the player-king and the king-as-player forces the king to recognize the possible distinction between his person and his kingship,[16] the enforced playing of a part awakens several of George Eliot's characters to the distinction between inner and outer reality. We have already examined Savonarola's growing awareness of the theatricality of his position. Arthur Donnithorne, Stephen Guest, Tito Melema, and Mrs. Transome are similar examples, as, of course, is Gwendolen Harleth. Further, for all but Savonarola and Tito from *Romola,* the inner reality that must be masked is associated with passion and sexuality, fundamental energies that are clearly at variance with the social roles each character has chosen to play. For some of these characters—Savonarola, Stephen Guest, Arthur Donnithorne, and Gwendolen Harleth—the result of the conflict is a self transformed. For Tito and Mrs. Transome, that result is a self entrapped and finally destroyed, although Eliot's images for that entrapment (the enchanted thorn-bush at the end of the "Introduction" to *Felix Holt the Radical* and the shirt of mail in *Romola*) show that the entrapping role nevertheless expresses a reality about the ego within it.[17]

All of the actors and actresses mentioned thus far must in some way bring others to play their appropriate parts in the plays they have written for themselves. Rosamond combines passive resistance with simple stratagems, like preventing Ned Plymdale from hearing of the proposed sale of her house (*Middlemarch,* ch. 64, pp. 477-80). With an increase in intelligence comes an increase in the ability to devise and carry out stratagems that do, for a time, determine the actions of the human drama. Tito is the obvious exemplar of this capacity. Classed with him must be Madame Laure, who acts her role so thoroughly that she is able to make the play she is in become a reality in order that she may achieve her own personal ends. Her act simultaneously asserts and denies the reality of the stage; in fact, her ability to get away with murder is the most potent example in George Eliot's fiction of the result of not taking stage reality seriously enough. Because acting out a part requires bodily movement, it is real in a way that other forms of illusion or artistry are not—the actor or actress is *there* in a way that the lyrics of a song or the scene in a painting is not. He or she has an undeniable physical reality. It is only because Madame Laure is aware of this, and also of the conventional refusal to grant reality to the stage, that she knows she can rid herself of her husband. She plays upon the same stupidity about artistry that Becky Sharp does in *Vanity Fair.* Her conscious actions accomplish what Rosamond achieves through instinctive role playing.

Several figures from George Eliot's last two novels are similar to Madame Laure in their double roles as actors in, and creators of, real-life dramas. On the one hand we have the rather innocuous Will Ladislaw and Hans Meyrick and on the other Alcharisi and Lapidoth. Will and Hans are both associated with the drama by means of the language used in the novels, and both are fond of getting up theatrical entertainments. The passages that seriously present Will's casting of himself in passionate dramas have already been quoted. Hans, having used stage directions to dramatize Daniel's response to his "impertinent" letter about loving Mirah, is (according to Daniel) "beginning to play at love: he is taking the whole affair as a comedy" (ch. 52, pp. 485, 486). This insouciant attitude toward life as a drama is also characteristic, to a degree, of Will. His approach to Miss Noble (they are like figures from "romantic comedy," ch. 50, p. 364) and to Mr. Brooke (whose political speeches he tries to stage-manage) combines real sympathy with a sense of comic roles. His relationship to the children of Middlemarch is a further manifestation of his attitude:

> He had a fondness, half artistic, half affectionate, for little children. . . . This troop he had led out on gypsy excursions to Halsell Wood at nutting-time, and since the cold weather had set in he had taken them on a clear day to gather sticks for a bonfire in the hollow of a hillside, where he drew out a small feast of gingerbread for them, and improvised a Punch-and-Judy drama with some private home-made puppets. (Ch. 46, p. 339)

Similarly, Hans manages to make even Mirah laugh by his flamelike impersonations of comic characters from the stage (ch. 37, p. 349).

Because this capacity to entertain is somewhat similar to Lapidoth's "repeating quirks, and stories, and plots of the plays he used to adapt, in the belief that he could at will command the vivacity of his earlier time" (*Daniel Deronda,* ch. 67, p. 589), distinctions between the more admirable Will and Hans and the less admirable Lapidoth and Alcharisi are not easy to make. Lapidoth has, not a faulty theatricality, but a lack of respect for the truth-telling capacities of dramatic art, which is as damning as his adoption of various roles in order to manipulate his children. In contrast, Alcharisi far exceeds Lapidoth in stature. Even Will's and Hans's comedies are only part of their response to the potential energies of art, including the actor's art. In order to perceive the full implications of seeing the drama as an art form (in addition to seeing the actor as an artist), we must return to the other novels to examine a final element: those moments when the artistry of the constructed drama—including the various forms of the play within the larger play that is the novel itself—is crucial to a revelation of meaning.

Various forms of entertainment in George Eliot's novels might be classed as a kind of "play within a play." Some we have already touched upon in chapter 4: the singing of parts by Tina Sarti, by the quartet of characters in *The Mill on the Floss,* and by Ladislaw and Rosamond; and the speaking of sermons by Dinah Morris, Savonarola, Rufus Lyon (really a failed dialogue or debate), and Mordecai Cohen. These performances are intended to affect the audience in either directly rhetorical or indirectly dramatic ways—whether that audience is the larger public in *Adam Bede* and *Felix Holt the Radical,* the private gatherings of the Dean and Lydgate drawing rooms in *The Mill on the Floss* and *Middlemarch,* or a combination of the public and private in the various episodes of *Daniel Deronda.* A scene like Mr. Brooke's speech at the hustings in *Middlemarch* partakes of some of the rhetorical directness and significance of these public sermons. In chapter 51 of that novel, we see clearly that Mr. Brooke's failure as a speaker (a failure of art) derives from an inability to hide his essentially rambling mind within the role that Will Ladislaw and his other political backers have tried to construct for him. Further, an effigy that embodies the perceptions of at least a part of his audience is made visible before him. This scene, then, underscores simultaneously the illusion and the truth of dramatizations. Brooke's role as liberal candidate is pure fabrication, and it breaks down quite easily under the influence of nerves and alcohol. Yet the effigy dramatically, if cruelly, announces anew the symbolic truth about the falsity of role, so we must accept that theatrical representation is both true and false to human nature. Finally, the entire chapter effectively incarnates or "dramatizes" the political currents that determine events in Middlemarch society.

Several other kinds of public ritual in George Eliot's novels might be classified as pageants or theatrical spectacles. In the celebration of Arthur Donnithorne's birthday in *Adam Bede* (chs. 22-26), the New

Year's Eve dance in *Silas Marner* (ch. 11), the public ceremonies of Florence in *Romola* (chs. 8, 49, 60, 65), and the trial in *Felix Holt the Radical* (ch. 46), certain collective beliefs and emotions are confirmed in the performing of certain gestures in a public arena. The very regularity, even artificiality, of the activities is intended to enforce the embodied truth. This is especially true of rituals, like those in *Romola,* that have quasi-religious significance; even the rituals in *Adam Bede* can be considered quasi religious: Arthur Donnithorne's tenants see him as solely and even spiritually important because of his role as future lord of the manor, and would be horrified by his failure to live within that role. The dance in *Silas Marner* and the trial in *Felix Holt the Radical* are more provocative, because in each an unexpected break in the ritual suddenly alters the sense of reality of the watching audience. In the former, Silas Marner suddenly appears to announce Molly Farren's condition to the assembled company; the effect of this is to alter radically Godfrey's relationship to the dance and the dancers. Godfrey's sense of reality, like Mr. Brooke's, shifts in contradictory ways: On the one hand, he is reminded of the interior reality he has tried to forget in Nancy Lammeter's company; on the other, the truth Silas announces will indeed now make his courtship of Nancy real. Equally, Esther's sudden break with tradition—her choice to speak at Felix's trial—permits true justice, not simply the bare forms of justice, to be done. She affirms a reality about Felix Holt which people present at the trial, especially Sir Maximus Debarry, come to believe in and act on, even though the trial itself never denies the opposing reality of Felix's crime. If his impulsive actions during the riot were disastrous, her similar act here restores the balance, so the trial, instead of being only a ritual of punishment, becomes a means to reveal truth.

Other dramatizations in George Eliot's novels do not possess the dignity or significance of public ritual. In some ways, Arthur's birthday party is related to these other theatricals, for it is based upon Arthur's individuality, being a celebration of his birth on a particular day; although the surrounding society wants to and must recognize Arthur's significance for all of them, his birthday is not truly a public ritual. More telling is Arthur's choice to add certain dramatic episodes to the more general ritual of the day. He tells the Irwines that, since Adam has agreed to manage the estate woods, "I mean to announce the appointment to them, and ask them to drink Adam's health. It's a little drama I've got up in honour of my friend Adam" (ch. 22, p. 218). Soon after this we recognize the full falsity of Arthur's friendship and the inadequacy of his acts as lord of the manor to make up for his acts as private and passionate man. Yet, his favors, as well as the public drama he "gets up" to bring glory to both himself and Adam, are chief elements in the discovery of truth for each. The public announcement of Adam's appointment becomes the yardstick by which Adam gauges Arthur's deception, even while it remains as a symbol of the real good will Arthur bears for Adam.

Much the same kind of breaking through to reality by means of dramatic illusion can be seen in Tom Tulliver's swordplay before Maggie in *The Mill on the Floss* (bk. 2, ch. 5, pp. 159-61); Tessa's false wedding in *Romola* (ch. 14, vol. 1, pp. 228-30); the Casaubons' visit to Naumann's studio in *Middlemarch* (ch. 22, pp. 158-62); and the Archery meeting and Hermione episode in *Daniel Deronda* (ch. 10, pp. 71-78; ch. 6, pp. 37-45). In each case, the would-be dramatist, like the sorcerer's apprentice, manages to unleash real powers and energies by playing with apparently petty stratagems. Despite the playlike quality of each episode—and tangential even to the self-aggrandizement that is often the motive for the spectacle—the effects are real enough: Tom's bloody foot, Tessa's spousal role, Casaubon's self-concept, and Gwendolen's sudden terrors, despite her preeminence.

The dramatic joke that Scales the butler plays upon Christian in *Felix Holt the Radical* is even more thoroughly and self-consciously contrived. George Eliot makes a satirical, practical joke depend upon a playbill in "Janet's Repentance," but there the message appears to be the fairly conventional assertion of religion and preachers as untrustworthy theatricalities (ch. 9, pp. 314-15). When Scales chooses to cut off the sleeping Christian's coattail in order to gain ascendancy below stairs, his actions echo one of the most famous of plays within a play: "The Murder of Gonzago" in *Hamlet*.

Like the elder Hamlet and like the king in Hamlet's play, Christian chooses a most unfortunate time to go to sleep. In that unprotected state, he provides a perfect opportunity for his enemy to gain an ascendancy over him. Scales wishes that "Mr. Christian's comb would be cut so effectually that it would take a long time to grow again" (ch. 12, p. 151). He even sees his joke in theatrical terms: "Exit Scales, laughing, and presenting a fine example of dramatic irony to any one in the secret of Fate" (p. 151). Scales's little drama is, of course, an enactment rather than a reenactment of a true event, unlike Hamlet's presentation of "The Murder of Gonzago" to the Danish court. Nevertheless, from this enactment Scales, too, hopes to elicit a public expression of "guilt" by means of the play he has devised: he intends to watch Christian's return, as Hamlet will watch Claudius, in order to gauge the reality of his stratagem. Like Hamlet's, his bit of play has its effect in a discomfiture beyond even the expectations of the amateur dramatist.

Further, like the truth unleashed in the other playlets we have mentioned, this truth has energies far greater (and perhaps more potentially destructive) than any the perpetrator had expected. Gertrude's request that Hamlet visit her in her bedroom, the ensuing death of Polonius, and the dispatching of Rosencrantz and Guildenstern to capture Hamlet and take him off to death in England all result from the enacting of "The Murder of Gonzago." Likewise, the discovery of Esther's parentage and potential inheritance, the interest of the Debarrys in Rufus Lyon's fate, and the final exposure of Matthew Jermyn (and, consequently, of Harold Transome) all derive from Scales's innocent prank. Contrived though it may be, Scales's joke seems to be Eliot's sole means to truth in the novel most clearly associated with her interest in the drama.[18]

By the time she wrote *Middlemarch,* Eliot had so thoroughly incorporated the implications of the drama into her narrative techniques that there is no sense of contrivance about her shifting of actor and spectator roles, her construction of a play within a play, or the degree of disguise necessary in ordinary social intercourse. Chapter 34 of *Middlemarch,* which describes Featherstone's funeral, exemplifies her success.

The chapter begins (following an epigraph written in dialogue by George Eliot) with the apparent setting of the Lowick churchyard, where various people have gathered to watch the pageantry of the Featherstone funeral. There is an immediate contrast between the "prosaic" and thus realistic May weather and Peter Featherstone's extravagant desires to command his relatives to certain obsequies (p. 236). In discussing Featherstone's intentions, Eliot speaks in dramatic terms that remind us comically of the necessity for a standpoint outside life if we are fully to appreciate the "play of life":

> In writing the programme for his burial he certainly did not make clear to himself that his pleasure in the little drama of which it formed a part was confined to anticipation. In chuckling over the vexations he could inflict by the rigid clutch of his dead hand, he inevitably mingled his consciousness with that livid stagnant presence, and so far as he was preoccupied with a future life, it was with one of gratification inside his coffin. Thus old Featherstone was imaginative, after his fashion. (P. 237)

George Eliot goes on to speak of Featherstone's resentment of Mr. Casaubon, who is a preacher to whom he must listen, as opposed to Mr. Cadwallader, before whom he can play the part of generous landowner. With this reference to Mr. Cadwallader, Eliot shifts the focus of the drama from the churchyard to the upper room of Lowick Manor, from which Dorothea, the Chettams, and Mrs. Cadwallader are watching the watchers of the Featherstone funeral. Their attitude as audience seems at first to have much in common with that of the gentry in *Adam Bede* who watch the birthday dance or of the people in *Daniel Deronda* who listen to Mirah sing. Here, however, Eliot presents even more completely the various complexities of their situations as spectators. First, because Dorothea has been called from the library by visitors, her watching brings her to focus on something more, rather than less, related to life. Further, she has a sense of the rather mysterious influence that the scene she watches will have upon her: "Scenes which make vital changes in our neighbours' lot are but the background of our own, yet, like a particular aspect of the fields and trees, they become associated for us with the epochs of our own history, and make a part of that unity which lies in the selection of our keenest consciousness" (p. 238).

Yet, immediately after having invested the Featherstone funeral with a reality by showing us its influence on the consciousness of one in whom we are interested, George Eliot reminds us that part of Dorothea's difficulty is that she is only a spectator—that she, too, enacts the empty female social role we have associated with the amateur actress: "The country gentry of old time lived in a rarified social air: dotted apart on their stations up the mountain they looked down with imperfect discrimination on the belts of thicker life below" (p. 238). Because she is not at ease with such distance, Dorothea continues to watch the scene before her with interest, while Celia hides behind Sir James.

Mr. Brooke's entrance prepares for further dramatic development in the chapter. Mrs. Cadwallader has been treating the cast below her, including her husband, like a fit opportunity for entertainment, but Mr. Brooke reminds her that the ritual does have its solemnity and significance (p. 239). When Dorothea begins to expand upon this, her husband's arrival silences her: he is an audience whose presence makes a difference in her performance (p. 240). Then, just when it appears that renewed attention to the Featherstone funeral will dissipate the growing dramatic tension in the room, that exterior drama breaks open in such a way as to reveal the truth about difficulties in Lowick Manor:

> "Positively," exclaimed Mrs. Cadwallader, "there is a new face come out from behind that broad man queerer than any of them: a little round head with bulging eyes—a sort of frog-face—do look. . . . "
>
> "Let me see!" said Celia, with awakened curiosity, standing

> behind Mrs. Cadwallader and leaning forward over her head. "Oh, what an odd face!" Then with a quick change to another sort of surprised expression, she added, "Why, Dodo, you never told me that Mr. Ladislaw was come again!" (P. 240)

This interchange, and its effect, make Mrs. Cadwallader turn her attention from the drama without the room to that within, a "dumb show" she wishes to be able to interpret. George Eliot's transformation of the unknown young man whose birth and behavior will redirect the Vincy/Lydgate/Bulstrode plots into the young man who will introduce new drama into the supposedly completed Casaubon plot is plausible as well as artistically economical. Further, Dorothea's discomfiture at this sudden appearance is doubled by her need to play a part before her assembled guests; she is aware that her husband does not speak as he feels, either (p. 241). The chapter closes with the suggestion that Will has a part to play in yet another drama, the political one that Mr. Brooke is getting up (p. 241). Mr. Brooke, who has the last word in the chapter, offers the reader a comic commentary on the issues that are pertinent here. He explains the picture by Naumann which he has brought and asserts along the way that the painter's art has captured the truth of Mr. Casaubon (however much our awareness of Casaubon's consciousness at this point may belie this). He bases his sense of that truth upon the element most significant for actors as well as painters—fleshly presence:

> There you [Casaubon] are to the life: a deep subtle sort of thinker with his forefinger on the page, while Saint Bonaventure or somebody else, rather fat and florid, is looking up at the Trinity. Everything is symbolical, you know—the higher style of art: I like that up to a certain point, but not too far—it's rather straining to keep up with, you know. But you are at home in that, Casaubon. And your painter's flesh is good—solidity, transparency, everything of that sort. (P. 241)

Despite Mr. Brooke's assertions about Casaubon's bodily presence and aesthetic sensibilities, relatively few characters in George Eliot's novels are aware of the capacity of the dramatic art form to reveal truth. Alcharisi and Herr Klesmer are directly aware; Will Ladislaw and Mirah only indirectly. I include Will (the man Brooke offers to the reader at the close of chapter 34) primarily because of a remark he makes, not about drama, but about poetry. When he and Dorothea discuss possible artistic futures for him, he defines the poet primarily by means of his consciousness:

> To be a poet is to have a soul so quick to discern that no shade of quality escapes it, and so quick to feel, that discernment is but a hand playing with finely-ordered variety on the chords of emotion—a soul in which knowledge passes instantaneously into feeling, and feeling flashes back as a new organ of knowledge. (*Middlemarch,* ch. 22, p. 166)

But when Dorothea reminds him of the necessity for a physical manifestation of such sensitivity—the poems—Will opts instead for the physical manifestation of the dramatic art—the person: "You [Dorothea] *are* a poem" (p. 166). Nevertheless, Will's description of the artistic personality is useful for the light it sheds upon the play of energy and intention in the actor's art. Little Jacob Cohen of *Daniel Deronda* offers comic confirmation of this when Mordecai tries to teach him to recite portions of Hebrew poetry; after Jacob's lapse into stroller's tricks evokes Mordecai's scorn, "the shock resolved itself into tears; Jacob lifted up his small patriarchal countenance and wept aloud. . . . On [Mordecai's returning gentleness] Jacob, feeling the danger well-nigh over, howled at ease, beginning to imitate his own performance and improve upon it—a sort of transition from impulse into art often observable" (ch. 38, p. 360).

It is in the light of this that Alcharisi's artistic abilities must be seen.[19] The passage about her art is significant:

> The varied transitions of tone with which this speech was delivered were as perfect as the most accomplished actress could have made them. The speech was in fact a piece of what may be called sincere acting: this woman's nature was one in which all feeling—and all the more when it was tragic as well as real—immediately became matter of conscious representation: experience immediately passed into drama, and she acted her own emotions. In a minor degree this is nothing uncommon, but in the Princess the acting had a rare perfection of physiognomy, voice, and gesture. It would not be true to say that she felt less because of this double consciousness: she felt—that is, her mind went through—all the more, but with a difference: each nucleus of pain or pleasure had a deep atmosphere of the excitement or spiritual intoxication which at once exalts and deadens. (*Daniel Deronda,* ch. 51, p. 472)

In fact, it is not Alcharisi's artistry as an actress which condemns her morally, but her lapses from it, when she leaves the stage for domestic and then for social drama. First her father forces her to use marriage as a means to artistic freedom; then her own fear of artistic failure leads her to turn to the same empty social role to which such amateur actresses as Miss Assher and Hetty aspired. Indeed, even Mirah's revulsion from the stage is dependent not upon its falsity but upon her failure to recognize its significance. She dislikes the actresses because their real lives are paltry when compared to the great emotions, which they act upon the stage without being touched by them (ch. 20, p. 157).

Mirah has more positive beliefs about performance when that performance is primarily musical. One of the first indications that she is more complex than the demure angel she appears is her singing for Herr Klesmer (ch. 39). Her ease before a knowledgeable audience, her lack of self-consciousness about her art, her ability to separate her art from her self, and her ability to discipline that self in order to improve her art—all of these things are in direct contrast with Gwendolen's behavior before Klesmer during a similar interview. Mirah does lapse at the close of the chapter into a more naive attitude toward her dress as an expression of her self rather than of her talent, but luckily the more conscious artist Hans assures her that acting out the role of poor Jewess would hardly be appropriate for an accomplished singer; he is right in knowing that her role as artist is really more her "self" than is her private poverty.

Although Klesmer, the supreme artist of George Eliot's novels, is not a dramatist, his portrayal of himself in the role of musician on the social stage of the novel makes him perhaps even more suitable for our purposes. He reminds people who do not take the stage and art seriously that the artistic world is potent and real: "A creative artist is no more a mere musician than a great statesman is a mere politician. We are not ingenious puppets, sir, who live in a box and look out on the world only when it is gaping for amusement. We help to rule the nations and make the age as much as any other public men" (ch. 22, p. 180). This greatness of the world of art is the point of the comedy during Klesmer's examination of Mirah's singing. When Klesmer appears, the little home in Chelsea is a quasi-comic version of the reflexiveness of the arts: the girls are doing needlework while Mirah amuses them by reading aloud; she, meanwhile, is the object of Kate's drawing for an undoubtedly artificial illustration. Suddenly, when Klesmer entered, "the rooms shrank into closets, the cottage piano . . . seemed a ridiculous toy, and the entire family existence as petty and private as an establishment of mice in the Tuileries." This is because Klesmer's personality and gaze "suggested vast areas and a multitudinous audience, and probably they made the usual scenery of his consciousness" (p. 362). Klesmer as artist does indeed create his own "locus," and a later passage from the chapter implies what that locus is:

> Altogether it was an amusing picture—the little room with so much of its diagonal taken up in Klesmer's magnificent bend to the small feminine figures like images a little less than life-size, the grave Holbein faces on the walls, as many as were not otherwise occupied, looking hard at this stranger who by his face seemed a dignified contemporary of their own, but whose garments seemed a deplorable mockery of the human form. (P. 365)

The drawing-room of social comedy is small indeed when compared to the realities contained within art—dramatic or musical. Of course, Klesmer, like Will Ladislaw before him, accepts the equal reality of that miniature stage and even suggests that some dramas and some singing are most appropriate for its dimensions. He manages, as his incongruous face and apparel announce, to accede to two realities: the social world and art. It is only by recognizing their reality that he can perceive their distinctness. As Daniel Deronda said of the sculptor's art in relation to nature, each permits an awareness of the other.

In discussing Herr Klesmer and Will Ladislaw, we have drifted from the drama to other arts—painting, poetry, and music. Nevertheless, when George Eliot consciously draws upon examples from these sister arts, she does seem to focus upon elements common to drama as well. The connections between music and the speaker/audience relationship have already been discussed. One instance from *Adam Bede* regarding painting (an art form frequently used to explain Eliot's technique) will suggest similar likenesses between its metaphoric implications and those of the drama:

> For all who saw them through a less mythical medium, the Miss Irwines were quite superfluous existences; inartistic figures crowding the canvass of life without adequate effect. Miss Anne, indeed, if her chronic headaches could have been accounted for by a pathetic story of disappointed love, might have had some romantic interest attached to her; but no such story had either been known or invented concerning her, and the general impression was quite in accordance with the fact, that both the sisters were old maids for the prosaic reason that they had never received an eligible offer. (Ch. 5, p. 58)

The lack of reality accorded to the Miss Irwines, then, is the result of their having failed to have any part to play in the drama of life; although the passage speaks of a canvas rather than a stage, terms like "pathetic" and "story" hint at the necessity for a plot of some sort in order that these women be the focus of attention. As is usual in George Eliot's novels, the story requisite for such a focus would be a romantic or marital one. Without that story, there cannot be even the interesting discrepancy between appearances and reality ("impression" and "fact") upon which the tensions of the drama metaphor are based.

But there remains the question of the relationship between dramatic and narrative art, if we shift from the term *poetry* to the more general term *writing.* In the passage about the Miss Irwines as well as the later, more famous passage about Dutch realism from chapter 17 of *Adam Bede,* George Eliot's ostensible purpose is to discuss the significance of point of view. It is immediately clear that, whereas viewing a picture and watching a play place strict limits on the spectator's point of view, reading a story permits a whole range of new possibilities for shifts in focus, attention, and perspective. To a degree, the drama is an advance upon painting because it permits bodily movement and thus a sense of bodily reality. It also allows degrees of shift in focus, a concept apparent to George Eliot from the beginning of her novel-writing career, for she remarks in "Amos Barton" that "Mr. Bridmain, and Jet the spaniel, looked on with the air of actors who had no idea of by-play" (ch. 3, p. 69). In the ensuing plot, both Mr. Bridmain and Jet the spaniel are permitted enough significance that Eliot is justified in turning our attention toward them. The writer must do without this sense of bodily presence; characters cannot call attention to themselves either through gesture or through some less tangible kind of intensity. Or, rather, the functions of this bodily presence must be taken over by the only means at the writer's command: narrative voice and its language.

That these last resources are George Eliot's best strength seems obvious enough from the failure of her attempt at dramatic art. She was unable to write *The Spanish Gypsy* as a play for performance,[20] and it does not really succeed as a closet drama. The subtlety that Shakespeare is able to achieve through the manipulation of his plots, his stage business, and his figurative language escapes Eliot when she attempts to limit herself to a small cast of characters who seem more intent upon affecting the audience by means of their speech than upon affecting one another. Like the controlled rhetoric of Shakespeare's early plays,[21] the rhetoric of *The Spanish Gypsy* implicitly denies the moving power of dramatization itself. Further, it is only after this unsuccessful play that the great increase in Eliot's novelistic complexity of voice and of language occurs.[22]

This increased complexity is exemplified in the chapter epigraphs for the three works George Eliot wrote during and after *The Spanish Gypsy.*[23] The epigraphs often come from plays, especially the plays of Shakespeare; even when they are written by Eliot herself, these epigraphs often appear as dramatic dialogues. In addition, the narrator in these novels becomes increasingly allusive, making the reader aware in this way, too, that the work exists not simply in the "reality" of mimesis but in the "reality" of the arts as well. Indeed, this seems to be the by-product of Eliot's growing awareness of the significance of conscious illusion and perhaps most justifies Herbert Spencer's designation of her as "the female Shakespeare."[24] As Ann Righter explains, Shakespeare had exploited the physical reality of the actor on the stage who was nevertheless but the shadow of a man playing a part in order to explore the degree to which dreams and reality—and the play and its audience—implicate each other. Eliot achieves much the same end through blatantly metaphoric language, through an intrusive narrator who is of interest in his own right (because of his intelligence rather than his apostrophes), and through allusions that place characters in both the real world and the world of art: she makes her reader comprehend by means of the interplay, rather than the opposition, between reality and illusion.

To a degree, we have ended where we began, if George Eliot's abilities as a narrator depend upon her abilities to use language. There remains one unanswered question, however. In giving up the unavoidable presence of the actor whose reality the audience must take cognizance of, even when they know he may only be "acting," and in giving up the directly rhetorical appeals to the sensibilities of the audience which are so much more frequent in the early novels, Eliot did not mean to give up the power to move her own audience. Having examined in this and preceding chapters wordplay, setting, plot, character, and point of view, we have nevertheless not yet addressed directly the question of the effects upon the reader achieved through these means. How do these conventional patterns or units of perception unleash the laughter or the tears of the reader, proving finally thereby that the novel itself is no illusion?

7

FROM INSIDE TO OUTSIDE THE BOOK: HUMOR AND PATHOS

THE FINAL PORTION of my argument requires that we step "outside" the novels themselves in order to examine their relationship to the reader, implicated though that reader may have been in the foregoing discussions. Crucial to any definition of such a relationship between reader and work are the energies that characterize it—humor and pathos—and the structures that generate and control those energies. Many discussions of the "effects" of George Eliot's fiction focus upon tragedy and pathos;[1] nevertheless, as the preceding chapters suggest, her art also depends heavily upon the structures and energies of comedy and humor, for her awareness of the double perspective and the double meaning is apparent at every level of her fiction, from wordplay to double plot.

One might conclude initially that George Eliot's fictional "structures" derive from humor, whereas their significant "content" is intended to be pathetic. It is certainly true that much of her content is emotionally charged, her consideration of sexuality and self-display being but the most prominent topics of this sort. Yet even these subjects may be the cause of humor as well as pathos, so such a simple discrimination of elements in her art is not really workable. In the passage in "Notes on Form in Art" (see chapter 1 above), Eliot tried a slightly different version of such a discrimination by associating the energy behind art with emotion in general and the structures developed from it with intellect. How this might be true in specific novels, as well as how energy and structure are related to humor and pathos, requires further examination of Eliot's other statements, both fictional and extra-fictional.

Traditionally, the emphasis in any explanation of George Eliot's theory of art has been placed upon the impact of that art on the reader. Eliot's assertion in "The Natural History of German Life"

(1856) about "the greatest benefit we owe to the artist" defines her own aesthetic and moral intentions: "The extension of our sympathies . . . [,] a picture of human life such as a great artist can give, surprises even the trivial and the selfish into that attention to what is apart from themselves, which may be called the raw material of moral sentiment" (*Essays,* p. 270). The very language of this statement reveals information about her techniques as well as her intentions. She uses the terms "picture" and "surprise," which suggests that, although realistic observation may be important in her work, some element of the unusual is necessary to awaken the habit-dominated reader. Often that surprise is dependent on a humorous way of telling the story or providing the picture. Yet, most theories of humor assert that laughter and sympathy are antithetical,[2] so it remains crucial to determine how Eliot's humor is related to her avowed commitment to a sympathetic art.

The difficulty in arriving at such a determination is fundamental: how are the energies of fiction related to its structures? In earlier chapters, I discussed the degree to which each seems to generate the other, or at least to be implicated in evoking the other. Two brief but significant remarks George Eliot made in her essays about literature will help us arrive at a more general description of the manner whereby the energies of art (humorous or pathetic) are generated or limited by its ordering elements (plot, setting, point of view). In "Silly Novels by Lady Novelists" (1856), she defines almost offhandedly this very concept:

> No educational restrictions can shut women out from the materials of fiction, and there is no species of art which is so free from rigid requirements. Like crystalline masses, it may take any form, and yet be beautiful; we have only to pour in the right elements—genuine observation, humour, and passion. (*Essays,* p. 324)

The importance given to humor in this short list of elements may seem surprising. Yet George Eliot singles out this quality for praise in her evaluations of other writers during her reviewing years. She speaks of Carlyle's "rich humour," complains of Kingsley's failures at humor, and remarks that Harriet Beecher Stowe is saved from the excesses of her own feelings in part by a sense of humor.[3] Her most extensive discussion of the importance of humor is the essay "German Wit: Heinrich Heine" (1856).

The placement of humor in the passage above provides a starting point for analyzing Eliot's broader conception of artistic practice in general. If observation, humor, and passion are the three elements an artist needs most, then observation may be seen to relate to the outer world and passion to inner being, while humor represents that very interface between the outer world and the inner being that George Eliot referred to some thirteen years later ("Notes on Form in Art") as the shell. To a degree, these designations are valid. The other language of the passage, however, presents another difficulty: how does one "pour" elements into a novel so that "crystalline masses" result?

Another of George Eliot's assumptions about art, revealed in a second telltale remark, helps to answer this question. Here, the reference to aesthetics is even more offhand, for Eliot is ostensibly explaining the true task of philosophy in a scientific age: "In its function of determining logic or method, it [philosophy] is still the centre and heart of human knowledge, and it has to apply this method to the investigation of *Psychology, with its subordinate department Aesthetics;* to Ethics; and to the principles of Jurisprudence" ("The Future of German Philosophy" [1855], *Essays,* p. 153, emphasis mine). If aesthetics is a branch of psychology, then Eliot's beliefs about the actual functioning of the human mind ought to be directly relevant to her own artistic theory and practice. In other words, the relationship between energy and order which obtains in mental processes should have a direct bearing on the relationship between those elements in Eliot's fiction.

In order to understand the relationship between the processes of mind and the processes of art we must pursue a double line of argument, for although we may be able to determine how an individual is brought to sympathetic awareness, it does not necessarily follow that art must simply duplicate that process in order to bring about the desired result. In the last analysis, the bridge between mind and art is language, both in general and in particular. George Eliot's beliefs about language—and the actual terms and even metaphors she uses to explain mind and art—will incarnate most adequately the means by which her fictional structures have power over the reader.

George Eliot did not write extensively about psychology, so much of our description of her beliefs must be inferential. She did, however, spend one of the last years of her life preparing her husband's work on that topic for publication. Her editing of the last two volumes of *Problems of Life and Mind* was intended, of course, to carry out G. H. Lewes's authorial intentions following his death in 1878; and, as K. K. Collins points out, most of her alterations of his text were stylistic in nature.[4] One of her two most extensive revisions, however, concerns a topic of crucial importance for her own art; in completely rewriting two paragraphs on the origins of emotions ("The Affective States,"

Problems of Life and Mind, vol. 5, problem 3, sections 158–59), she provides us with the opportunity to consider her own beliefs about those origins. Indeed, the passage as a whole is a succinct description of the process whereby such "original" vital energies ("instincts") gradually develop their "sequent emotions and sentiments, [which] constitute a large province of the affective sphere" (p. 492). This is the principal characteristic of Eliot's revision of Lewes's language here, for she subordinates his specific examples from animal behavior to her own more explicit delineation of the development of human affections and sentiments from primitive emotion. A closer examination of the stages she describes will best expose those principles by which raw human emotion becomes the sympathy so important to her art.

The passage begins by stating that all emotions "in the beginning are egoistic, and their root-manifestation is probably a form of Fear, which in the reaction of its relief is the initiation of that emotional ease called gladness or joy" (p. 491). Lewes had begun this section with the more ambiguous statement that "emotions are egoistic & sympathetic" (p. 491). The primacy of fear is echoed in other statements by Eliot. For instance, in "The Influence of Rationalism" (1865), she declares that "Fear is earlier born than hope, lays a stronger grasp on man's system than any other passion, and remains master of a larger group of involuntary actions" (*Essays,* p. 403). Further, in "The Affective States" she places the impulses resulting from fear—aggression and defense—before all others as the initial egoistic impulses deriving from the creature's placement in a world of other egoistic creatures: "In the collision of appetites, whether of hunger or sexuality, arise the aggressive and defensive impulses, which would remain fiercely and solely egoistic but for that sense of dependence on individual beings or other-selves which lies implicitly in the sexual and parental relations" (p. 491).

The assertions here about eating and procreating correlate clearly with George Eliot's presentation of those appetites in her fiction. What can also be discovered in this passage is the necessary element for the development of such primitive instincts and impulses into "sympathy." Eliot speaks here of the "sense" of dependence; later she uses "mental range" and "consciousness" to explain the transmutation. In other words, she ascribes the power to move beyond egoism to intellect: "With the enlargement of the *mental range* in the human being, and under that influence of the social medium which raises emotions into sentiments, the *consciousness* of dependence is the continual check on the egoistic desires, and the continual source of that interest in the experience of others which is the wakener of sympathy" (p. 491, emphasis mine). Thus, to certain primitive emotional ties generated by appetite must be added mind, the capacity to observe and understand, which then permits the "awakening" of sympathy.

The subject matter of George Eliot's fiction supports this assertion, being often based on the more fearful aspects of appetite and aggression of both the "nutritive" and "reproductive" sorts, although her avowed intention in examining these appetites is the generation of sympathy. Equally, the distinctive structures of her work on both the large and the small scale form a pattern in which the discrepancy between the emotion generated and the intellectual relationship perceived (between egoistic desire and observed fact) results not only in the capacity for sympathy but also in the surprise of humor or wit.

Although George Eliot does make comments in her essays about art and artists which reinforce the assertions made in "The Affective States," her most explicit (and most often quoted) remarks derive from her essays about the development of sympathy in the moral or religious sphere. The following passages from two such essays appear to contradict each other, but in relationship to each other they constitute the crucial condition for the development of sympathy:

> There is not a more pernicious fallacy afloat in common parlance, than the wide distinction made between intellect and morality. [Amiable impulses without intellect, man may have in common with dogs and horses; but morality, which is specifically human, is dependent on the regulation of feeling by intellect. All human beings who can be said to be in any degree moral have their impulses guided, not indeed always by their own intellect, but by the intellect of human beings who have gone before them, and created traditions and associations which have taken the rank of laws. . . .] ("Evangelical Teaching: Dr. Cumming" [1855], *Essays,* p. 166)*

> On its theoretic and perceptive side, morality touches Science; on its emotional side, [Art. Now, the products of Art are great in proportion as they result from the immediate prompting of innate power which we call Genius, and not] from laboured obedience to a theory or rule; and the presence of genius or innate prompting is directly opposed to the perpetual consciousness of a rule.... In the same way, in proportion as morality is emotional, [*i.e.*, has affinity with Art,] it will exhibit itself in direct sympathetic feeling and action, and not as

*Material in brackets was omitted from the 1884 edition of George Eliot's essays; it is provided in this manner by Mr. Pinney in his edition of those essays and will be so reproduced in any subsequent quotations from them.

the recognition of a rule. ("Worldliness and Other-Worldliness: The Poet Young" [1857], *Essays,* p. 379)

The first passage reinforces the assumptions of George Eliot's version of "The Affective States" by emphasizing the importance of intellect to human moral development.[5] The second, however, suggests that Art has less to do with this intellectual development than with the more primitive impulses that precede it. In "Woman in France," Eliot had already asserted that fiction was peculiarly free from rigid requirements, although her intention, of course, was not to suggest that there are no standards for literary production. Rather, she has chosen, in discussing artistic greatness, to return to the element of energy rather than to any single ordering principle. This emphasis on energy, which becomes but another word for genius, is characteristic of her other pronouncements about art as dependent upon the quality of mind of the artist. It is by means of her definition of genius that we may begin to understand the reasons for her choice of particular energies to animate her own fiction.

In order to discuss genius, George Eliot must have recourse to metaphor; even in the somewhat abstract passage from "Worldliness and Other-Worldliness" quoted above, she adds an alternative phrase ("innate prompting") in order to delimit the term. The metaphors she chooses reinforce the energetic quality of genius, as well as its intangibility and even moral ambiguity. Most prominent in the essays is the electrical image:

> To those who saw only the splendour of his genius, and the nobility of his sentiments, his childhood and youth seemed to promise a brilliant career; but any who were capable of a more discriminating estimate and refined analysis of [Macarthy's] character, must have had a foreboding that it contained elements which would too probably operate as non-conductors, interposed between his highly-charged mind and the negatively electrified souls around him. ("Poetry and Prose, From the Notebook of an Eccentric" [1846–1847], *Essays,* p. 15)

> But [Sterling's] intellect was active and rapid, rather than powerful, and in all his writings we feel the want of a stronger electric current to give that vigour of conception and felicity of expression, by which we distinguish the undefinable something called genius. ("[The Life of Sterling]" [1852], *Essays,* p. 47)

> In France alone the mind of woman has passed like an electric current through the language, making crisp and definite what is elsewhere

> heavy and blurred. ("Woman in France: Madame de Sablé" [1854], *Essays,* p. 54)

These passages primarily reinforce the conception that genius is a form of energy; the quotations even assert that this genius is "undefinable," although its result can be "crisp and definite." The use of the electrical image in the following quotation from *Adam Bede* extends our understanding somewhat by suggesting the effect of such energy: "Our love is inwrought in our enthusiasm as electricity is inwrought in the air, exalting its power by a subtle presence" (ch. 33, p. 299). Presence, as we have seen in earlier chapters, is a crucial condition in George Eliot's fiction. But more clearly helpful in discovering how that presence affects the reader is a passage describing the genius of Thomas Carlyle which moves from an implicit "energetic"—if not electrical—metaphor to a different, more inclusive image. This passage is particularly helpful because Eliot did not always agree with Carlyle's specific intellectual conclusions, although she maintained her admiration for his genius.

> It has been well said that the highest aim in education is analogous to the highest aim in mathematics, namely, to obtain not *results* but *powers,* not particular solutions, but the means by which endless solutions may be wrought. . . . On the same ground it may be said that the most effective writer is . . . he who rouses in others the activities that must issue in discovery. . . . The influence of such a writer is dynamic. . . . He does not, perhaps, convince you, but he strikes you, undeceives you, animates you. You are not directly fed by his books, but you are braced as by a walk up to an alpine summit, and yet subdued to calm and reverence as by the sublime things to be seen from that summit. ("Thomas Carlyle" [1855], *Essays,* p. 213)

The more abstract terms of this passage ("rouse," "dynamic," "strikes," "animates") allow us to see certain similarities between the function of genius as electrical energy and the function of music as discussed in chapter 4: impulse has called forth impulse, and animation has responded to animation. In addition, George Eliot consciously rejects the image of books as food to be ingested, apparently moving beyond the satisfaction of a more simple, primitive appetite in her convictions about mental stimulation. Finally, by using the image of the alpine climb (perhaps an echo of Wordsworth), she not only prefers animation to plenitude but adds to that animation the capacity for insight. It is apparently the combination of these last two conditions which brings about the superficially incongruous results (for the reader) of being braced and yet subdued. That is, the effect of genius includes both the reader's participation in the experience and the external truths he or she observes by means of this participation—Carlyle, in this case, offers both a climb and a view.

The visual element in the passage about Carlyle adds a vital third factor to the emerging relationship between genius and audience: we have now the fervor of the writer, the animation of the reader, and the expanse of the world displayed to the reader in the process. It is at this juncture that George Eliot's frequent use of a second kind of metaphoric language gains significance: often the power or energy of genius is associated with conditions of light, although in this case, as with electricity, it is usually not light itself, but the effect of its presence, which announces genius. That is, although in her early "Poetry and Prose, From the Notebook of an Eccentric," Eliot used the traditional conception of the artist animated by "the good, the true, the beautiful, which outlive every generation, and are all-pervading as the light which vibrates from the remotest nebula to our own sun" ([1846-1847], *Essays,* pp. 18-19), the vital word that connects genius, imaginative susceptibility, and (most importantly) artistic technique is *shadow.*

A hint of the crucial importance of shadow as a means to explain the presence of mind, genius, or power in art can be found in a passage from George Eliot's criticism of Dr. Cumming. Here, as in the passage about Carlyle, she modulates from the language of force to a new kind of language: "His writings have, indeed, no high merit: they have no originality or *force* of thought, no *striking* felicity of presentation, no *depth* of emotion" ("Evangelical Teaching: Dr. Cumming" [1855], *Essays,* p. 163, emphasis mine). Emotion, the human quality that provided the original energy that (in art) becomes genius, is presented here in spatial terms. To understand the implications of this, we must focus on the means whereby the individual becomes aware of "depth"—namely, through shadow, or, more exactly, through the relationships among light, object, and shadow. Shadow is the most provocative of these elements for a number of reasons. In the literal, optical sense, shadow is less a thing in itself than the announcement of relationship between two other things (light and object). In this there is an echo of the other "third terms" Eliot uses in her fiction: shell, child, humor. Furthermore, shadow has distinct psychological associations that connect it with Eliot's primal emotion of fear. Thus, when she uses shadow as a metaphor, not only for genius but also for language and its functions, these joint influences—from the science of optics and from the emotional tonalities of human psychology—provide us with a means to understand how pathos and humor come to be present in the factually structured, three-dimensional world of her fiction.

Three quotations from her novels indicate how George Eliot makes use of the relationship between light and shadow to announce distinctions of place, consciousness, and time such that the characters concerned become aware of their existence in a world of depths:

> I recall with a fond sadness Shepperton Church as it was in the old days. . . . No low partitions allowing you, with a dreary absence of contrast and mystery, to see everything at all moments; but tall dark panels, under whose *shadow* I sank with a sense of retirement through the Litany, only to feel with more intensity my burst into the conspicuousness of public life when I was made to stand up on the seat during the psalms or the singing. ("Amos Barton," ch. 1, p. 42, emphasis mine)

> And all the while the *dark shadow thus cast* on the lot of a woman [Mrs. Glasher] destitute of acknowledged social dignity, spread itself over her visions of a future that might be her [Gwendolen's] own, and made part of her dread on her own behalf. (*Daniel Deronda,* ch. 48, p. 456, emphasis mine)

> Nay, the involuntary loss of any familiar object almost always brings a chill as from an evil omen; it seems to be the first *finger-shadow of advancing death.* ("Janet's Repentance," ch. 10, p. 318, emphasis mine)

Each of these passages attests to the optical and emotional implications of shadow. The shadow makes the perceiver more aware of its contrary, whether that contrary is the light of public attention, the light of social acceptability, or the light of life itself. The shadow also makes the perceiver aware of the external object that interrupts that light, from the neutral panels of Shepperton Church, to Mrs. Glasher's ominous presence, to the ultimate objective reality of death itself. The means whereby the last passage announces death's reality is a kind of double shadowing, for it is the absence of the object capable of casting a shadow which announces the ultimate absence that is death itself. This is undoubtedly the root cause of the association of shadow with fear. The effect of such fears of absence, however, is often an intenser sense of the light or life that opposes them. George Eliot uses as an epigraph a poem by Mrs. Browning which portrays succinctly the psychological condition inherent in this metaphor:

> Go from me. Yet I feel that I shall stand
> Henceforward in thy shadow. Never more

Alone upon the threshold of my door
Of individual life, I shall command
The uses of my soul, nor lift my hand
Serenely in the sunshine as before
Without the sense of that which I forebore—
Thy touch upon the palm.
(*Felix Holt the Radical,* ch. 32, p. 314)

George Eliot makes the same point more abstractly when she describes Dorothea's emergence from early "stupidity" in taking the world as "an udder to feed our supreme selves": Dorothea must begin to "conceive with that distinctness which is no longer reflection but feeling—an idea wrought back to the directness of sense, like the solidity of objects—that [Casaubon] had an equivalent centre of self, whence the lights and shadows must always fall with a certain difference" (*Middlemarch,* ch. 21, pp. 156-57). Here the "objects" connected with shadow exist upon two levels: Dorothea must be aware of Casaubon as an objective fact in her own perceptual world, and she must also be aware that the objects that present themselves to Casaubon are sufficiently differently placed that their shadows (and his sense of light) must always appear "with a certain difference."

The language of shadow, then, provides a fairly consistent pattern of interpretation for emotional life, although the relationship between that life (including the energies it manifests) and the functioning of art is not yet apparent. Two other passages that rely upon this language while extending its implications can help clarify that relationship. These passages reveal that shadow can, on the aesthetic as well as the psychological level, generate apparently opposed results. Its significance can lie in its capacity to announce either presence or loss. Each of these capacities is in turn related to the actions of pathos and of humor, although that relationship is by no means straightforward.

> There was no line of silvery willows marking the course of a stream—no group of Scotch firs with their trunks reddening in the level sunbeams—nothing to break the flowerless monotony of grass and hedgerow but an occasional oak or elm, and a few cows sprinkled here and there. A very commonplace scene, indeed. But what scene was ever commonplace in the descending sunlight, when colour has awakened from its noonday sleep, and the long shadows awe us like a disclosed presence? ("Janet's Repentance," ch. 26, p. 405)

> The quality . . . which will be held to have placed [Macarthy] not above, but simply out of, the sphere of his fellow men . . . was a

> morbid sensitiveness in his feeling of the beautiful, which I can compare to nothing but those alleged states of mesmeric lucidity, in which the patient obtains an unenviable cognizance of irregularities, happily imperceptible to us in the ordinary state of our consciousness. His ideal was not, as with most men, an enshrined object of worship, but a beautiful shadow which was ever floating before him, importunately presenting itself as a twin object with all realities, whether external or mental, and turning all their charms into mockery. ("Poetry and Prose, From the Notebook of an Eccentric" [1846-1847], *Essays,* p. 15)

In the passage from "Janet's Repentance," the light of the "descending" sun raises a "commonplace" scene to one with distinct emotional overtones; the shadows awe by announcing "presence," although it is not entirely clear whether that presence is the light itself or the distinct objects that become more intense through the play of light and shadow, which brings out their color. The second passage does not describe awe—perhaps itself a term for the state of sympathetic emotion intended to be the ultimate effect of art. Rather, it suggests how shadow can begin to explain, if not justify, a state of mind conducive to mockery, which is a "darker" aspect of humor. Macarthy does indeed perceive objects with great distinctness, but the "shadow" of the quotation derives not from their presence but from the absence of some ideal that they fail to incarnate fully. This distinction between ideal and real, rather than between one real object in space and another, could make Macarthy a misanthrope; instead, his capacity for benevolence makes him a humorist. Likewise, George Eliot suggests that La Rouchefoucauld's satire, based upon that "condition of human nature in which the selfish instincts are still dominant," rises above mere antagonism because "it occasionally struck him that the shadow of virtue must have a substance, but had he never grasped that substance—it had never been present to his consciousness" ("Woman in France: Madame de Sablé" [1854], *Essays,* pp. 75-76).

The inference from shadow to substance which La Rouchefoucauld makes only imperfectly is essential for understanding George Eliot's fiction. On the moral level, the darker aspects of human emotion and action call up their substantial counterparts, at least for those who are conscious or awakened:

> No doubt wickedness hath its rewards to distribute; but whoso wins in this devil's game must needs be baser, more cruel, more brutal than the order of this planet will allow for the multitude born of woman, the most of these carrying a form of conscience—*a fear*

> *which is the shadow of justice, a pity which is the shadow of love*—that hindereth from the prize of serene wickedness, itself difficult of maintenance in our composite flesh. (*Daniel Deronda,* ch. 35, p. 301, emphasis mine)

Shadow can permit the individual to deduce the existence of light, so that, in mundane terms, the darker aspects of existence can provide indirect evidence (by their effects) of certain positive alternatives; shadow, in the sense of shading, can also permit more subtle discriminations, which are relevant on both the moral and the aesthetic level. This is implied in the earlier passage from "Janet's Repentance" when the colors "sleep" in the brightness of the noonday sun. In other words, too much light bleaches out color, whereas shadow permits distinctness and discrimination. Adding George Eliot's metaphors of color to those of shadow, then, we begin to evolve a conception of moral perception which will eventually illuminate aesthetic perception and the necessary (for Eliot) relationship between them.

In several places George Eliot plays upon the similarities between seeing color and seeing moral tone:

> Nice distinctions are troublesome. It is so much easier to say that a thing is black, than to discriminate the particular shade of brown, blue, or green, to which it really belongs. It is so much easier to make up your mind that your neighbour is good for nothing, than to enter into all the circumstances that would oblige you to modify that opinion. ("Amos Barton, ch. 4, p. 76)

> [Evangelicals] might give the name of piety to much that was only puritanic egoism; they might call many things sin that were not sin; but they had at least the feeling that sin was to be avoided and resisted, and colour-blindness, which may mistake drab for scarlet, is better than total blindness, which sees no distinction of colour at all. ("Janet's Repentance," ch. 10, p. 320)

> Nature seemed to have coloured [Bates's face] when she was in a hurry, and had no time to attend to *nuances,* for every inch of him visible above his neckcloth was of one impartial redness; so that when he was at some distance your imagination was at liberty to place his lips anywhere between his nose and chin. ("Mr. Gilfil's Love-Story," ch. 4, p. 154)

In each of these quotations distinctions of shade permit the eye to perceive exactly. The last passage, however, appears to qualify the direct relationship between precision and insight, for it implies that the absence of distinction permits the action of imagination—the term for mind most clearly associated with aesthetic perception. Further, the very room in which the reader first meets the red-faced Mr. Bates is described as "a space of chiaroscuro for the imagination to revel in" (p. 153), primarily because the contrasts between regions of darkness and objects that loom out from those regions are so "suggestive." This ambiguity is really no more than the doubled aspect of literary art itself, as the use of the shadow metaphor for fiction and language reveals. In that use as well, the capacities of shadow to enforce intensity, as a means both to a clear outline and to an emotionally charged atmosphere, become apparent.

George Eliot defines story itself as a "shadow" of truth:

> And Mr. Barton this morning succeeded in carrying the pauper imagination to the dough-tub, but unfortunately was not able to carry it upwards from that well-known object to the unknown truths which it was intended to shadow forth. ("Amos Barton," ch. 2, p. 63)

> [Mordecai's] inward need for the conception of this expanded, prolonged self was reflected as an outward necessity. The thoughts of his heart (that ancient phrase best shadows the truth) seemed to him too precious, too closely inwoven with the growth of things not to have a further destiny. (*Daniel Deronda,* ch. 38, p. 356)

> [Said Mordecai,] It is the lingering imperfection of the souls already born into the mortal region that hinders the birth of new souls and the preparation of the Messianic time:—thus the mind has given shape to what is hidden, as the shadow of what is known, and has spoken truth, though it were only in parable. (*Daniel Deronda,* ch. 43, p. 406)

The first passage is clearly comic and suggests the perennial difficulty that the "darkness" of shadows and of stories can often result in their misinterpretation. The second defines even the relationship between the single linguistic phrase and the reality it refers to as one that partakes of the shadow/substance dichotomy. The last passage, interestingly, seems to reverse the associations of shadow and substance, finding the invisible to be the shadow of the *visible* and the real to be the shadow of the spoken, in an unplatonic fashion. Nevertheless, all three of these passages describe attempts to communicate truth by means of "shadowy" language or story, so the very capacities of language to "cast a shadow" need to be examined.

Extensive explanations of the peculiar powers of "shadowy" language appear twice in George Eliot's essays. In "The Future of German

Philosophy," the discussion of the functioning of language is a segment of a larger explanation of the functioning of mind, so we can see here a consistency in her beliefs about the necessary correlation between mental process and aesthetic process:

> The true object of investigation is the formation of ideas from judgments, and in order to ascertain the law of their formation, we must direct our observation to those cases in which a new judgment or perception occurs, and is embodied in language, to the mental process which takes [place when] * a discovery in natural science is made and is expressed in words, to the . . . * development of language, and to the application of language by children. . . . According to these tests, every judgment exhibits itself as a comparison, or perception of likeness in the midst of difference: the metaphor is no mere ornament of speech, but belongs to its essence, though usage gradually dispenses with it. . . . Again, when we hear a child call the neighbour's dog, not a dog, but *Caro,* because its own dog is named Caro, we see the origin of the idea of species, or of general ideas. . . . The true statement is, that every analytical judgment has previously been synthetic, and every synthetic judgment is such only once, and immediately becomes analytic. . . . Thus, from the simple act of judgment we ascend to the formation of ideas, to their modification, and their generalisation. And by a series of ascending generalisations we are led to the most comprehensive, abstract ideas. But by the side of these abstract ideas, to which we attain by an ascent from positive particulars, there is another set of ideas which owe their origin to unprecise expressions and mere devices of language, by which we bridge over our ignorance or eke out our limitation, and singularly enough these are the very ideas which have been enthroned as the *absolute.* ([1855], *Essays,* pp. 151-52)

Most pertinent here are George Eliot's assertions that metaphor is the essence of language and that the embodiment of judgment in language is the essence of mental development. Yet even here we have the "darker" aspect of language as only the shadow cast by truth, not perception or truth itself; for Eliot concludes with a warning that some metaphors are merely "devices" of language—manifestations of lack of perception rather than precise ("distinct") expressions of that perception. Determining which metaphors are true and which are false, of

*The original text of the essay is obviously garbled, and this insertion and ellipsis are the editor's [Mr. Pinney's] attempt to reconstruct the sense of George Eliot's remarks.

course, is the whole purpose of Eliot's fiction and of my examination of it.

For all the ambiguity of language, which derives from its shadowy, metaphoric, or device-ridden character, Eliot prefers it as a medium to anything more clear-cut:

> Suppose, then, that the effort which has been again and again made to construct a universal language on a rational basis has at length succeeded, and that you have a language which has no uncertainty, no whims of idiom, no cumbrous forms, no fitful shimmer of many-hued significance, no hoary archaisms 'familiar with forgotten years' —a patent de-odorized and non resonant language, which effects the purpose of communication as perfectly and rapidly as algebraic signs. Your language may be a perfect medium of expression to science, but will never express *life,* which is a great deal more than science. With the anomalies and inconveniences of historical language, you will have parted with its music and its passion, with its vital qualities as an expression of individual character, with its subtle capabilities of wit, with everything that gives it power over the imagination; . . . The sensory and motor nerves that run in the same sheath, are scarcely bound together by a more necessary and delicate union than that which binds men's affection, imagination, wit, and humour, with the subtle ramifications of historical language. ("The Natural History of German Life" [1856], *Essays,* pp. 287-88)

The language of this passage echoes both the metaphors we have been examining in George Eliot's essays and those that are so important in her novels. From the "fitful shimmer of many-hued significance" to the resonance of music, Eliot emphasizes qualities in historical language —that is, the metaphor-ridden language used by men and women to "eke out their limitation"—which give it depth, intensity, energy. Further, the connection between these qualities of language and the more complex conceptions crucial to Eliot's art ("affection, imagination, wit, and humour") is grounded in man's physical being by the concluding image of the nerves in their sheaths. This correspondence between nervous system and aesthetic system was our starting point, but the implications that I have traced out by means of Eliot's language can help to explain the significance and structures of humor and pathos in her fiction. Indeed, both humor and pathos come into being by means of language or, more specifically, style.

My initial separation of humor and pathos from the other elements of George Eliot's fiction was based upon their condition as "energies" or emotions generated by the fiction rather than as "orders" perceived by the intellect within that fiction. Yet, to say that the distinction between elements of order and those of energy can be explained by the distinction between intellect and emotion raises fundamental issues far more complex than can be treated adequately here. There is one point of view, however, that is useful in illuminating Eliot's aesthetic practices and successes vis-à-vis both the structure and the impact of her novels. That point of view is grounded in certain assumptions about the physical basis of mind and the essential humanness of laughing and weeping. Central to my explanation is Arthur Koestler's argument in *Insight and Outlook: An Inquiry into the Common Foundations of Science, Art, and Social Ethics.*[6] Two quotations from his work suggest the overarching conclusions that link his theory of humor and pathos to Eliot's art:

> We may now express the emotional dynamics of the comic in the following terms:
>
> *The abrupt transfer of a train of thought from one operative field to another leads to its separation from its original emotional charge.* An idea or situation seen in a sudden new light casts off its affective shadow. . . .
>
> [Laughter] is obviously a new reflex, for which the *need* arises at a high evolutionary level by the gradual increase of the security of existence, and for which the *possibility* arises at the stage when reasoning has gained a certain degree of autonomy from emotion. (Pp. 65, 69)

> The development of the germ cell into the completed organism shows at every step that differentiation of structure and integration of function are related aspects of one unitary process.
>
> When the differentiative-integrative process is completed, this double aspect of development is continued as the relation of part to whole in the mature organism. The part has to maintain its individuality, otherwise the organism would lose its articulation and revert to amorphous homogeneity; at the same time, it has to behave as a *part* in the whole, that is, in functional subordination. (P. 135)

On the surface, these remarks echo George Eliot's own. In the first passage, Koestler draws upon metaphors of electricity ("charge") and shadow to explain the presence of emotion. In the second, he states a belief about organic wholes which is congruent with Eliot's remarks, not only in "Notes on Form in Art," but also in "The Natural History of German Life"; in the latter she quotes approvingly Riehl's description of the social organism:

> In modern society the divisions of rank indicate *division of labour,* according to that distribution of functions in the social organism which the historical constitution of society has determined. In this way *the principle of differentiation and the principle of unity are identical.* ([1856], *Essays,* p. 296, emphasis mine)

It is the fundamental intention of George Eliot's fiction to demonstrate that whereas intellect and emotion are "differentiable" aspects of the human psyche (as the surprise of humor so frequently announces), recognition of their relation and final "unity" is essential to the health of the individual. Pathos, in its highest form, represents this unity of intellect and emotion.

In order to explain fully the implications of Koestler's remarks on humor and pathos, as well as the correlation of those remarks with George Eliot's own assertions or practices, some extended quotation and summary are necessary. We may begin, as Koestler does, with the structure of humor. Koestler defines that structure in geometric terms as the sudden intersection of two distinct "logical" or "associative" chains of thought, each with its own emotional charge, which has as its result the release of a "flash" of laughter (pp. 20, 26). The success of the humor depends significantly on the nature of the junction, which may be a common word, idea, or situation, and on the nature of the two "chains" or "fields" of thought or association thus joined, or, in Koestler's term, "bisociated." The effect of this bisociation is not simply ambiguity or double meaning: it is a mental phenomenon in which a concept is simultaneously associated with two different and habitually (but not logically) incompatible contexts (and their attendant emotional valencies) (pp. 24, 37). Appropriately for my purposes, Koestler relies on the metaphor of the tuning fork to embody this: a certain element capable of becoming a junction between two contexts begins to "vibrate"—not according to the "affective or habit-preferred" pitch of the first context, but according to the pitch of the new context, with which it is now also associated (p. 48).

We have already discussed George Eliot's fondness for the metaphors of sound and vibration; she also recognizes this geometric structure for humor, although she distinguishes between a different kind of response, which she calls humor, and "Wit," which is her term for Koestler's comic geometry. She presents her beliefs in "German Wit: Heinrich Heine" (1856):

> Wit seizes on unexpected and complex relations. . . . It detects an unsuspected analogy or suggests a startling or confounding inference. . . . This affinity of Wit with ratiocination is the more obvious in proportion as the species of wit is higher and deals less with words and with superficialities than with the essential qualities of things. Some of Johnson's most admirable witticisms consist in the suggestion of an analogy which immediately exposes the absurdity of an action or proposition; and it is only their ingenuity, condensation, and instantaneousness which lift them from reasoning into Wit—they are *reasoning raised to a higher power.* (*Essays,* p. 218)

In addition to the description of the junction of two different contexts as an "unsuspected analogy," this passage provides evidence that Eliot finds the capacity to perceive relations to be fundamental to all other mental processes. As she says in "The Future of German Philosophy," judgment is always "a comparison, or perception of likeness in the midst of difference" (*Essays,* p. 151). The "higher power" or "charge" that lies behind the analogy of a witticism is, for both Koestler (p. 54) and Eliot, connected with conditions of aggression or defense; in "German Wit," Eliot writes that "strange as the genealogy may seem, the original parentage of that wonderful and delicious mixture of fun, fancy, philosophy, and feeling which constitutes modern humour, was probably the cruel mockery of a savage at the writhings of a suffering enemy" (*Essays,* p. 219). According to Koestler, the delight of humor comes when those aggressive/defensive energies become redundant by the separation brought about through bisociation: the new context makes them unnecessary, and the result is a de-tension or liberation from the "fetters" of their original "biological purpose" (self-preservation). The emotional tension is "annihilated," not by action, but by the "aimless muscular activity" of laughing, which "explodes anger, greed, envy," thereby "punctur[ing] any instinctual drive" (pp. 57–58).[7] Thus, although laughter may be grounded in the aggressive emotions, it can be a sign of their being superseded or at least rechanneled.

The modulation from both Koestler's and George Eliot's definitions of the phenomenon of humor as an element of the aggressive/defensive activities of mind to the alternate phenomenon of sympathetic tears begins at the moment when humor fails of its effect. This occurs, not when there is no longer the geometric structure of wit (which, indeed, is intended by both writers to be the fundamental process of all creative thought), but when, in Koestler's words, the onlooker's attitude toward the contexts or fields of thought joined by the bisociation is different (p. 75). As Eliot writes, "'Nothing,' says Goethe, 'is more significant of men's character than what they find laughable.' . . . The last thing in which the cultivated man can have community with the vulgar is their jocularity" ("German Wit: Heinrich Heine" [1856], *Essays,* p. 217). Later in the same essay she remarks that what defeats "the sense of the ludicrous" in Voltaire's *Candide* is "disgust" (p. 220). It is clear, then, that the presence of an alternative emotion changes the nature of the bisociation from comic to tragic. This fact is not explicitly stated in Eliot's essay on "German Wit," primarily because she wishes to elucidate the distinction between wit and humor rather than that between comedy and tragedy. But even in the former distinction—wherein humor is the "*sympathetic* presentation of incongruous elements in human nature and life" (p. 219)—the crucial element for humor's unlikeness to wit is the attitude of the onlooker toward the incongruity placed before him. The onlooker, then, reintroduces the figure of the reader. At least in part, the energy associated with the narrative derives from him or her. Horace Kallen, another analyst of humor and pathos, expresses the personal, and thus extraliterary, cause for the reader's particular response, whether in the form of laughter or tears, as the effect provided by the "dynamic relevancy" of the bisociation: "For laughter and tears never cease to be sudden functions of the actual present, liberations from actually felt bondage. Without this present relevancy, no object, no phrase, no action, however perfect its style, gets laughed at or wept over. It is their unexpected pertinence, their relation, that renders them comic or tragic."[8]

Of course, this assertion becomes the justification for realism, the presentation in art of those elements that the reader can be made to see and to feel as actual and present. From this we can now extrapolate a theory of the comic and the pathetic which is comprised of three parts: the sudden conjunction of apparently incongruent items; their reality or relevance for the reader; and the resulting emotional charge, whether laughter or tears. In a sense, these are no more than an extension of George Eliot's three elements of fictional art: humor, observation, and passion.

Although this theory accounts for the capacity of narrative art to generate humor or pathos, it does not reveal the personal sources for the pathetic, as opposed to the comic, response to the bisociation that occurs. Both Koestler and Eliot account for the tearful response by asserting the existence of certain emotions that are neither aggressive nor defensive. Koestler calls these emotions "self-transcending" because activities associated with them tend to expand the range of awareness beyond the limits of self, making that self aware that it is a part of a higher functional whole.[9] Crying, then, becomes the response to the decomposition or loss of any relation that satisfies this "integrative" or "participatory" tendency (p. 120). It appears, from her many remarks on the moral value of art, that Eliot considers art to serve the "self-transcending" emotions, being a means by which we become aware that we are indeed part of a larger human and social whole. Yet, the characters within her fiction who seem most able to call up states of self-transcendence—Dinah Morris and Mordecai Cohen, especially—seem unconnected with, if not detrimental to, the most powerful effects of her art. Koestler's remarks on the achievement of "self-transcendence" in art may explain why this is so.

Koestler grounds his comments about the effects of art in a distinction between the physiology of laughing and the physiology of weeping. Laughing "explodes" emotion through muscular activity and puffs of exhaled breath; weeping permits emotion to drain away gradually through the overflow of tears and "sighing expirations."[10] Although we may laugh as we read, the overriding emotional effect of literature is less the explosion of emotion than its gradual and continual internal evolution during the process of reading—hence the belief that art in the end satisfies self-transcending rather than aggressive emotional needs. As the various fields of association, with their elements of image, idea, memory, and expectation, "feed" emotion into the narrative, that narrative's bisociations and transformations help to channel and finally consummate those emotions by "earthing" them in the absolutes that art provides (pp. 283, 331). Koestler summarizes this psychological event by means of the now familiar metaphors of the flash of light and the flood of water, although their common ground continues to be his fundamental geometric pattern:

> Its *intellectual* aspect is the sudden perception of the object in a new, brighter, and more relevant light, a new and deeper understanding of the objects of trivial experience, in short a eureka process which is the positive counterpart of the malicious eureka process of the joke. Its *emotional* aspect is the result of the transfer of the integrative charge from the narrow associative [context of one field] to the wider associative [context of the second], with its greater emotion-absorbing capacity, in which it can suddenly expand—like water drained from a pipe into a wide system of irrigation channels. *In this simultaneous occurrence of* intellectual illumination *and* emotional expansion, *which are but two aspects of the same bisociative process, lies the essence of the aesthetic experience.* (Pp. 287–88)

Here we have a clear description of the manner by which constructions dependent on intellect are related to (and even help to generate) the emotional energies so important to the production and consumption of art. Bisociation—the perception that two apparently distinct elements can implicate each other—becomes in art a means of channelling emotion more successfully in order to satisfy one's psychic needs as well as a means of seeing more clearly.

Koestler's use of terms that have metaphoric possibilities in George Eliot's fiction underscores the congruency between his and Eliot's conceptions of aesthetic experience. Eliot's belief in the importance of "illumination" is well recognized, so Koestler's addition of the concept of "expansion" of the self is a useful reinforcement of the significance of that fundamental, yet dangerously egoistic need so apparent in Eliot's fiction (see chapter 3, above). Conversely, Koestler's insistence that the effect of art is not simply an expansion of the self, or, more conventionally, a catharsis for the observer but also an intellectual illumination explains a great deal about the large- and small-scale elements of George Eliot's novels. For instance, Dinah Morris's moments of oceanic transcendence, although they satisfy the self-transcending impulse of human nature for her, are virtually devoid of intellectual penetration; her status as a kind of moral ideal is thus rightly lessened in *Adam Bede,* and she must learn a different kind of knowledge during the course of the novel. As Koestler remarks,

> with the development of the conscious individuality and the increasing importance of abstract thought, the integrative [self-transcending] instinct . . . can no longer be satisfied by the raptures and trances evoked by primitive ritual; these would only earth the older layers of the psyche. To achieve self-transcendence, the newer, intellectual layers have also to be engaged. (P. 353)

Put more simply, Eliot wishes to bring about through her fiction the exercise of our sympathies without the sacrifice of our intellect.

George Eliot's conception of the function and form of art—as it is described in her essays and embodied in her fictional language—follows out the full implications of her commitment to a sophisticated model of the psychic/organic whole. She comprehends the distinction between the intellect and the emotions within the whole of the self, just as she comprehends the distinction between the self and the other within the whole of the human community. As the earlier quotation from Koestler explains, there can be no complex unity without such a distinction of parts. Eliot's response to such distinctness is a rejection of the univocal —the narrowed consciousness of only a single point of view, be it intellectual or emotional, commonplace or fanciful, selfish or social—as well as of the divergent—the capacity to perceive both the intellectual and the emotional, the commonplace and the fanciful, the selfish and the social, only in order to insist upon their lack of relationship. Rather, she finds that each of these elements implicates the other; their distance from each other only serves to generate the energy (humorous or pathetic) that announces their mutuality. Herein lies the potency of all of Eliot's "Janus-faced" language,[11] from the doubleness of metaphor per se, to the doubleness implicit in specific terms such as the shell or the child. The validity of this theory as an explanation of Eliot's success as a novelist can be shown through an examination of her manipulation of these potencies in her novels.

A distinction must be made between those aspects of George Eliot's narratives which take as their avowed topic the sense of the humorous or the pathetic and those that are intended to generate humor or pathos. Unlike earlier distinctions between the "self-conscious" and the "implicit" presentation of a subject, here the self-conscious is the more conventional and less significant presentation. That is, although Eliot's novels include several extensive scenes devoted to the development of a practical joke or the evocation of pathos at a deathbed, the effect of these scenes is fairly predictable and self-contained within the larger dynamics of the novels. Some degree of subtlety emerges as Eliot begins to focus more directly on the psychological implications for her characters of the capacity to laugh or to cry, but it is only when the arousal of these emotions is an issue between narrator and reader, through, among other means, a kind of dramatic irony, that the heart of Eliot's success as a writer is apparent.

Virtually every one of George Eliot's stories has a moment when the characters participate in the generation of a humorous situation. The first extended example is Dempster's playbill joke ("Janet's Repentance," ch. 9, pp. 314–15), which is clearly an act of aggression intended to emphasize the distance between Tryan's exalted conception of himself and the physical reality of his congregation's needs. The laughter at Seth Bede's expense over his failure to remember the panels in his door (*Adam Bede,* ch. 1, pp. 6–7) is triggered by the same kind of "bisociation" of spiritual and physical seeing, although here the joke is somewhat better humored. The barber's joke on Tacco in *Romola* (ch. 16, vol. 1, pp. 256–66), the joke on Christian concerning his coattail in *Felix Holt the Radical* (ch. 12, pp. 150–52), and the effigy of Mr. Brooke during the hustings in *Middlemarch* (ch. 51, pp. 370–71) are similar humorous situations. These episodes are all examples of what the "vulgar" find jocular, as Eliot notes in "German Wit." As such they characterize a state of mind in the individual and in the society he represents which is closer to "barbarism" than civilization, although Eliot has been careful to indicate that the enduring elements of the comic are present even here:

> A great deal of humour may co-exist with a great deal of barbarism, as we see in the Middle Ages; but the strongest flavour of the humour in such cases will come, not from sympathy, but more probably from triumphant egoism or intolerance; at best it will be the love of the ludicrous exhibiting itself in illustrations of successful cunning and of the *lex talionis,* as in *Reineke Fuchs,* or shaking off in a holiday mood the yoke of a too exacting faith, as in the old Mysteries. ("German Wit: Heinrich Heine" [1856], *Essays,* p. 219)

Egoism and cunning—the aggressive and defensive (yet liberating) intelligence of the self—are undoubtedly intended to predominate in such moments.

In addition to such scenes of humor, usually planned at the expense of a single individual for the sake of group/social superiority, there are also scenes of humorous combat. George Eliot appears to take more unalloyed pleasure in these, perhaps because of the more equal matching of individual wit. Mrs. Poyser, in *Adam Bede,* takes on many opponents, although her debate with schoolmaster Bartle Massey (ch. 53, pp. 438-39) probably suits our purposes best. Classed with their exchange must be Bob Jakin's bargaining with Mrs. Glegg in *The Mill on the Floss* (bk. 5, ch. 2, pp. 279-83). Similar, but more unequal, are the battles between Scala and Politian in *Romola* (ch. 7, vol. 1, pp. 114-20), between Christian and Scales in *Felix Holt the Radical* (ch. 7, pp. 103-8), and between Dagley and Mr. Brooke in *Middlemarch* (ch. 39, pp. 289-91). In each case, Eliot complicates the humor by making a joke of aggressive egoism itself. For most of the combatants, superior cunning has only brought about superior exposure. Here we begin to see a shift in the intended response of the reader toward a sense of the ludicrous derived from, but not identical to, that which they would perceive themselves. Perhaps a further twist upon this construction is the combat of wits which fails to take place in *Felix Holt the Radical;* the inability of Rufus Lyon and the unfortunate Mr. Sherlock to appear in the same room together provides its own humorous point (ch. 24). Additional dramatic irony undoubtedly derives from the fact that "Lion's" real antagonist is not the religious establishment represented by Mr. Sherlock, but "Christian," who is really a false father figure.

The scenes just mentioned take as their subject matter the elements of the humorous as we outlined them earlier: one kind suggests that the attitude of the audience determines what that audience will find funny;[12] the other suggests that the bisociation of two points of view or kinds of cunning can generate humor for the reader. Proof that the humorous response is not always "barbaric" also exists in George Eliot's briefer remarks about the sense of humor as it is manifested by her various characters. From Mr. Cleves's initial cameo appearance in "Amos Barton" to Mary Garth's primary importance in *Middlemarch,* the ability to laugh is associated with mental and moral health:

> Look at [Mr. Cleves] more attentively, and you will see that his face is a very interesting one—that there is a great deal of humour and feeling playing in his grey eyes, and about the corners of his roughly-cut mouth: a man, you observe, who has most likely sprung from the harder-working section of the middle class, and has hereditary sympathies with the checkered life of the people. (Ch. 6, p. 93)

> [Mary's] shrewdness had a streak of satiric bitterness continually renewed and never carried utterly out of sight, except by a strong current of gratitude towards those who, instead of telling her that she ought to be contented, did something to make her so. . . . For honesty, truth-telling fairness, was Mary's reigning virtue: she neither tried to create illusions, nor indulged in them for her own behoof, and when she was in a good mood she had humour enough in her to laugh at herself. (Ch. 12, p. 84)

Conversely, Gwendolen Harleth and Esther Lyon are distinguished from Hetty Sorrel and Rosamond Vincy by their ability to laugh even though they dislike looking ridiculous as much as Hetty and Rosamond do (see *Daniel Deronda,* ch. 3, p. 17; *Felix Holt the Radical,* ch. 10, p. 126; *Adam Bede,* ch. 18, p. 169; *Middlemarch,* ch. 16, p. 117). The only other character who seems to match Mary Garth's capacity to laugh at the world and the self is, interestingly enough, Will Ladislaw, who manages to survive extended periods of contact with Mr. Brooke by means of "a tickling vision of a sheep-stealing epic written with Homeric particularity" (*Middlemarch,* ch. 39, p. 284). This private joke is interrupted by Dorothea's abrupt appearance at the Grange, and Will's contrary capacity for awe is immediately apparent in his response to her. It is Dorothea herself, however, who represents far more completely the alternative capacity for sympathetic self-transcendence. Although she shows a touch of the satiric in her conversations with Celia, her dominant mood is often self-transcending, or "oceanic,"[13] in nature.

The list of those characters who, like Dorothea, are primarily oceanic is a familiar one: Janet Dempster, Dinah Morris, Seth Bede, Silas Marner, Dino Bardi, Rufus Lyon, Daniel Deronda, Mordecai Cohen, and Mirah Lapidoth. Each is associated with religious experience, and each seems born to such tendencies rather than educated into them. Further, while George Eliot admires their selflessness, the evidence of the novels—and of readers' reactions to them—is that this capacity to lose the self in a sense of the other is an imperfect and sometimes dangerous state. With the exception of Janet Dempster (who is really only included because of her starlight walk in chapter 25, p. 398), each learns in the course of his or her narrative to recognize the necessary existence of certain "selfish" needs identifiable only by means of one's inescapable separate flesh. Indeed, their entanglements in selfish need derive from passion or passion-once-removed: Dinah's love for Adam, and Seth's love for her; Silas's love for Sarah and then for Godfrey and Molly's child; Rufus and Annette, Dorothea and Will, Mirah and Daniel Deronda. Even Dino and Mordecai (the most celibate representatives) recognize passion through their responsibilities to the sister who marks their parents' passionate union.

One cannot learn much about the generation of the state of self-transcendence from Eliot's novels, since the ability to transcend the self is so innate a quality for the characters concerned. One hint of its origins is derivable, however, from those scenes—the contrary of the humorous set-pieces—in which weeping signals the loss of that sense of oceanic union whch these characters are capable of calling up. The pathetic scene *par excellence* is, of course, the deathbed scene. We see it enacted in each of the three stories in *Scenes of Clerical Life* (the deaths of Milly Barton, Tina Sarti, and Edgar Tryan), in *Felix Holt the Radical* (the death of Annette), and in *Daniel Deronda* (the death of Mordecai). Three of these five deaths are the deaths of mothers, and Tryan and Mordecai are both priestly figures who are identified with mothers (Janet's and Mirah's) in the novels. Even Seth Bede's love for Dinah has maternal echoes:

> [He] had only just learned what it is to love—to love with that adoration which a young man gives to *a woman whom he feels to be greater and better than himself.* Love of this sort is hardly distinguishable from religious feeling. What deep and worthy love is so? whether of woman *or child,* or art or music. Our caresses, our tender words, our still rapture under the influence of autumn sunsets, or pillared vistas, or calm majestic statues, or Beethoven symphonies, all bring with them the consciousness that they are mere waves and ripples in an unfathomable ocean of love and beauty; our emotion in its

keenest moment passes from expression into silence, our love at its highest flood rushes beyond its object, and loses itself in the sense of divine mystery. (*Adam Bede,* ch. 3, p. 33, emphasis mine)

In addition to the references to maternal figures and maternal love, this description relies upon oceanic imagery as well as the more familiar imagery of music and light. If we add Romola's Madonna-like activities in *Romola* to this class of "mother-related" moments of transcendence and pathos, it seems logical to assume that the fundamental structure for the generation of pathos is the loss of that primary integrative relation symbolized by the union of mother and child. Those who remain capable of recreating that sense of union are, provocatively enough, often orphan figures themselves—for reasons of most concern to psychoanalytic critics. A revelation of the capacity to face the loss of that relationship inherent in the death of the mother seems to be the primary intention behind those deathbed scenes in the novels. Indeed, the pathos of such moments is so absolute and thus so conventional that, in dealing with them, critics are usually far less concerned with their content than with the linguistic means George Eliot uses to mediate that content. These linguistic means, by which Eliot generates laughter as well as tears in the reader, deserve attention.

I asserted earlier that the nature of the humor or pathos generated depends upon the nature of the fields of thought or association brought into relation with each other and upon the item that provides the junction between them. In Chapters 4 and 5, I examined extensively the most basic fields of experience that George Eliot uses in her fiction: the fear of annihilation, and sexual desire. Virtually every story reenacts either the plot of "The Legend of Jubal" or the sexual plot or both. Certainly both topics carry strong emotional charges for the reader—they are likely to be considered relevant to his or her present situation. The nature of the junctions between Eliot's various fields of association is less obvious.

The humor in *Scenes of Clerical Life* is often restricted to the single word or single line. In "Amos Barton," for instance, the narrator remarks that Mrs. Patten "used to adore her husband, and now she adores her money" (ch. 1, p. 46); and that Barton's hat "shows no symptom of taking to the hideous doctrine of expediency, and shaping itself according to circumstances" (ch. 1, p. 44). Mr. Dunn's remarks on the consumption of his linen and woollen goods in chapter 10 of "Janet's Repentance" (see Chapter 2, above) are equally dependent upon the junction a single word makes between a conventionally dignified and a conventionally low topic. Such local jokes, usually made by the narrator rather than by a character, persist even in George Eliot's most accomplished narratives. For instance, in *Silas Marner,* she remarks that "Mrs. Kimble was the Squire's sister, as well as the doctor's wife—a double dignity, with which her diameter was in direct proportion" (ch. 11, p. 145). Here a subliminal part of the fun is the punlike alliteration of "d" sounds, from dignity to diameter, although the key junction is the difference between a spiritual and physical magnitude represented simultaneously by the single word-junction "double." This joke about Mrs. Kimble is not very different from the one about Mr. Casson in *Adam Bede* (see Chapter 2, above). This suggests the way in which the single witticism begins to have implications for more extended narrative. Not only does the voice of the narrator—and the quality of mind or tone ascribed to that narrator as a result of such witticisms—persist in an extended narrative,[14] but the possibility of a more extended juxtaposition of the two fields of association, most frequently the physical and spiritual fields, persists as well. Indeed, as we have seen in the joke on Mr. Casson, the essence of that joke becomes a fundamental issue for all of Eliot's fiction.

The jokes about Mr. Casson and Mrs. Kimble both draw attention to proportion (a conception crucial to the structure of humor) as the hidden junction between the high and the low; and George Eliot herself speaks mockingly about the significance of this sort of proportion as the essence of her own fictional choices:

> And here I am naturally led to reflect on the means of elevating a low subject. Historical parallels are remarkably efficient in this way. The chief objection to them is, that the diligent narrator may lack space, or (what is often the same thing) may not be able to think of them with any degree of particularity, though he may have a philosophical confidence that if known they would be illustrative. It seems an easier and shorter way to dignity, to observe that—since there never was a true story which could not be told in parables where you might put a monkey for a margrave, and *vice versa*—whatever has been or is to be narrated by me about low people, may be ennobled by being considered a parable; so that if any bad habits and ugly consequences are brought into view, the reader may have the relief of regarding them as not more than figuratively ungenteel, and may feel himself virtually in company with persons of some style. Thus while I tell the truth about loobies, my reader's imagination need not be entirely excluded from an occupation with lords; and the petty sums which any bankrupt of high standing would be sorry to retire upon, may be lifted to the level of high commercial

transactions by the inexpensive addition of proportional ciphers. (*Middlemarch,* ch. 35, pp. 249-50)

Although critics might object that this passage fails to be humorous for the reader because George Eliot has intentions behind the joke which make it a wheedling sort of performance,[15] the linguistic techniques displayed and the dominant preoccupations apparent make the passage important. First, the plays upon words or single concepts derive from two kinds of language, the arithmetic/geometric and the visual/artistic. From "elevate" and "parallel" to "sums" and "ciphers," Eliot reminds us of the tendency to use relations of quantity in dealing with matters of quality. Or, through words like "illustrative," "brought into view," and "figuratively," she reminds us of the more dignified interpretation of narrative as a transposition of the seen into the imagined.

Second, once the reader has been alerted by both overt statement and obvious "punning" that the language of the passage is to be understood in two senses, a second level of humor becomes apparent—humor at the expense of humor itself (much like the humor at the expense of humorous combat discussed earlier). For, if "proportion" is the starting point for perceiving the underlying junction between apparently unconnected fields of experience—in this case, loobies and lords—then the passage finally undercuts the appropriateness of proportionality itself.[16] This is most obvious in the final joke, in which "high standing" really only represents a greater degree of nothingness, ciphers being entirely incapable of mathematical proportionality. Yet this reversal of correlation (rather than the parallelism asserted early in the passage) is the hidden point of the parenthetical remark George Eliot makes about narrators who indulge in historical parallels: when she asserts that lack of space and lack of particular knowledge may be the same thing, she reminds us that it is often "articulation" rather than "space" which announces "fullness" or content. On the moral level, she also reinforces this concept of reversal rather than proportion: there is the obvious emphasis of "*vice versa*" (which makes a margrave into a monkey and a lord into a loobie) as well as the more indirect implication that "ennobling" the bad and the ugly by the literal expedient of ascribing bad behavior to a noble only increases the badness. Of course, this last "reversal" is really the reversal of a reversal and so returns us to proportionality with a new sense that morally low behavior committed by the socially high is actually proportionally lower.

We have already seen that the concepts that serve as junctions for the humor of this passage are significant for George Eliot's moral and aesthetic beliefs: she is preoccupied with space and proportionality on the physical, moral, and artistic levels. Further, the passage just analyzed comes at the end of the chapter in *Middlemarch* devoted to the "Christian Carnivora" present at the reading of Peter Featherstone's will. The issues and effects of that will are of the utmost seriousness in the novel; as Fred Vincy discovers at the conclusion of the chapter, the junction of "the stranger's [Joshua Rigg's] face" and the thought of a "love-child" is not really ludicrous at all (p. 244). As he well knows, his own love relations with Mary will be affected by his failure to inherit from the dead uncle. Thus, Eliot appears to be able to treat a conventionally pathetic or sympathetic subject comically—in this case, she literally brackets the serious content of the chapter by humorous paragraphs at its beginning and end. Yet even this is not an entirely accurate description of her technique, for the voice of the narrator actually modulates between humor and pathos throughout the scene at Stone Court. Herein lies the essential quality of Eliot's fictional success. The reader's capacity to pursue the thread of narrative as it shifts from comic to pathetic depends upon a degree of intellectual awareness and emotional commitment which guarantees the perpetual generation and transmutation of psychic energy. Further, since that narrative frequently turns round upon itself, much as the implications of parallelism do in the previous passage, the reader's energy is renewable—even, perhaps especially, upon rereading the text.

What happens on the local level—sentence by sentence—also happens on the most extended level in George Eliot's fiction. It is really no more than a step from considering that the actual tale about the Featherstone legatees is but a parable for another, more ennobled, tale to realizing that that tale may be a parable about the Casaubon legatees or (more distantly) the Brooke legatees. Indeed, the sentence preceding the narrator's remarks in chapter 35 hints at that likelihood: "No soul was prophetic enough to have any foreboding as to what might appear on the trail of Joshua Rigg" (p. 249). As we noted earlier, Joshua is the unrecognized junction between the various ("bisociated") plots of the novel, a junction that lifts the rather broad humor about his froglike face to the level of dramatic irony. And dramatic irony, despite its dependence upon the structure of humor as we have defined it, is frequently associated in plot with loss (future or unrecognized) and thus with pathos.

The assertions about George Eliot's art which I might now make convincingly are really no different from those that critics have been making for decades. The topic just concluded—the significance of the multiple plots in the aesthetic success of her fiction—supports the accepted critical view that Eliot is least successful in her two short stories and her poetry. In both cases the restriction to a single plot is attended by a restriction to a single tone—comic or pathetic. Indeed, one might imagine a novel worthy of George Eliot which tempered the humor of "Brother Jacob" with the morbid pathos of "The Lifted Veil." Certainly some of the poetry might be improved by an infusion of that "play of humour" she felt to be inappropriate to that genre (see *Letters,* 3: 382).

The assignation of a particular style to a particular kind of plot or narrative form is the first major qualification, then, that must be made when assessing George Eliot's work. Of course, critics have already spoken extensively about her style as one of the possible defects of otherwise successful novels and as the hallmark of the triumph of *Middlemarch.*[17] That style is the result of the series of issues we have examined: the desire to engage the reader in the fiction; the commitment to a language that is "shadowy" (i.e., metaphorical); the resultant development of a tone that modulates between the humorous and the pathetic. Eliot herself, in the essays she wrote about fiction, turned most frequently to failures of style at the level of the sentence and word as the sign of more general artistic failure.[18] Style becomes the nodus where almost all other elements meet; it defines the narrative voice, it generates the bisociations upon which the reader's energetic engagement depends, and it embodies the conceptions which become the structure for the narratives themselves. "Consumption," "expansion," and "generation" all come into being at the level of style, although they are terms used equally to define Eliot's largest fictional units.

Even George Eliot's propensity to prologues, epilogues, epigraphs, and asides reminds the reader and critic that the voice of the narrator as it is embodied in the style is concerned not simply with telling a story but also with telling that story to the reader who exists in a world outside the story itself. The most effective means for bringing about the involvement of that reader returns us to language once again, for Eliot's most potent stylistic technique is the artistic allusion, direct or implicit. Such allusions remind the reader that language is by tradition shadowy and that the text they are reading, for all its realism of observation, exists within that shadowy tradition. Further, allusions draw upon the energies embodied in that language as it has been used by authors in the past to generate humor and pathos—especially the latter. When her language resonates with that of past authors, even her deathbed scenes become powerful for the reader:

> "There," said Dinah, "now the kitchen looks tidy, and now, dear mother—for I'm your daughter to-night, you know—I should like you

> to wash your face and have a clean cap on. Do you remember what David did, when God took away his child from him? While the child was yet alive he fasted and prayed to God to spare it, and he would neither eat nor drink, but lay on the ground all night, beseeching God for the child. But when he knew it was dead, he rose up from the ground and washed and anointed himself, and changed his clothes, and ate and drank; and when they asked him how it was that he seemed to have left off grieving now the child was dead, he said, 'While the child was yet alive, I fasted and wept; for I said, Who can tell whether God will be gracious to me, that the child may live? But now he is dead, wherefore should I fast? can I bring him back again?'" (*Adam Bede,* ch. 10, p. 98)

Proving that George Eliot's novels *do,* sentence by sentence or event by event, generate laughter and tears in the reader would require methods of analysis beyond the focus of my argument here. Nevertheless, the discussions contained in each of the preceding chapters have spoken, at least indirectly, of the humor and pathos inherent in the language of her fiction. This appears to justify my initial inference that language, especially language as metaphor, can indeed be shown to both constitute and generate the reality for which her fiction is so famous. I shall use Eliot's own method, including her incorporation of biblical phrasing as a means of communication, to summarize the perceptions expressed heretofore: I offer a metaphor for Eliot's artistic means and ends that is derived from the opening of her most successful novel, *Middlemarch.* There, Eliot wishes to "place" Dorothea through her manner of dress—which is itself "placed" by its relationship to her sister's manner of dress. Style being the dress of thought, the analogy between the two sisters "shadows forth" Eliot's own manner of narrative dress:

> [Dorothea] was usually spoken of as being remarkably clever, but with the addition that her sister Celia had more common-sense. Nevertheless, Celia wore scarcely more trimmings; and it was only to close observers that her dress differed from her sister's, and had a shade of coquetry in its arrangements; for Miss Brooke's plain dressing was due to mixed conditions, in most of which her sister shared. (Ch. 1, p. 5)

Whether one finally prefers George Eliot's clever (if rather self-transcending) style or her commonsensical (and sometimes sarcastic) style—or the mixed conditions that the sisters' styles together embody—the ultimate effect of Eliot's art today is akin to the effect of Dorothea Brooke's appearance:

> Miss Brooke had that kind of beauty which seems to be thrown into relief by poor dress. Her hand and wrist were so finely formed that she could wear sleeves not less bare of style than those in which the Blessed Virgin appeared to Italian painters; and her profile as well as her stature and bearing seemed to gain the more dignity from her plain garments, which by the side of provincial fashion gave her the impressiveness of a fine quotation from the Bible,—or from one of our elder poets,—in a paragraph of to-day's newspaper. (Ch. 1, p. 5)

In other words, although Eliot's novels may not be models of the plain style—Italianate or otherwise—they undoubtedly remain impressive.

NOTES

CHAPTER 1

1. Although only a single example from a large body of work, George Eliot's passage regarding the difficulty of "reading" the natural order makes explicit the connection between reality and language: "Every man under such circumstances is conscious of being a great physiognomist. Nature, he knows, has a language of her own, which she uses with strict veracity, and he considers himself an adept in the language. . . . Nature has her language, and she is not unveracious; but we don't know all the intricacies of her syntax just yet, and in a hasty reading we may happen to extract the very opposite of her real meaning" (*Adam Bede*, ch. 15, pp. 130–31).

2. Martin Price's discussion of the terms *energy* and *order* and their mutual implications in *To the Palace of Wisdom: Studies in Order and Energy from Dryden to Blake* (Garden City, N.Y.: Doubleday & Co., 1964) is a valuable context for my argument.

3. Nicolas Abraham, "The Shell and the Kernel," *Diacritics* 9, no. 1 (1979): 17.

4. These notes by George Eliot are provided in Thomas Pinney's "More Leaves from George Eliot's Notebook," *Huntington Library Quarterly* 29 (1966): 364.

5. Pinney, "More Leaves from George Eliot's Notebook," p. 371.

6. *The Complete Writings of William Blake*, ed. Geoffrey Keynes (London: Oxford University Press, 1966), p. 155.

CHAPTER 2

1. See, for instance, David R. Carroll's "Unity Through Analogy: An Interpretation of 'Middlemarch,'" *Victorian Studies* 2 (1959): 305–16; and Mark Schorer's "Fiction and the 'Matrix of Analogy,'" *Kenyon Review* 11 (1949): 550–59.

2. W. J. Harvey provides an excellent discussion of this aspect of George Eliot's natural language in "Idea and Image in the Novels of George Eliot," *Critical Essays on George Eliot*, ed. Barbara Hardy (London: Routledge & Kegan Paul, 1970), pp. 151–98. More recently, David Carroll has discussed the combination of the organic movement and a dialectical movement, with conclusions similar to my own, although he seems to contend that the belief in organicism precedes a fairly straightfoward attempt to "embody" it in the fiction. See "'Janet's Repentance' and the Myth of the Organic," *Nineteenth-Century Fiction* 35 (1980): 331–48.

3. Barbara Hardy, *The Novels of George Eliot: A Study in Form* (New York: Oxford University Press, 1967), pp. 206–9.

4. George Clark, "Henryson and Aesop: The Fable Transformed," *ELH* 43 (1976): 5.

5. See Gordon S. Haight, ed., *The George Eliot Letters* 2: 473; 3: 177.

6. See K. K. Collins, "G. H. Lewes Revised: George Eliot and the Moral Sense," *Victorian Studies* 21 (1978): 492.

7. See, for instance, Nina Auerbach, "The Power of Hunger: Demonism and Maggie Tulliver," *Nineteenth-Century Fiction* 30 (1975): 150–71.

8. Ludwig Feuerbach, in *Das Wesen des Christenthums,* which George Eliot translated in 1854, also emphasizes the significance of real animal appetite in his discussion of the sacrament of the last supper. See *The Essence of Christianity,* trans. George Eliot (New York: Harper & Bros., 1957), pp. 276–78.

9. U. C. Knoepflmacher presents a careful analysis of this chapter with regard to its historical and literary analogues in "*Middlemarch:* An Avuncular View," *Nineteenth-Century Fiction* 30 (1975): 53–81; esp. pp. 60–66.

10. Wallace Stevens, "Effects of Analogy," *The Necessary Angel: Essays on Reality and the Imagination* (New York: Random House, 1951), p. 114.

11. Ibid., p. 118.

12. Walker Percy, "Metaphor as Mistake," *Sewanee Review* 66 (1958): 81.

13. Morton W. Bloomfield, "The Syncategorematic in Poetry: From Semantics to Syntactics," *To Honor Roman Jakobson* (The Hague: Mouton & Co., 1967), 1: 312.

14. See Bloomfield, "Syncategorematic in Poetry," p. 312.

15. Henry James, "Daniel Deronda: A Conversation," *Atlantic Monthly,* December, 1876, as reprinted in *George Eliot: The Critical Heritage,* edited by David Carroll (New York: Barnes & Noble, 1971), pp. 417–33.

CHAPTER 3

1. *The Complete Poetical Works of Samuel Taylor Coleridge,* ed. E. H. Coleridge (Oxford: Clarendon Press, 1912), 1: 197.

2. Angus Fletcher discusses this sort of "liminal" anxiety in "'Positive Negation': Threshold, Sequence, and Personification in Coleridge," *New Perspectives on Coleridge and Wordsworth,* ed. Geoffrey H. Hartman (New York: Columbia University Press, 1972), pp. 140–41.

3. N. N. Feltes, "George Eliot's 'Pier-Glass': The Development of a Metaphor," *Modern Philology* 67 (1969): 69–71.

4. Ibid., p. 69.

5. In "Optic and Semiotic in *Middlemarch,*" in *The Worlds of Victorian Fiction,* ed. Jerome H. Buckley (Cambridge: Harvard University Press, 1975), pp. 125–45, J. Hillis Miller discusses this image as Narcissus-like in its implications (p. 141). He also remarks on the etymology of *parable* as descriptive of the ideal course of a narrative through space, like a comet (p. 139), but he does not see his own geometric figure to be of consequence for George Eliot.

6. Feltes, "George Eliot's 'Pier-Glass,'" p. 71.

7. The examination in *Adam Bede* of man's place in the natural order is the subject of extensive analysis in U. C. Knoepflmacher's book, *George Eliot's Early Novels: The Limits of Realism* (Berkeley and Los Angeles: University of California Press, 1968), pp. 116–27.

8. See Barbara Hardy, *The Novels of George Eliot: A Study in Form* (New York: Oxford University Press, 1967), pp. 218–21; and Brian Swann, "*Middlemarch:* Realism and Symbolic Form," *ELH* 39 (1972): 296.

9. John Arthos, "George Eliot: 'The Art of Vision,'" *Rivista di Letterature Moderne e Comparate* 3 (1952): 270.

10. David R. Carroll carefully explains this aspect of the abbey stable section in "*Mansfield Park, Daniel Deronda,* and Ordination," *Modern Philology* 62 (1965): 217–26.

CHAPTER 4

1. For a more extensive discussion of Wordsworth's "On the Power of Sound" in relation to George Eliot's conceptions, see an earlier version of this chapter in "George Eliot and Wordsworth: The Power of Sound and the Power of Mind," *Studies in English Literature* 20 (1980): 675–94.

2. This quotation forms the conclusion of Reva Stump's *Movement and Vision in George Eliot's Novels* (Seattle: University of Washington Press, 1959) and indicates that, despite the cogency of Stump's analysis, George Eliot's imagination cannot be completely defined as the power of vision. Sensibility in Eliot's novels is often too subtle to be expressed in visual terms, or, as Eliot herself puts it, we shouldn't "put on . . . spectacles to discern odours" (*Adam Bede,* ch. 18, p. 170). Frequently, sound and smell are meant to suggest that greater subtlety.

3. For a fuller discussion of the association of plot and temporality, see chapter 5.

4. In *Movement and Vision,* Reva Stump discusses extensively the implications of the language of sight and vision, and many of her insights are easily applicable to the language of sound. See that book for a discussion of complementary terms from the two kinds of language, such as rhythm and outline, tonal quality and color, volume and space, and so forth.

5. Additional discussions of the relevance of past and future to George Eliot's consolation in the face of mortality are presented by U. C. Knoepflmacher, in *George Eliot's Early Novels,* pp. 89–127, and by Edward T. Hurley, in "Death and Immortality: George Eliot's Solution," *Nineteenth-Century Fiction* 24 (1969): 222–27.

6. Most previous critical attention to such aural susceptibilities has focused on Gwendolen Harleth and Maggie Tulliver. Albert R. Cirillo, in "Salvation in *Daniel Deronda:* The Fortunate Overthrow of Gwendolen Harleth," *Literary Monographs* 1, edited by Eric Rothstein and Thomas K. Dunseath (Madison: University of Wisconsin Press, 1967), pp. 201–43, discusses the importance of music in characterizing Gwendolen's fate and also notes the centrality of music to George Eliot's work as a whole. Shirley Frank Levenson, in "The Use of Music in *Daniel Deronda,*" *Nineteenth-Century Fiction* 24 (1969): 317–34, also discusses Gwendolen and music. William J. Sullivan examines the same issue in "Music and Musical Allusion in 'The Mill on the Floss,'" *Criticism* 16 (1974): 232–46.

7. Both U. C. Knoepflmacher, in "*Daniel Deronda* and William Shakespeare," *Victorian Newsletter* 19 (1961): 27–8, and Shirley Frank Levenson, in "The Use of Music in *Daniel Deronda,*" (see note 6, above), note this event in the novel.

8. Wordsworth, *The Prelude,* ed. Ernest de Selincourt, corrected by Stephen Gill (London: Oxford University Press, 1970), pp. 77–78.

9. One can see echoed in Eliot's preachers the many monitory voices of Wordsworth's poems, especially those of the Wanderer and the Pastor of *The Excursion.* For a sample of discussions of the larger issues of language and speech per se, see Robert Kiely, "The Limits of Dialogue in *Middlemarch,*" in *The Worlds of Victorian Fiction,* edited by Jerome H. Buckley (Cambridge: Harvard University Press, 1975), pp. 103–23; J. Hillis Miller, "Nature and the Linguistic Moment," in *Nature and the Victorian Imagination,* edited by U. C. Knoepflmacher and G. B. Tennyson (Berkeley and Los Angeles: University of California Press, 1977), pp. 440–51; Eve Marie Stwertka, "The Web of Utterance: *Middlemarch,*" *Texas Studies in Literature and Language* 19 (1977): 179–87; and Tony Tanner, *Adultery in the Novel: Contract and Transgression* (Baltimore: Johns Hopkins University Press, 1979), pp. 3–112. See also chapter 6, below.

10. Christopher Herbert, in his article "Preachers and the Schemes of Nature in *Adam Bede,*" *Nineteenth-Century Fiction* 29 (1975): 412–27, for example, argues against the validity of Dinah Morris's sermon.

11. The significance of Savonarola's story is discussed by Gennaro A. Santangelo in "Villari's *Life and Times of Savonarola:* A Source for George Eliot's *Romola,*" *Anglia* 90 (1972): 118–31; and Janet K. Gezari in "*Romola* and the Myth of Apocalypse," in *George Eliot: Centenary Essays and an Unpublished Fragment,* edited by Anne Smith (Totowa, N.J.: Barnes & Noble, 1980), pp. 77–102. See also Judith Wilt, *Ghosts of the Gothic: Austen, Eliot, and Lawrence* (Princeton: Princeton University Press, 1980), pp. 187–88, 197–203; and Felicia Bonaparte, *The Triptych and the Cross: The Central Myths of George Eliot's Poetic Imagination* (New York: New York University Press, 1979), passim.

CHAPTER 5

1. René Girard discusses at length the degree to which "simple" desire is in reality an expression of the self's need for a sense of power through another in *Deceit, Desire, and the Novel,* trans. Yvonne Freccero (Baltimore: Johns Hopkins Press, 1966).

2. Several critics have spoken of the relation between adoption and sexuality in George Eliot's plots. Walter Naumann, in "The Architecture of George Eliot's Novels," *Modern Language Quarterly* 9 (1948): 37–50, notes the recurrence of adoption and subsequent sexual tensions. The most extensive recent discussion is the psychoanalytic one in Laura Comer Emery's *George Eliot's Creative Conflict: The Other Side of Silence* (Berkeley and Los Angeles: University of California Press, 1976).

3. Angus Fletcher, *Allegory: The Theory of a Symbolic Mode* (Ithaca, N.Y.: Cornell University Press, 1964), p. 151.

4. Charles Altman, "Medieval Narrative vs. Modern Assumptions: Revising Inadequate Typology," *Diacritics* 4 (1974): 16–17.

5. Ibid., p. 17.

6. Ibid., pp. 16, 18.

7. Peter K. Garrett, *The Victorian Multiplot Novel: Studies in Dialogical Form* (New Haven: Yale University Press, 1980), pp. 139–40.

8. Tony Tanner, *Adultery in the Novel: Contract and Transgression* (Baltimore: Johns Hopkins University Press, 1979). Although I have pursued my own ideas about George Eliot independently, Mr. Tanner's many insights dovetail significantly with my concepts, including his use at several points of the language of appetite, of absence, and of music and his sense of the importance of language itself.

9. Ibid., pp. 11–12, 87.

10. Jonathan Arac, "Rhetoric and Realism in Nineteenth-Century Fiction: Hyperbole in *The Mill on the Floss,*" *ELH* 46 (1979): 688.

11. "Blind rut" is Robert L. Caserio's term (derived from Stephen Dedalus) for the moment of sexual gratification. See his discussion in *Plot, Story, and the Novel: From Dickens and Poe to the Modern Period* (Princeton: Princeton University Press, 1979), p. 241.

12. Steven Marcus, "Human Nature, Social Orders, and Nineteenth-Century Systems of Explanation: Starting In with George Eliot," *Salmagundi* 28 (1975): 20–42.

13. Mason Harris discusses the convention of the servant girl debauched by the gentleman with regard to *Adam Bede* in "Arthur's Misuse of the Imagination: Sentimental Benevolence and Wordsworthian Realism in *Adam Bede,*" *English Studies in Canada* 4 (1978): 41–59.

14. Alexander Welsh presents an extensive discussion of this pattern of choice in Sir Walter Scott's fiction in *The Hero of the Waverley Novels* (New Haven: Yale University Press, 1963).

15. Alan Mintz, in *George Eliot and the Novel of Vocation* (Cambridge: Harvard University Press, 1978), pp. 54–56, asserts that the vocation plot replaces the sexual plot in George Eliot's fiction.

16. The word *possibilities* is used by Barbara Hardy in *The Novels of George Eliot: A Study in Form* (New York: Oxford University Press, 1967), p. 135, to express the iridescent quality of George Eliot's characters, a quality that keeps the reader in suspense about the outcome (plot resolution) of her characters' lives.

17. For example, Russell M. Goldfarb discusses these incestuous possibilities in "Robert P. Warren's Tollivers and George Eliot's Tullivers," *University Review* 36 (1970): 209–13.

18. Tanner discusses this point extensively in *Adultery in the Novel,* chapter 1 ("Passion"), esp. pp. 18–24.

19. See Tanner, *Adultery in the Novel,* pp. 66-72, for a complete discussion of Maggie's decision.

20. See, for example, David R. Carroll's discussion of marrying in *Silas Marner* in "*Silas Marner:* Reversing the Oracles of Religion," *Literary Monographs* 1, edited by Eric Rothstein and Thomas K. Dunseath (Madison: University of Wisconsin Press, 1967), pp. 192–93.

21. Deronda's circumcised penis is an important aspect of Cynthia Chase's discussion of the novel in "The Decomposition of the Elephants: Double-Reading *Daniel Deronda,*" *PMLA* 93 (1978): 215–27.

22. Significant discussions of "The Lifted Veil" include U. C. Knoepflmacher's study in *George Eliot's Early Novels: The Limits of Realism* (Berkeley and Los Angeles: University of California Press, 1968), pp. 128–61; Gillian Beer's "Myth and the Single Consciousness: *Middlemarch* and *The Lifted Veil,*" in *This Particular Web: Essays on 'Middlemarch,'* edited by Ian Adam (Toronto: University of Toronto Press, 1975), pp. 91–115; and Charles Swann's work, "Déjà vu: Déjà lu: 'The Lifted Veil' as an Experiment in Art," *Literature and History* 5 (1979): 40–57.

23. See Swann's "Déjà vu: Déjà lu" (note 22 above).

24. Discussions of *The Mill on the Floss* from a feminist perspective focus particularly on this issue. See, for instance, Elizabeth Ermarth, "Maggie Tulliver's Long Suicide," *Studies in English Literature* 14 (1974): 587–601; Patricia Meyer Spacks, "Us or Them," *Hudson Review* 31 (1978): 34–52; and Elizabeth Weed, "*The Mill on the Floss* or the Liquidation of Maggie Tulliver," *Genre* 11 (1978): 427–44.

25. Tanner, *Adultery in the Novel,* p. 16.

26. This aspect of George Eliot's novel is explained in U. C. Knoepflmacher's "*Middlemarch:* An Avuncular View," pp. 53–81.

27. Tony Tanner discusses various forms of willing in *Clarissa,* including the written will "inserted from death into the present . . . and thus not open to dialogue or question" for the child. See *Adultery in the Novel,* p. 101.

28. The sexual implications of the Gwendolen Harleth plot are outlined in Jerome Thale's "'Daniel Deronda': The Darkened World," *Modern Fiction Studies* 3 (1957): 119–26; its implications can be pursued through Joseph Wiesenfarth's analysis of the similarities between that plot and the Medea plot in "The Medea in 'Daniel Deronda,'" *Neueren Sprachen* 72 (1973): 103–8.

29. There is a provocative echo of George Eliot's brutal men in Mr. Davilow, who, like Lawyer Dempster and Latimer's brother Alfred (and perhaps ultimately Dunsey Cass), dies from a mishap involving a horse.

30. Peter K. Garrett, *The Victorian Multiplot Novel,* p. 168.

31. Leon Gottfried, "Structure and Genre in *Daniel Deronda,*" in *The English Novel in the Nineteenth Century,* edited by George Goodin (Urbana: University of Illinois Press, 1972), p. 168.

32. Cynthia Chase, "The Decomposition of the Elephants," p. 223.

33. See J. Hillis Miller, *Charles Dickens: The World of His Novels* (Bloomington: Indiana University Press, 1958).

34. Discussions of the place of motherhood in George Eliot's fiction include

Bonnie S. Zimmerman, "'Radiant as a Diamond': George Eliot, Jewelry and the Female Role," *Criticism* 19 (1977): 212–22; Eve Marie Stwertka, "The Web of Utterance: *Middlemarch*," *Texas Studies in Literature and Language* 19 (1977): 179–87; Judith M. Hughes, "Self-Suppression and Attachment: Mid-Victorian Emotional Life," *Massachusetts Review* 19 (1978): 541–55; and Nina Auerbach, "Artists and Mothers: A False Alliance," *Women and Literature* 6, no. 1 (1978): 3–15. Interestingly, the first three critics find George Eliot's attitude to be positive, whereas Auerbach finds it negative.

35. See Robert L. Caserio, *Plot, Story, and the Novel,* and Patricia Drechsel Tobin, *Time and the Novel: The Genealogical Imperative* (Princeton: Princeton University Press, 1978).

36. See Knoepflmacher, "*Middlemarch:* An Avuncular View."

37. Several persons have written about the relationship between George Eliot's fiction and the concept of tragedy, Aristotelian or otherwise. See, for example, Fred C. Thomson, "*Felix Holt* as Classic Tragedy," *Nineteenth-Century Fiction* 16 (1961): 47–58; Darrel Mansell, Jr., "George Eliot's Conception of Tragedy," *Nineteenth-Century Fiction* 22 (1967): 155–71; U. C. Knoepflmacher, *George Eliot's Early Novels: The Limits of Realism,* pp. 162–220; David Moldstad, "*The Mill on the Floss* and *Antigone,*" *PMLA* 85 (1970): 527–31; and Jeannette King, *Tragedy in the Victorian Novel: Theory and Practice in the Novels of George Eliot, Thomas Hardy, and Henry James* (Cambridge: Cambridge University Press, 1978), pp. 70–96.

38. Interestingly, George Eliot asserted that, in composing *Adam Bede,* her originating point and thus the climax for her developing plot was the conversation between Dinah and Hetty in prison, when Hetty is brought to recognize and speak of the reality of her child (see Haight's *Letters,* 2: 502).

39. Irving Massey, *The Gaping Pig: Literature and Metamorphosis* (Berkeley and Los Angeles: University of California Press, 1976), pp. 1, 35.

CHAPTER 6

1. Several articles have been written about dramatic form and George Eliot's novels. For general discussions, see Darrel Mansell, Jr., "George Eliot's Conception of Tragedy," *Nineteenth-Century Fiction* 22 (1967): 155–71; Felicia Bonaparte, *Will and Destiny: Morality and Tragedy in George Eliot's Novels* (New York: New York University Press, 1975); and Jeannette King, *Tragedy in the Victorian Novel: Theory and Practice in the Novels of George Eliot, Thomas Hardy, and Henry James* (Cambridge: Cambridge University Press, 1978). In addition, several articles have been written about the forms of drama in individual novels: Michael Edwards, "A Reading of *Adam Bede,*" *Critical Quarterly* 14 (1972): 205–18; Ian Adam, "The Structure of Realisms in *Adam Bede,*" *Nineteenth-Century Fiction* 30 (1975): 127–49; U. C. Knoepflmacher, "Tragedy and the Flux: *The Mill on the Floss,*" *George Eliot's Early Novels: The Limits of Realism* (Berkeley and Los Angeles: University of California Press, 1968), pp. 162–220; David Moldstad, "*The Mill on the Floss* and *Antigone,*" *PMLA* 85 (1970); 527–31; John Hagan, "A Reinterpretation of *The Mill on the Floss,*" *PMLA* 87 (1972): 53–63; Brian Swann, "'The Mill on the Floss' and the Form of Tragedy," *English Miscellany* 24 (1973–74): 199–232; Sara M. Putzell, "'An Antagonism of Valid Claims': The Dynamics of *The Mill on the Floss,*" *Studies in the Novel* (North Texas State University) 7 (1975): 227–44; Fred C. Thomson, "The Theme of Alienation in *Silas Marner,*" *Nineteenth-Century Fiction* 20 (1965): 69–84; Fred C. Thomson, "Felix Holt as Classic Tragedy," *Nineteenth-Century Fiction* 16 (1961): 47–58; Neil D. Isaacs, "*Middlemarch:* Crescendo of Obligatory Drama," *Nineteenth-Century Fiction* 18 (1963): 21–34; and Brian Swann, "George Eliot and the Play: Symbol and Metaphor of the Drama in *Daniel Deronda,*" *Dalhousie Review* 52 (1972): 191–202. With the exception of the works of Ian Adam, Neil D. Isaacs, and Brian Swann (on *Daniel Deronda*),

these discussions focus upon the form of tragedy in relationship to George Eliot's construction rather than on the kind of structure acted drama implies. Such work is exhaustive and yet not so helpful in understanding Eliot's evaluation of the drama as is a closer look at the language of theatricality itself in the novels.

2. A thorough discussion of this convention, especially in relationship to Shakespeare, is contained in Anne Righter's *Shakespeare and the Idea of the Play* (New York: Barnes & Noble, 1962).

3. Chief proponents of the belief that acting and the stage embody evils in George Eliot's fiction are W. J. Harvey, in *The Art of George Eliot* (New York: Oxford University Press, 1962), p. 59; Brian Swann, in "George Eliot and the Play"; and Thomas P. Wolfe, in "The Inward Vocation: An Essay on George Eliot's *Daniel Deronda*," *Literary Monographs* 8, edited by Eric Rothstein and Joseph Anthony Wittreich, Jr. (Madison: University of Wisconsin Press, 1976), pp. 1–46.

4. Judith Wilt, in "George Eliot: The Garment of Fear," *Ghosts of the Gothic: Austen, Eliot and Lawrence* (Princeton: Princeton University Press, 1980), p. 228, asserts that acting, even more than music or novel-writing, was a form of exhibitionism that George Eliot both feared and desired.

5. See *Letters,* 4: 300.

6. See Wilt, "George Eliot," pp. 173–230, for a full discussion of the need to grasp one's own visions of fear.

7. Several critics have pointed out the importance of action as opposed to passivity in George Eliot's novels. This has been most extensively examined in relationship to *Daniel Deronda:* Jerome Thale discusses it in "River Imagery in 'Daniel Deronda,'" *Nineteenth-Century Fiction* 8 (1954): 300–6, as does Peter K. Garrett, in *The Victorian Multiplot Novel: Studies in Dialogical Form* (New Haven: Yale University Press, 1980), pp. 167–79. Judith Wilt, in "George Eliot," and Henry Alley, in "New Year's at the Abbey: Point of View in the Pivotal Chapters of *Daniel Deronda,*" *Journal of Narrative Technique* 9 (1979): 147–59, link Deronda's achievement of the active state to psychological events associated with acting and drama.

8. See Righter, *Shakespeare and the Idea of the Play,* pp. 13–42.

9. Robert Y. Turner, in *Shakespeare's Apprenticeship* (Chicago: University of Chicago Press, 1974), discusses at length the shift in the dramatic speeches of Shakespeare's plays from the directly rhetorical to the internally dramatic as Shakespeare discovered the power of poetry itself to move.

10. Both Peter K. Garrett, in *The Victorian Multiplot Novel,* pp. 135–79, and J. Hillis Miller, in "Nature and the Linguistic Moment," *Nature and the Victorian Imagination,* edited by U. C. Knoepflmacher and G. B. Tennyson (Berkeley and Los Angeles: University of California Press, 1977), pp. 440–51, explain how important an awareness of the need to interpret meaning (especially meaning contained within forms of language) is in George Eliot's later novels.

11. See Turner's *Shakespeare's Apprenticeship,* note 9, above.

12. The discussion of Nelly Dean as that most archetypal of all actors, the villain, is contained in James Hafley's "The Villain in *Wuthering Heights,*" *Nineteenth-Century Fiction* 13 (1958): 199–215.

13. Sandra M. Gilbert and Susan Gubar, in *The Madwoman in the Attic: The Woman Writer and the Nineteenth-Century Literary Imagination* (New Haven: Yale University Press, 1979), note that George Eliot associates the theatrical metaphors with the emptiness engendered in women's lives through a lack of definition supplied by work; they also note the insight such a condition can produce (p. 532).

14. See especially chapters 17–19, in which Jane watches from the curtained window seat as the elegant ladies and gentlemen emerge from the curtain separating the drawing room from the dining room, as they play charades, and as Rochester performs his little drama as the gypsy fortune teller.

15. Another Victorian novel that seems to make the entire plot a mere performance to effect the moral regeneration of a social butterfly is *Our Mutual Friend,* in which Dickens makes John Harmon and Noddy Boffin deny their true selves and act parts in order for Bella Wilfer to give up her pretensions to a social role for a "truer" one.

16. See Righter, *Shakespeare and the Idea of the Play,* pp. 113-38.

17. Discussions of the characters mentioned in this paragraph are too numerous to list here. The best single discussion of the general dilemma of acting and will is Felicia Bonaparte's, in *Will and Destiny: Morality and Tragedy in George Eliot's Novels* (see note 1, above).

18. For a discussion of the connections between *Felix Holt the Radical* and the drama, see Fred C. Thomson, "*Felix Holt* as Classic Tragedy" (note 1, above), as well as the discussion of the writing of the novel in Gordon S. Haight's *George Eliot: A Biography,* pp. 374-86.

19. Judith Wilt, on pp. 226-29 of "George Eliot," gives an excellent discussion of Alcharisi's positive as well as negative qualities, seeing her to be, like Mordecai and Klesmer, a royal genius.

20. See Haight, *George Eliot: A Biography,* p. 379.

21. See Turner, *Shakespeare's Apprenticeship,* for a discussion of Shakespeare's early interest in "the way people respond [i.e., the audience] rather than . . . the way they talk [i.e., the actors]" (p. 31).

22. Eric S. Rabkin, in *Narrative Suspense* (Ann Arbor: University of Michigan Press, 1973), p. 141, discusses the distinctions between the voice of narrative and the physical presence of drama, stating the continuing presence of the suspense of language is necessary in order to carry the reader forward in a story that does not have actors still on stage. David Daiches, in *George Eliot: Middlemarch* (Great Neck, N.Y.: Barron's Educational Series, 1963), also notes that, unlike the drama, the novel must be "poetic" (using all the resources of language), because the narrator cannot speak in person (p. 24).

23. See David Leon Higdon's "George Eliot and the Art of the Epigraph," *Nineteenth-Century Fiction* 25 (1970): 127-51, for a complete listing of sources for her epigraphs.

24. See Haight, *George Eliot: A Biography,* p. 468.

CHAPTER 7

1. For a list of essays on George Eliot's novels and tragic form, see Chapter 6, note 1.

2. The most famous formulations of the antithesis of laughter and sympathy are those of Thomas Hobbes in *The Leviathan* (1651), Henri Bergson in *Laughter* (1900), and Sigmund Freud in *Jokes and Their Relation to the Unconscious* (1905). The nineteenth century, however, was dominated by "sympathetic" humor; see Robert Bernard Martin, *The Triumph of Wit: A Study of Victorian Comic Theory* (Oxford: Clarendon Press, 1964), pp. 25-46.

3. See Eliot's *Essays,* pp. 127, 128, 327.

4. See Collins's article "G. H. Lewes Revised: George Eliot and the Moral Sense," *Victorian Studies* 21 (1978): 465-66. The text of Lewes's "The Affective States" and of George Eliot's revision is provided on pp. 491-92.

5. This assertion by George Eliot tends to refute I. T. Ker's claim that Eliot's moral bias favored spontaneous enthusiasm at the expense of intellect; see I. T. Ker, "George Eliot's Rhetoric of Enthusiasm," *Essays in Criticism* 26 (1976): 134-55.

6. Koestler, *Insight and Outlook* (Lincoln: University of Nebraska Press, 1949). Koestler repeats and expands his arguments in *The Act of Creation* (New York: Macmillan, 1964).

7. Koestler points out here that Herbert Spencer, in "The Physiology of Laughter," was the first to assert this evolutionary connection. Horace M. Kallen, in *Liberty, Laughter, and Tears: Reflections on the Relations of Comedy and Tragedy to Human Freedom* (DeKalb: Northern Illinois University Press, 1968) asserts that there is a "wide consensus that laughter and tears punctuate critical moments of an individual's personal history and diverse turning points in his pursuit of liberty": laughter in particular permits the individual to turn a transaction with the world into a transaction within one's own psychosomatic sovereignty—the body (see pp. 40, 53).

8. Kallen, Ibid., p. 79.

9. Steven Marcus presents an excellent summary of George Eliot's conception of sympathy in "Human Nature, Social Orders, and 19th Century Systems of Explanation: Starting In with George Eliot," *Salmagundi* 28 (1975): 32. He suggests that sympathy is the logical extension of self-transcending emotions.

10. Koestler, *The Act of Creation*, p. 272.

11. Koestler uses "Janus-faced" to describe the situation of a "part" that is subordinate to the larger whole and yet is a whole in relationship to its own subparts (*Insight and Outlook*, p. 135).

12. A number of critics have noted the topics that George Eliot usually finds to be comic per se: See May Tomlinson, "The Humor of George Eliot," *Southwest Review* 5 (1920): 243-48; William J. Hyde, "George Eliot and the Climate of Realism," *PMLA* 72 (1957): 156-57; W. J. Harvey, *The Art of George Eliot* (New York: Oxford University Press, 1962), p. 156; John Killham, "The Idea of Community in the English Novel," *Nineteenth-Century Fiction* 31 (1977): 381; Patricia Shaw, "Humour in the Novels of George Eliot," *Filologia Moderna* 13 (1973) 305-35.

13. Koestler explains the oceanic feeling at length in *The Act of Creation*, pp. 292-95.

14. Eric S. Rabkin, in *Narrative Suspense* (Ann Arbor: University of Michigan Press, 1973), p. 140, notes that the continued presence of the narrative voice is essential to the development of a narrative line from a single bisociation or joke.

15. In "The Morality of Wilhelm Meister" (1855), *Essays*, p. 145, George Eliot herself complains about writers who have direct intentions regarding the response of the hearer.

16. John Holloway, in "Thought, Style, and the Idea of Co-Variance in Some Mid-Nineteenth-Century Prose," *Studies in the Literary Imagination* 8, no. 2 (1975): 1-14, discusses the presence in George Eliot's work of locutions expressing proportion.

17. Critics such as Barbara Hardy, in *The Novels of George Eliot: A Study in Form* (New York: Oxford University Press, 1967), pp. 201-14; W. J. Harvey, in *The Art of George Eliot*, pp. 84-87; and Rachel Trickett, in "Vitality of Language in Nineteenth-Century Fiction," *The Modern English Novel: The Reader, the Writer and the Work*, ed. Gabriel Josipovici (London: Open Books Publishing, 1976), pp. 37-53, all complain of failures of tone that are related to failures of style in George Eliot's novels. More recent critics have begun to examine the degree to which Eliot's style, especially her use of images and metaphors, reveals a complex awareness of the subject of language itself as a creator of reality. See J. Hillis Miller, "Nature and the Linguistic Moment," *Nature and the Victorian Imagination*, ed. U. C. Knoepflmacher and G. B. Tennyson (Berkeley and Los Angeles: University of California Press, 1977), pp. 440-51; Elizabeth Weed, "*The Mill on the Floss* or the Liquidation of Maggie Tulliver," *Genre* 11 (1978): 427-44; Cynthia Chase, "The Decomposition of the Elephants: Double-Reading *Daniel Deronda*," *PMLA* 93 (1978): 215-27; and Jonathan Arac, "Rhetoric and Realism in Nineteenth-Century Fiction: Hyperbole in *The Mill on the Floss*," *ELH* 46 (1979) 673-92. See

also Mark Schorer, "Fiction and the 'Matrix of Analogy,'" *Kenyon Review* 11 (1949): 550–59; and Robert B. Heilman, "Return to Raveloe: Thirty-Five Years After," *English Journal* 46 (1957): 1–10. On the other hand, George Levine argues cogently for Eliot's equal interest in a reality that is not constituted by language in *The Realistic Imagination: English Fiction from Frankenstein to Lady Chatterley* (Chicago: University of Chicago Press, 1981), pp. 6–12.

18. George Eliot's most extensive analysis of the failure of style at the level of sentence and word is her essay, "Lord Brougham's Literature" (1855), *Essays,* pp. 139–41.

BIBLIOGRAPHY

WORKS FREQUENTLY CITED

The following editions of George Eliot's works and other central texts have been referred to in this book.

Adam Bede. Boston: Houghton Mifflin Co., 1968.

"Brother Jacob." *Works of George Eliot, Volume 3.* New York: P. F. Collier, n.d.

Daniel Deronda. New York: Harper & Row, 1960.

Essays of George Eliot. Edited by Thomas Pinney. New York: Columbia University Press, 1963.

Felix Holt the Radical. New York: W. W. Norton & Co., 1970.

George Eliot: A Biography. Gordon S. Haight. New York: Oxford University Press, 1968.

The George Eliot Letters. Edited by Gordon S. Haight. 9 vols. New Haven: Yale University Press, 1954–78.

"The Legend of Jubal." *The Works of George Eliot.* Edinburgh: William Blackwood & Sons, 1879.

"The Lifted Veil." *Works of George Eliot, Volume 3.* New York: P. F. Collier, n.d.

Middlemarch. Boston: Houghton Mifflin Co., 1956.

The Mill on the Floss. Boston: Houghton Mifflin Co., 1961.

Romola. The Works of George Eliot. 2 vols. Edinburgh: William Blackwood & Sons, n.d.

Scenes of Clerical Life. Harmondsworth, Middlesex: Penguin Books, 1973.

Silas Marner. Harmondsworth, Middlesex: Penguin Books, 1967.

SELECTED BIBLIOGRAPHY

The following works do not comprise a complete listing of significant scholarship on narrative and on George Eliot. Rather, they are those items that have become standard in any discussion of George Eliot, those that have directly influenced this book, and those that have been cited in the notes.

Abraham, Nicolas. "The Shell and the Kernel." *Diacritics* 9, no. 1 (1979): 16–28.

Adam, Ian. "The Structure of Realisms in *Adam Bede.*" *Nineteenth-Century Fiction* 30 (1975): 127–49.

——, ed. *This Particular Web: Essays on 'Middlemarch'.* Toronto: University of Toronto Press, 1975.

Allen, Walter. *George Eliot.* New York: Macmillan Co., 1964.

Alley, Henry. "New Year's at the Abbey: Point of View in the Pivotal Chapters of *Daniel Deronda." Journal of Narrative Technique* 9 (1979): 147–59.

Altman, Charles. "Medieval Narrative vs. Modern Assumptions: Revising Inadequate Typology." *Diacritics* 4 (1974): 12–19.

Arac, Jonathan. "Rhetoric and Realism in Nineteenth-Century Fiction: Hyperbole in *The Mill on the Floss." ELH* 46 (1979): 673–92.

Arthos, John. "George Eliot: 'The Art of Vision.'" *Rivista di Letterature Moderne e Comparate* 3 (1952): 260–70.

Auerbach, Nina. "Artists and Mothers: A False Alliance." *Women and Literature* 6, no. 1 (1978): 3–15.

——. "The Power of Hunger: Demonism and Maggie Tulliver." *Nineteenth-Century Fiction* 30 (1975): 150–71.

Auster, Henry. *Local Habitations: Regionalism in the Early Novels of George Eliot.* Cambridge, Harvard University Press, 1970.

Baumgarten, Murray. "From Realism to Expressionism: Toward a History of the Novel." *New Literary History* 6 (1975): 415–27.

Beaty, Jerome. *"Middlemarch" from Notebook to Novel: A Study of George Eliot's Creative Method.* Urbana: University of Illinois Press, 1960.

Bedient, Calvin. *Architects of the Self: George Eliot, D. H. Lawrence, and E. M. Forster.* Berkeley and Los Angeles: University of California Press, 1972.

Beer, Gillian. "Myth and the Single Consciousness: *Middlemarch* and *The Lifted Veil.*" In *This Particular Web,* edited by Ian Adam.

Bellringer, Alan W. "The Study of Provincial Life in *Middlemarch.*" *English* 28 (1979): 219–47.

Bennett, Joan. *George Eliot: Her Mind and Her Art.* Cambridge: Cambridge University Press, 1948.

Blake, Kathleen. "*Middlemarch* and the Woman Question." *Nineteenth-Century Fiction* 31 (1976): 285–312.

Bloomfield, Morton W. "The Syncategorematic in Poetry: From Semantics to Syntactics." In *To Honor Roman Jakobson.* Vol. 1. The Hague: Mouton & Co., 1967.

Bonaparte, Felicia. *The Triptych and the Cross: The Central Myths of George Eliot's Poetic Imagination.* New York: New York University Press, 1979.

——. *Will and Destiny: Morality and Tragedy in George Eliot's Novels.* New York: New York University Press, 1975.

Buckley, Jerome H., ed. *The Worlds of Victorian Fiction.* Cambridge: Harvard University Press, 1975.

Burke, Kenneth. *Language as Symbolic Action.* Berkeley and Los Angeles: University of California Press, 1966.

Burstein, Janet. "Victorian Mythography and the Progress of the Intellect." *Victorian Studies* 18 (1975): 309–24.

Carroll, David, ed. *George Eliot: The Critical Heritage.* New York: Barnes & Noble, 1971.

——. "'Janet's Repentance' and the Myth of the Organic." *Nineteenth-Century Fiction* 35 (1980): 331–48.

——. "*Mansfield Park, Daniel Deronda* and Ordination." *Modern Philology* 62 (1965): 217–26.

——. "*Middlemarch* and the Externality of Fact." In *This Particular Web,* edited by Ian Adam.

——. "*Silas Marner:* Reversing the Oracles of Religion." *Literary Monographs* 1, edited by Eric Rothstein and Thomas K. Dunseath. Madison: University of Wisconsin Press, 1967.

——. "The Unity of 'Daniel Deronda.'" *Essays in Criticism* 9 (1959): 369–80.

——. "Unity through Analogy: An Interpretation of 'Middlemarch.'" *Victorian Studies* 2 (1959): 305–16.

Caserio, Robert L. *Plot, Story, and the Novel: From Dickens and Poe to the Modern Period.* Princeton: Princeton University Press, 1979.

Chase, Cynthia. "The Decomposition of the Elephants: Double-Reading *Daniel Deronda.*" *PMLA* 93 (1978): 215–27.

Christ, Carol. "Aggression and Providential Death in George Eliot's Fiction." *Novel* 9 (1976): 130–40.

Cirillo, Albert R. "Salvation in *Daniel Deronda:* The Fortunate Overthrow of Gwendolen Harleth." *Literary Monographs* 1, edited by Eric Rothstein and Thomas K. Dunseath. Madison: University of Wisconsin Press, 1967.

Clark, George. "Henryson and Aesop: The Fable Transformed." *ELH* 43 (1976): 1–18.

Clayton, Jay. "Visionary Power and Narrative Form: Wordsworth and *Adam Bede.*" *ELH* 46 (1979): 645–72.

Collins, K. K. "G. H. Lewes Revised: George Eliot and the Moral Sense." *Victorian Studies* 21 (1978): 463–92.

Collins, Philip. *From Manly Tear to Stiff Upper Lip: The Victorians and Pathos.* Wellington, New Zealand: Victoria University Press, 1974.

Conway, Richard. "*Silas Marner* and *Felix Holt:* From Tale to Feminism." *Studies in the Novel* (North Texas State University) 10 (1978): 295–304.

Craig, George. "Reading: Who Is Doing What to Whom?" In *The Modern English Novel: The Reader, the Writer and the Work,* edited by Gabriel Josipovici.

Creeger, George R. "An Interpretation of *Adam Bede.*" *ELH* 23 (1956): 218–38.

Daiches, David. *George Eliot: Middlemarch.* Great Neck, N.Y.: Barron's Educational Series, 1963.

de Man, Paul. "The Rhetoric of Temporality." In *Interpretation: Theory and Practice,* edited by Charles S. Singleton. Baltimore: Johns Hopkins Press, 1969.

Deneau, Daniel P. "Imagery in the *Scenes of Clerical Life.*" *Victorian Newsletter* 28 (1965): 18–22.

——. "A Note on George Eliot's 'Amos Barton'—Reticence and Chronology." *Notes and Queries* n.s. 6 (1959): 450–51.

Derrida, Jacques. "Structure, Sign, and Play in the Discourse of the Human Sciences." In *The Languages of Criticism and the Sciences of Man,* edited by Richard Macksey and Eugenio Donato. Baltimore: John Hopkins Press, 1970.

Dessner, Lawrence Jay. "The Autobiographical Matrix of *Silas Marner.*" *Studies in the Novel* (North Texas State University) 11 (1979): 251–82.

Doyle, Mary Ellen. *The Sympathetic Response: George Eliot's Fictional Rhetoric.* London: Associated University Presses, 1981.

Dunham, Robert H. "*Silas Marner* and the Wordsworthian Child." *Studies in English Literature* 16 (1976): 645–59.

Edwards, Michael. "A Reading of *Adam Bede.*" *Critical Quarterly* 14 (1972): 205–18.

Emery, Laura Comer. *George Eliot's Creative Conflict: The Other Side of Silence.* Berkeley and Los Angeles: University of California Press, 1976.

Ermarth, Elizabeth. "Maggie Tulliver's Long Suicide." *Studies in English Literature* 14 (1974): 587–601.

——. "Method and Moral in George Eliot's Narrative." *Victorian Newsletter* 47 (1975): 4–8.

Fast, Robin Riley. "Getting to the Ends of *Daniel Deronda.*" *Journal of Narrative Technique* 7 (1977): 200–17.

Feltes, N. N. "George Eliot's 'Pier-Glass': The Development of a Metaphor." *Modern Philology* 67 (1969): 69–71.

Feuerbach, Ludwig. *The Essence of Christianity*. Translated by George Eliot. New York: Harper & Brothers, 1957.

Fleishman, Avrom. "'Daniel Charisi': An Assessment of *Daniel Deronda* in the History of Ideas." In *Fiction and the Ways of Knowing: Essays on British Novels.* Austin: University of Texas Press, 1978.

Fletcher, Angus. *Allegory: The Theory of a Symbolic Mode.* Ithaca, N.Y.: Cornell University Press, 1964.

——. "'Positive Negation': Threshold, Sequence, and Personification in Coleridge." In *New Perspectives on Coleridge and Wordsworth,* edited by Geoffrey H. Hartman. New York: Columbia University Press, 1972.

Frank, Joseph. "Spatial Form in Modern Literature." *Sewanee Review* 53 (1945): 221–40, 433–56, 643–53.

Fricke, Douglas C. "Art and Artists in *Daniel Deronda.*" *Studies in the Novel* (North Texas State University) 5 (1973): 220–28.

Frye, Northop. "Myth, Fiction, and Displacement." In *Fables of Identity: Studies In Poetic Mythology.* New York: Harcourt, Brace & World, 1963.

——. "The Road of Excess." In *Myth and Symbol: Critical Approaches and Applications,* edited by Bernice Slote. Lincoln: University of Nebraska Press, 1963.

Garrett, Peter K. *The Victorian Multiplot Novel: Studies in Dialogical Form.* New Haven: Yale University Press, 1980.

Gezari, Janet K. "The Metaphorical Imagination of George Eliot." *ELH* 45 (1978): 93–106.

——. "*Romola* and the Myth of Apocalypse." In *George Eliot: Centenary Essays and an Unpublished Fragment,* edited by Anne Smith.

Gilbert, Sandra M., and Gubar, Susan. *The Madwoman in the Attic: The Woman Writer and the Nineteenth-Century Literary Imagination.* New Haven: Yale University Press, 1979.

Ginsburg, Michal Peled. "Pseudonym, Epigraphs, and Narrative Voice: *Middlemarch* and the Problem of Authorship." *ELH* 47 (1980): 542–58.

Girard, René. *Deceit, Desire, and the Novel: Self and Other in Literary Structure.* Translated by Yvonne Freccero. Baltimore: Johns Hopkins Press, 1966.

Goldfarb, Russell M. "Robert P. Warren's Tollivers and George Eliot's Tullivers." *University Review* 36 (1970): 209–13; 275–79.

Goode, John. "'Adam Bede.'" In *Critical Essays on George Eliot,* edited by Barbara Hardy.

Goodin, George, ed. *The English Novel in the Nineteenth Century.* Urbana: University of Illinois Press, 1972.

Gordon, Jan B. "Origins, *Middlemarch,* Endings: George Eliot's Crisis of the Antecedent." In *George Eliot: Centenary Essays and an Unpublished Fragment,* edited by Anne Smith.

Gottfried, Leon. "Structure and Genre in *Daniel Deronda.*" In *The English Novel in the Nineteenth Century,* edited by George Goodin.

Greenberg, Robert A. "Plexuses and Ganglia: Scientific Allusion in *Middlemarch.*" *Nineteenth-Century Fiction* 30 (1975): 33–52.

Greenstein, Susan M. "The Question of Vocation: From *Romola* to *Middlemarch.*" *Nineteenth-Century Fiction* 35 (1981): 487–505.

Haddakin, Lilian. "'Silas Marner.'" In *Critical Essays on George Eliot,* edited by Barbara Hardy.

Hafley, James. "The Villain in *Wuthering Heights.*" *Nineteenth-Century Fiction* 13 (1958): 199–215.

Hagan, John. "A Reinterpretation of *The Mill on the Floss.*" *PMLA* 87 (1972): 53–63.

Hardy, Barbara, ed. *Critical Essays on George Eliot.* London: Routledge & Kegan Paul, 1970.

——. *The Novels of George Eliot: A Study in Form.* New York: Oxford University Press, 1967.

Harris, Mason. "Arthur's Misuse of the Imagination: Sentimental Benevolence and Wordsworthian Realism in *Adam Bede.*" *English Studies in Canada* 4 (1978): 41–59.

Hartman, Geoffrey. *Beyond Formalism: Literary Essays, 1958–1970.* New Haven: Yale University Press, 1970.

——. *Criticism in the Wilderness: The Study of Literature Today.* New Haven: Yale University Press, 1980.

——. *Wordsworth's Poetry 1787–1814,* New Haven: Yale University Press, 1964.

Harvey, W. J. *The Art of George Eliot.* New York: Oxford University Press, 1962.

——. "Idea and Image in the Novels of George Eliot." In *Critical Essays on George Eliot,* edited by Barbara Hardy.

Heilman, Robert B. "Return to Raveloe: Thirty-Five Years After." *English Journal* 46 (1957): 1–10.

Herbert, Christopher. "Preachers and the Schemes of Nature in *Adam Bede.*" *Nineteenth-Century Fiction* 29 (1975): 412–27.

Higdon, David Leon. "George Eliot and the Art of the Epigraph." *Nineteenth-Century Fiction* 25 (1970): 127–51.

Holland, Norman N. *The Dynamics of Literary Response.* New York: Oxford University Press, 1968.

Holloway, John. "Narrative Process in *Middlemarch.*" In *Narrative and Structure: Exploratory Essays.* Cambridge: Cambridge University Press, 1979.

——. "Thought, Style and the Idea of Co-Variance in Some Mid-Nineteenth-Century Prose." *Studies in the Literary Imagination* 8, no. 2 (1975): 1–14.

Hornback, Bert G. "The Organization of *Middlemarch.*" *Papers on Language and Literature* 2 (1966): 169–75.

Horowitz, Lenore Wisney. "George Eliot's Vision of Society in *Felix Holt the Radical.*" *Texas Studies in Literature and Language* 17 (1975): 175–91.

Hughes, Judith M. "Self-Suppression and Attachment: Mid-Victorian Emotional Life." *Massachusetts Review* 19 (1978): 541–55.

Hulme, Hilda M. "*Middlemarch* as Science Fiction: Notes on Language and Imagery." *Novel* 2 (1968): 36–45.

Hurley, Edward T. "Death and Immortality: George Eliot's Solution." *Nineteenth-Century Fiction* 24 (1969): 222–27.

——. "'The Lifted Veil': George Eliot as Anti-Intellectual." *Studies in Short Fiction* 5 (1967–1968): 257–62.

——. "Piero di Cosimo: An Alternate Analogy for George Eliot's Realism." *Victorian Newsletter* 31 (1967): 54–56.

Hyde, William J. "George Eliot and the Climate of Realism." *PMLA* 72 (1957): 147–64.

Isaacs, Neil D. "*Middlemarch:* Crescendo of Obligatory Drama." *Nineteenth-Century Fiction* 18 (1963): 21–34.

Iser, Wolfgang. *The Implied Reader: Patterns of Communication from Bunyan to Beckett.* Baltimore: Johns Hopkins University Press, 1974.

Jakobson, Roman. "The Cardinal Dichotomy in Language." In *Language: An Enquiry into Its Meaning and Function,* edited by Ruth Nanda Anshen. New York: Harper & Brothers, 1957.

Josipovici, Gabriel, ed. *The Modern English Novel: The Reader, the Writer and the Work.* London: Open Books Publishing, 1976.

Kahler, Erich. *The Inward Turn of Narrative.* Translated by Richard and Clara Winston. Princeton: Princeton University Press, 1973.

Kallen, Horace M. *Liberty, Laughter, and Tears: Reflections on the Relations of*

Comedy and Tragedy to Human Freedom. DeKalb: Northern Illinois University Press, 1968.

Kearney, John P. "Time and Beauty in *Daniel Deronda:* 'Was she beautiful or not beautiful?'" *Nineteenth-Century Fiction* 26 (1971): 286–306.

Ker, I. T. "George Eliot's Rhetoric of Enthusiasm." *Essays in Criticism* 26 (1976): 134–55.

Kermode, Frank. "Sensing Endings." *Nineteenth-Century Fiction* 33 (1978): 144–58.

Kiely, Robert. "The Limits of Dialogue in *Middlemarch.*" In *The Worlds of Victorian Fiction,* edited by Jerome H. Buckley.

Killham, John. "The Idea of Community in the English Novel." *Nineteenth-Century Fiction* 31 (1977): 379-96.

King, Jeannette. *Tragedy in the Victorian Novel: Theory and Practice in the Novels of George Eliot, Thomas Hardy, and Henry James.* Cambridge: Cambridge University Press, 1978.

Knoepflmacher, U. C. "*Daniel Deronda* and William Shakespeare." *Victorian Newsletter* 19 (1961): 27–28.

——. *George Eliot's Early Novels: The Limits of Realism.* Berkeley and Los Angeles: University of California Press, 1968.

——. "*Middlemarch:* Affirmation Through Compromise." In *Laughter and Despair: Readings in Ten Novels of the Victorian Era.* Berkeley and Los Angeles: University of California Press, 1971.

——. "*Middlemarch:* An Avuncular View." *Nineteenth-Century Fiction* 30 (1975): 53–81.

——. *Religious Humanism and the Victorian Novel: George Eliot, Walter Pater, and Samuel Butler.* Princeton: Princeton University Press, 1965.

Koestler, Arthur. *The Act of Creation.* New York: Macmillan Co., 1964.

——. *Insight and Outlook: An Inquiry into the Common Foundations of Science, Art and Social Ethics.* Lincoln: University of Nebraska Press, 1949.

Kropf, Carl R. "Time and Typology in George Eliot's Early Fiction." *Studies in the Novel* (North Texas State University) 8 (1976): 430–40.

Leavis, F. R. *The Great Tradition: George Eliot, Henry James, Joseph Conrad.* London: Chatto & Windus, 1962.

Levenson, Shirley Frank. "The Use of Music in *Daniel Deronda.*" *Nineteenth-Century Fiction* 24 (1969): 317–34.

Levine, George. "Determinism and Responsibility in the Works of George Eliot." *PMLA* 77 (1962): 268–79.

——. "George Eliot's Hypothesis of Reality." *Nineteenth-Century Fiction* 35 (1980): 1–28.

——. *The Realistic Imagination: English Fiction from Frankenstein to Lady Chatterley.* Chicago: University of Chicago Press, 1981.

Lévi-Strauss, Claude. *Structural Anthropology.* Garden City, N.Y.: Doubleday & Co., 1967.

Liebman, Sheldon. "The Counterpoint of Characters in George Eliot's Early Novels." *Revue des Langues Vivantes* 34 (1968): 9–23.

Mann, Karen B. "George Eliot and Wordsworth: The Power of Sound and the Power of Mind." *Studies in English Literature* 20 (1980): 675–94.

——. "George Eliot's Language of Nature: Production and Consumption." *ELH* 48 (1981): 190–216.

Mansell, Darrel, Jr. "George Eliot's Conception of Tragedy." *Nineteenth-Century Fiction* 22 (1967): 155–71.

Marcus, Steven. "Human Nature, Social Orders, and 19th Century Systems of Explanation: Starting In with George Eliot." *Salmagundi* 28 (1975): 20–42.

Marotta, Kenny. "*Adam Bede* as a Pastoral." *Genre* 9 (1976): 59–72.

Martin, Robert Bernard. *The Triumph of Wit: A Study of Victorian Comic Theory.* Oxford: Clarendon Press, 1964.

Massey, Irving. *The Gaping Pig: Literature and Metamorphosis.* Berkeley and Los Angeles: University of California Press, 1976.

McGowan, John P. "The Turn of George Eliot's Realism." *Nineteenth-Century Fiction* 35 (1980): 171–92.

Merleau-Ponty, Maurice. *Phenomenology of Perception.* Translated by Colin Smith. New York: Humanities Press, 1962.

Miller, J. Hillis. *Charles Dickens: The World of His Novels.* Bloomington: Indiana University Press, 1958.

——. *The Form of Victorian Fiction: Thackeray, Dickens, Trollope, George Eliot, Meredith, and Hardy.* Notre Dame, Ind.: University of Notre Dame Press, 1968.

——. "Narrative and History." *ELH* 41 (1974): 455–73.

——. "Nature and the Linguistic Moment." In *Nature and the Victorian Imagination,* edited by U. C. Knoepflmacher and G. B. Tennyson. Berkeley and Los Angeles: University of California Press, 1977.

——. "Optic and Semiotic in *Middlemarch.*" In *The Worlds of Victorian Fiction,* edited by Jerome H. Buckley.

——. "The Problematic of Ending in Narrative." *Nineteenth-Century Fiction* 33 (1978): 3–7.

Mintz, Alan. *George Eliot and the Novel of Vocation.* Cambridge: Harvard University Press, 1978.

Moldstad, David. "*The Mill on the Floss* and *Antigone.*" *PMLA* 85 (1970): 527–31.

Naumann, Walter. "The Architecture of George Eliot's Novels." *Modern Language Quarterly* 9 (1948): 37–50.

New Literary History ["On Narrative and Narratives"] 6 (1975).

Newton, K. M. *George Eliot: Romantic Humanist.* Totowa, N.J.: Barnes & Noble, 1981.

Noble, Thomas A. *George Eliot's 'Scenes of Clerical Life.'* New Haven: Yale University Press, 1965.

Oldfield, Derek and Sybil. "'Scenes of Clerical Life': The Diagram and the Picture." In *Critical Essays on George Eliot,* edited by Barbara Hardy.

Paris, Bernard J. *Experiments in Life: George Eliot's Quest for Values.* Detroit: Wayne State University Press, 1965.

——. "The Inner Conflicts of Maggie Tulliver: A Horneyan Analysis." *Centennial Review of Arts and Sciences* 13 (1969): 166–99.

——. "Toward a Revaluation of George Eliot's 'The Mill on the Floss.'" *Nineteenth-Century Fiction* 11 (1956): 18–31.

Pell, Nancy. "The Fathers' Daughters in *Daniel Deronda.*" *Nineteenth-Century Fiction* 36 (1982): 424–51.

Percy, Walker. "Metaphor as Mistake." *Sewanee Review* 66 (1958): 79–99.

Phelan, James. *Worlds from Words: A Theory of Language in Fiction.* Chicago: University of Chicago Press, 1981.

Pinney, Thomas. "The Authority of the Past in George Eliot's Novels." *Nineteenth-Century Fiction* 21 (1966): 131–47.

——. "More Leaves from George Eliot's Notebook." *Huntington Library Quarterly* 29 (1966): 353–76.

Pottle, Frederick A. "Synchrony and Diachrony: A Plea for the Use in Literary Studies of Saussure's Concepts and Terminology." In *Literary Theory and Structure,* edited by Frank Brady, John Palmer, and Martin Price. New Haven: Yale University Press, 1973.

Price, Martin. "The Fictional Contract." In *Literary Theory and Structure,* edited by Frank Brady, John Palmer, and Martin Price. New Haven: Yale University Press, 1973.

——. *To the Palace of Wisdom: Studies in Order and Energy from Dryden to Blake.* Garden City, N.Y.: Doubleday & Co., 1964.

Putzell, Sara M. "'An Antagonism of Valid Claims': The Dynamics of *The Mill on the Floss.*" *Studies in the Novel* (North Texas State University) 7 (1975): 227–44.

Rabkin, Eric S. *Narrative Suspense.* Ann Arbor: University of Michigan Press, 1973.

Righter, Anne. *Shakespeare and the Idea of the Play.* New York: Barnes & Noble, 1962.

Roberts, Lynne Tidaback. "Perfect Pyramids: *The Mill on the Floss.*" *Texas Studies in Literature and Language* 13 (1971): 111–24.

Roberts, Neil. *George Eliot: Her Beliefs and Her Art.* Pittsburgh: University of Pittsburgh Press, 1975.

Rubinstein, Elliot L. "A Forgotten Tale by George Eliot." *Nineteenth-Century Fiction* 17 (1962): 175–83.

Sadoff, Dianne F. "Nature's Language: Metaphor in the Text of *Adam Bede.*" *Genre* 11 (1978): 411–26.

Said, Edward W. *Beginnings: Intention and Method.* New York: Basic Books, 1975.

Santangelo, Gennaro A. "Villari's *Life and Times of Savonarola:* A Source for George Eliot's *Romola.*" *Anglia* 90 (1972): 118–31.

Schorer, Mark. "Fiction and the 'Matrix of Analogy.'" *Kenyon Review* 11 (1949): 550–59.

Sedgley, Anne. "Daniel Deronda." *The Critical Review* 13 (1970): 3–19.

Shaw, Patricia. "Humour in the Novels of George Eliot." *Filologia Moderna* 13 (1973): 305–35.

Smirlock, Daniel. "Rough Truth: Synecdoche and Interpretation in *The Egoist.*" *Nineteenth-Century Fiction* 31 (1976): 313–28.

Smith, Anne, ed. *George Eliot: Centenary Essays and an Unpublished Fragment.* Totowa, N.J.: Barnes & Noble, 1980.

Smith, Jane S. "The Reader as Part of the Fiction: *Middlemarch.*" *Texas Studies in Literature and Language* 19 (1977): 188–203.

Spacks, Patricia Meyer. "Us or Them." *Hudson Review* 31 (1978): 34–52.

Stevens, Wallace. *The Necessary Angel: Essays on Reality and the Imagination.* New York: Random House, 1951.

Stump, Reva. *Movement and Vision in George Eliot's Novels.* Seattle: University of Washington Press, 1959.

Stwertka, Eve Marie. "The Web of Utterance: *Middlemarch.*" *Texas Studies in Literature and Language* 19 (1977): 179–87.

Sudrann, Jean. "*Daniel Deronda* and the Landscape of Exile." *ELH* 37 (1970): 433–55.

Sullivan, William J. "Music and Musical Allusion in 'The Mill on the Floss.'" *Criticism* 16 (1974): 232–46.

——. "Piero di Cosimo and the Higher Primitivism in *Romola.*" *Nineteenth-Century Fiction* 26 (1972): 390–405.

Swann, Brian. "George Eliot and the Play: Symbol and Metaphor of the Drama in *Daniel Deronda.*" *Dalhousie Review* 52 (1972): 191–202.

——. "George Eliot's Ecumenical Jew, or, The Novel as Outdoor Temple." *Novel* 8 (1974): 39–50.

——. "*Middlemarch* and Myth." *Nineteenth-Century Fiction* 28 (1973): 210–14.

——. "*Middlemarch:* Realism and Symbolic Form." *ELH* 39 (1972): 279–308.

——. "'The Mill on the Floss' and the Form of Tragedy." *English Miscellany* 24 (1973–1974): 199–232.

——. "'Silas Marner' and the New Mythus." *Criticism* 18 (1976): 101–21.

Swann, Charles. "Déjà vu: Déjà lu: 'The Lifted Veil' as an Experiment in Art." *Literature and History* 5 (1979) 40–57.

Tanner, Tony. *Adultery in the Novel: Contract and Transgression.* Baltimore: Johns Hopkins University Press, 1979.

Thale, Jerome. "'Daniel Deronda': The Darkened World." *Modern Fiction Studies* 3 (1957): 119-26.

——. *The Novels of George Eliot.* New York: Columbia University Press, 1959.

——. "River Imagery in 'Daniel Deronda.'" *Nineteenth-Century Fiction* 8 (1954): 300-6.

Thomson, Fred C. "*Felix Holt* as Classic Tragedy." *Nineteenth-Century Fiction* 16 (1961): 47-58.

——. "The Theme of Alienation in *Silas Marner.*" *Nineteenth-Century Fiction* 20 (1965): 69-84.

Tobin, Patricia Drechsel. *Time and the Novel: The Genealogical Imperative.* Princeton: Princeton University Press, 1978.

Tomlinson, May. "The Humor of George Eliot." *Southwest Review* 5 (1920): 243-48.

Trickett, Rachel. "Vitality of Language in Nineteenth-Century Fiction." In *The Modern English Novel: The Reader, the Writer, and the Work,* edited by Gabriel Josipovici.

Turner, Robert Y. *Shakespeare's Apprenticeship.* Chicago: University of Chicago Press, 1974.

Van Ghent, Dorothy. *The English Novel: Form and Function.* New York: Rinehart, 1953.

Weed, Elizabeth. "*The Mill on the Floss* or the Liquidation of Maggie Tulliver." *Genre* 11 (1978): 427-44.

Welsh, Alexander. *The Hero of the Waverley Novels.* New Haven: Yale University Press, 1963.

Wiesenfarth, Joseph. "Adam Bede and Myth." *Papers on Language and Literature* 8 (1972): 39-52.

——. *George Eliot's Mythmaking.* Heidelberg: Carl Winter, Universitätsverlag, 1977.

——. "Legend in *The Mill on the Floss.*" *Texas Studies in Literature and Language* 18 (1976): 20-41.

——. "The Medea in 'Daniel Deronda.'" *Neueren Sprachen* 72 (1973): 103-8.

——. "*Middlemarch:* The Language of Art." *PMLA* 97 (1982): 363-77.

Wilt, Judith. "George Eliot: The Garment of Fear." In *Ghosts of the Gothic: Austen, Eliot, & Lawrence.* Princeton: Princeton University Press, 1980.

Wolfe, Thomas P. "The Inward Vocation: An Essay on George Eliot's *Daniel Deronda.*" In *Literary Monographs* 8, edited by Eric Rothstein and Joseph Anthony Wittreich, Jr. Madison: University of Wisconsin Press, 1976.

Zimmerman, Bonnie. "*Felix Holt* and the True Power of Womanhood." *ELH* 46 (1979): 432-51.

——. "'Radiant as a Diamond': George Eliot, Jewelry and the Female Role." *Criticism* 19 (1977): 212-22.

INDEX